Aunt Ruth:
The Queen of English and Her Reign of Error

Joel Schnoor

Gennesaret Press

Gennesaret Press
202 Persimmon Place
Apex, NC 27523

www.GennesaretPress.com

© *2017 Joel Schnoor. All rights reserved.*

No part of this book may be reproduced or transmitted by any means without the express written consent of the author.

ISBN: 978-0-9845541-7-1

Library of Congress Control Number: 2017948843

Printed in the United States of America
Apex, North Carolina

Front cover illustration by Doug Oglesby
Interior art and formatting by Joel Schnoor

To Michelle

Table of Contents

1 Aunt Ruth Loves Chocolate More Than Me 1
2 Aunt Ruth, QE-II 8
3 Aunt Ruth and Lou Gerund's Practicing 15
4 Aunt Ruth's Go-Cart Has Gone 20
5 Aunt Ruth Herself and Henry VIII 25
6 Aunt Ruth Is a Superlative Super Relative 31
7 Aunt Ruth Is a Historic Anomaly 37
8 Aunt Ruth Brings It 45
9 Aunt Ruth and the Okay Chorale 52
10 Aunt Ruth Is Only in a Quandary 59
11 Frankly, My Dear Aunt Ruth 63
12 Aunt Ruth and Metaphors 67
13 Queen Ruth Borrows Your Ear 73
14 Aunt Ruth Fishes Tight, Fishes Deep 81
15 Aunt Ruth Burned or Burnt the Toast 85
16 Aunt Ruth and Double Negatives 89
17 Aunt Ruth Passes the Pasta Pesto Test 92
18 Aunt Ruth by the Numbers 95
19 Aunt Ruth Fragments 102
20 Aunt Ruth Loves Her Transitive Radio 107
21 The Ripcord Was Pulled by Aunt Ruth 115
22 Intransitive Verbs Rock 121
23 Aunt Ruth and Verbs Ala Mode 125
24 Aunt Ruth and the Tense Predicament, Part I 133
25 Past Participle Guilt (Intermission) 139
26 Aunt Ruth and the Tense Predicament, Part II 144

27 Aunt Ruth Hunts the Subjunctive Beast 152
28 Aunt Ruth Wants a Cheeseburger Bad 160
29 Aunt Ruth and the Comma Splice 165
30 Iowa Ruth and the Lost Commas 172
31 Aunt Ruth and the Independent Santa Clause 182
32 Aunt Ruth Is a Short Short-Order Cook, etc. 190
33 Aunt Ruth Is Spaced Out 195
34 Aunt Ruthii 201
35 The Aunt Who Baked the Fruitcake 206
36 Aunt Ruth and the Queen's Baseball Card 211
37 Aunt Ruth Is Non-Nonplussed 216
38 Bored of Aunt Ruth 224
39 Aunt Ruth and the Solar ... Ellipsis 228
40 Aunt Ruth Letters from Aunt Iquity 234
41 Aunt Ruth and the Synonym Bun 238
42 Aunt Ruth Has Got to Be Kidding 244
43 Aunt Ruth and the Peach Cobbler's Kitten 249
44 Aunt Ruth in the Oval Office 253
45 Aunt Ruth and the Train to Gettysburg 260

46 Common Rough Spots in English 265
    Active Voice Verbs 265
    Adverse and Averse 266
    Antonyms 266
    Anxious and Eager 266
    Bad / Badly 267
    Beside / Besides 267
    Bored Of 268
    Borrow / Loan / Lend 268
    Breath / Breathe 269

Bring / Take.. 269
Colons and Semi-colons... 269
Commas... 270
Comparatives / Superlatives.. 272
Could / Couldn't Care Less.. 273
Deep / Deeply and Other Adjectives Used as Adverbs................. 274
Different Of / Different From / Different Than............................ 276
Double Negatives... 276
Double Possessives.. 277
Double Subjects... 277
Drier / Dryer... 278
Ellipses.. 279
Etc. Usage... 280
Fragment / Sentence Fragment... 280
Gerund.. 281
Get, Got, Have Got / Have Gotten... 282
Go / Went / Gone... 283
H- Words with Articles A / An... 283
Homographs / Homonyms / Homophones................................... 284
Hopefully, Frankly, Seriously, and Other Sentence Adverbs....... 284
Imminent / Eminent.. 285
Ingenious and Ingenuous.. 286
Into / In to.. 286
Intransitive Verbs... 287
Let's.. 287
Lightening and Lightning.. 288
Linking Verbs... 288
Masterful and Masterly.. 290
Metaphor.. 290
Modes / Moods of Verbs.. 291

Myself, Yourself, Himself, and Other -Selves 292
Neither 293
Nonplussed 294
Numbers 294
Only 295
Passive Voice Verbs 296
Past and Passed 296
Plurals Ending in -i or -ii 297
Possessives with Appositives 297
Plus 298
Precede and Proceed 298
Simile 298
Subjunctives 299
Synonyms 300
Than 300
That and Other Relative Pronouns 301
Transitive Verbs 302
Verb Tenses 303
Verbs Ending in -T or -ED 310
Wait For / Wait On 311
Way and Ways 311
While / Although 312

47 Relevant Grammar Points in Each Story 313

48 Find the Story for Each Grammar Point 318

Preface and Acknowledgements

I am not the grammar police! Indeed, I consider myself to be more the grammar detective, exploring and learning (just like you) how certain words and certain phrases have certain meanings and certain uses in certain contexts with certain rules. When we know "how it works," we can be both more precise and less ambiguous in our communication.

You're rolling your eyes. English is not drudgery! One can have fun with English usage and grammar. Writers from Chaucer to Shakespeare to Poe to Lederer—and even Monty Python—proved that years ago. Okay, by a quick show of hands: How many of you are reading this book because you read (and enjoyed) the first Aunt Ruth book, *I Laid an Egg on Aunt Ruth's Head*? See? I knew it could work. Thanks for coming back!

Writing *Aunt Ruth: The Queen* ... has required a steady effort over several years and has involved the eyes (and the time) of many people. To Richard Lederer, Jerry Laffey, Kristi Eskelund, and Olivia Green: THANK YOU! Your words were pivotal in helping me ratchet the quality of this book up a notch. To my parents (Jay and Connie), thank you for your corrections and for being my marketing department. To my siblings (Jennie Steinhauser and Barry Schnoor), thank you for your feedback and heart-warming laughter. To my children—Alex, Nathan, Laura, and Aaron—thanks for your thoughts, corrections, and for continuing to be *my* grammar police! You are keeping me honest.

Most of all, to my wife Michelle: You have spent almost as much time reading, reviewing, and correcting this as I have in writing it. Your "let it simmer awhile" approach has turned this into a marvelous smorgasbord with a panoply of flavor. Thank you for your thoroughness, your encouragement, your honesty, and for doing everything I would have been doing had I not been working on this book!

Joel Schnoor
September, 2017

1
Aunt Ruth Loves Chocolate More Than Me

And that, ladies and gentlemen, completes the tour of our gastronomic paradise," said the hostess. "We thank you for coming to Chocolate Bliss, and we invite you to stop by the gift shop on your way out—you will simply love our new Chocolate Grammar Crackers, though I seriously doubt you will love them more than me."

I coughed and then blushed. Did our tour hostess really think that we loved her, or was this merely an unfortunate and misguided choice of using *than* as a preposition rather than as a conjunction? Did she doubt that we would love the Chocolate Grammar Crackers more than we loved her, or did she doubt that we would love the Chocolate Grammar Crackers more than she did?

I sank deep into thought. Myriad misunderstandings have occurred because of the confusion surrounding the dual nature of *than*—is it a conjunction or is it a preposition? Back in the old days, *than* was only a conjunction. So, if I wanted to say that I like pork chops more than Albert likes pork chops, I would say:

>I like pork chops more than Albert (or more than Albert does).

If I wanted to say that I like pork chops more than I like Albert, I would say:

>I like pork chops more than I like Albert.

That could have been the end of the story, with no room for ambiguity. However, someone somewhere—maybe a bureaucrat in Washington—had the bright idea that perhaps *than* is entitled to more than life as a conjunction. The possibility of the prepositional *than* ushers our language into the dawn of a new era, the era of confusion and difficult situations.

The problem with using *than* as a preposition is possibly best described in the final journal entry of a certain linguist who encountered a tribe of cannibals deep in the Congo:

> My angst at thinking I am among grammatical imbeciles has been greatly assuaged. When the chief said, "Let's see if we like pork chops more than him," I assumed that he meant "more than he," or, "more than he does," and I was dismayed at his error.
>
> However, I have since come to realize that this innovative fellow is actually using *than* as a *preposition*. Well, isn't this clever? So, he really does mean what he says, or to paraphrase, "Let's see if we like pork chops more than we like him." Anyway, signing off for now. The chief has invited me for dinner.

"Please hurry along, but remember our motto," continued our tour hostess, snapping me out of my reverie. "*Better choco-late than choco-never.*" She smiled, waved good-bye, and disappeared in a cloud of smoke with a rather dramatic flourish.

After our tour group had exited the room, Aunt Ruth bent over, ostensibly to tie her shoelaces. She stayed down a long time. When she stood up, we were the only two left in the hallway. "Let's go back in there," she whispered.

"Back in where?" I asked, oblivious to my aunt's clandestine wishes. I was still mulling over the unfortunate coining of a new adverb, *choco-never.*

"In there," she said, pointing to the laboratory from which we had just exited, "back to Lake Chocolate."

A sign in large red letters, outlined by a black skull and crossbones, proclaimed: "Welcome to Lake Chocolate. Keep Out Under Penalty of Torture and Dismemberment. Have a Nice Day."

"Wonder what that means?" chuckled Aunt Ruth. "Surely, they wouldn't really torture you, and who cares if we lose our membership? I don't recall joining anything here at Chocolate Bliss anyway."

"You might be surprised to discover that dismemberment does not mean the same as losing a membership," I sighed, knowing I was about as likely to stop Aunt Ruth from going in there as I would be at stopping the band from playing *Freebird* as the final encore at a Lynyrd Skynyrd tribute concert.

"I've got to see that giant pool of chocolate one more time," she exclaimed, suddenly pushing through the double doors with no hesitation. She was a relative on a mission.

I shook my head and followed her through the doors. I had no choice, did I?

"Oh my, don't you just want to dive into the sea of chocolate?" she asked.

"Um, no, not really."

"Well, I do."

"Aunt Ruth, I know you're crazy about chocolate, but—"

"I love chocolate more than anybody in the whole world."

"Do you love chocolate more than you love anybody in the whole world, or do you love chocolate more than anybody in the whole world loves chocolate?"

"You know," Aunt Ruth began, ignoring my question, "the ancient Greeks had like 46 or 47 different words for love. One of them—I think in Greek it was *chocolust*—meant a love for chocolate."

"Really?"

"No, not really. Oh my, that liquid chocolate is so inviting."

"Listen, Aunt Ruth, I wouldn't—"

"I know you wouldn't, my non-adventurous nephew, but I certainly would."

"Aunt Ruth, do you love chocolate more than me?"

"How much do you love chocolate?"

"No, I asked if you love chocolate more than me. I'm asking if you love chocolate more than you love me. If I wanted to compare your love for chocolate with my love for chocolate, I would ask you if you love chocolate more than I."

"You're confusing me, Nettle-headed Nephew."

"Okay, it's like this, Aunt Ruth. When *than* is used as a conjunction, it connects two sentences or clauses. I could ask if you love chocolate more than I, where 'more than I' really implies 'more than I do,' or 'more than I love chocolate.'

"So," I continued, "suppose I can drink a gallon of hot chocolate *faster than he*; that's the same as saying I can drink it *faster than he can*. Are you with me so far?"

"I think I'm getting one of my sick grammar headaches," sighed Aunt Ruth.

"Just hear me out, if you would," I said, "for your edification."

"Oh, please," she moaned.

"In today's English, *than* is often used as a preposition, and that's where the confusion arises. Now, we all know that prepositions need objects."

"Undoubtedly," she groaned.

"So, when *than* is used as a preposition, it requires an object, right?"

"Indubitably," she gasped.

"And, in fact, we can go so far as to say that when *than* is followed by an object pronoun, we know that *than* is a preposition."

"You like living on the edge, don't you?" she opined.

I ignored her sarcasm. "It's obvious, therefore, that when I say, 'The piranhas can eat the hamburger faster than me,' we see the object pronoun *me* and we know automatically that *than* is a preposition, right?"

"Obviously," she muttered.

"Therefore, what I mean is that the piranhas can eat the hamburger faster than they can eat me, NOT that the piranhas can eat the hamburger faster than I can eat the hamburger."

"Yes, naturally," she whispered.

"But, then what?" I asked emphatically, coming to the climax of my argument with vim and vigor. I was at the peak of my game. "What happens if you can't determine whether *than* is followed by an object or the subject of a conjunctive clause?"

"I think I'm nauseous," she uttered.

"No, you don't nauseate me a bit, Aunt Ruth. I feel fine. I would say you're not nauseous, only mildly annoying."

She rolled her eyes and I continued, undaunted.

"What happens, say, if we stated, 'The piranhas can eat the hamburger faster than you?' Is *than* being used as a conjunction or as a preposition? We can't tell, because we don't know if *you* is a subject or an object! Do we mean the piranhas can eat the hamburger faster than you can, or do we mean that those vicious little fish can eat the hamburger faster than they can eat you?"

All I heard from Aunt Ruth was a gentle snore.

"And THAT," I shouted, snapping Aunt Ruth awake from her snooze with a start, "that is the issue with using *than* as a preposition. It leaves the door wide open for this obfuscation."

"Are you done?" Aunt Ruth yawned.

"Yes," I stated defiantly, if not obstreperously.

"Well, I can see how that might be confusing," offered Aunt Ruth. "When did people start using *than* as a preposition?"

"Oh, Shakespeare and Milton were known to use *than* as a preposition."

"Good heavens, are you just going to stand idly by while those upstarts from England destroy our language?" Aunt Ruth smiled. "So, what you're telling me is that *than* has been used as a preposition for over four hundred years."

"I guess it's something like that," I admitted.

"It's almost a trend then, isn't it?"

"I suppose so."

"Then," she whispered quietly, "I have a little suggestion that I hope is helpful for you." She leaned toward me and yelled, "GET OVER IT!"

While I was still in a stupor, she said, "You know, I can't imagine any better way of going than this."

"Going where?" I asked.

She didn't answer. Instead, Aunt Ruth leaped into the air and performed a spectacular swan dive into the center of the enormous lake of chocolate.

Five judges appeared out of nowhere and gave her ratings of 10.0, 10.0, 9.9, 10.0, and 9.8.

Aunt Ruth slowly rose to the top, gasping when she finally surfaced. With her mouth right at the chocolate level, it was apparent that she was trying to tread chocolate while at the same time drinking it.

"It's ... so ... creamy!" she panted, delighted. "Nauseating Nephew, I have something to tell you."

"Yes, dear aunt?"

"I do love chocolate more than you."

"I understand, Aunt Ruth," I pouted. "I know I haven't been the perfect nephew. I know that I have failed you at times, and I hope that—"

Splash! A wave of chocolate gushed from the pool, caused by Aunt Ruth's intentional redirection of the warm, liquid chocolate straight at me.

"What was that for?" I asked.

"You're being silly. Of course I don't love chocolate more than I love you, but I guarantee that I love chocolate more than you do."

I felt better.

At that moment, I saw a large, dark shape in the water moving toward Aunt Ruth.

"Aunt Ruth, there's something swimming toward you, and it doesn't look like it loves chocolate more than you."

She turned and looked. The mysterious object was rapidly drawing closer.

"This can't be good," she said. "I think I probably ought to get out now."

She swam to the side of the pool. Drenched in chocolate, her clothes weighed a ton, but I managed to help pull her out in the nick of time.

The animal bellowed. It had huge antlers and seemed intent on becoming good friends with Aunt Ruth. I don't know what it would have done had it reached her, but I'm glad we didn't find out.

"What kind of creature is that?" asked Aunt Ruth.

"You won't believe this, but I think it's a chocolate moose."

"Oh, my," sighed Aunt Ruth. "Well ... I guess that means we should skedaddle out of here. Otherwise, we risk getting our 'just desserts'!"

2

Aunt Ruth, QE-II

We were somewhere off the coast of Greece when our ship sailed directly into a storm of titanic proportions. I had been lying in my bunk reading up on the Greek thinkers and heroes of old—guys like Sophocles, Pericles, Barnacles, Hercules, and Molecules—when the ship took a sharp roll to the port side, throwing me out of bed. We had strayed into some seriously nasty weather!

I decided to go topside to see if I could somehow help. Besides, this being the first night of the cruise, I had not yet met the captain. After donning my raincoat, I clung for dear life to the ship's rail as I fought the howling wind and driving rain on my way to the bridge. Finally, I saw the captain standing at the helm, wearing a yellow rain-suit and clutching the wheel with both hands. A large hood hid the captain's face.

As I approached, I could hear the captain belting out a song. "Mine eyes have seen the glory of the coming of the—"

I cupped my hands and yelled, "Captain, do you need any help?" I wasn't sure if the captain could hear me through the torrential rain.

Likewise, with cupped hands, the captain shouted back, "Call ... me ... Ishmael." Why did that voice sound oddly familiar?

"Hello, Ishmael. I've never met anyone with that name before," I said.

"Oh, that's not my name. I've just always wanted somebody to call me that. In answer to your question: Maybe. I hadn't planned on heading in to a storm."

I was having a hard time hearing in the surrounding din. "I may have misunderstood you, but for a moment there I thought you said, 'heading in to a storm,' rather than, 'heading into a storm,' which is what you obviously meant. Now, many people do not realize that *in to* and *into* are not the same thing."

"Whoa, Nellie," said the captain. "They're not?"

"They're not."

"Okay, stick around, buddy. I could use your grammatical wherewithal. I need to get a handle on this *in to* / *into* thing. Do understand that I am battling a wild storm and will need to embark out orders to fight it."

"With all due respect, Captain, that's *bark* out orders, not *embark* out orders. *Embark* is what you do when you begin a journey, leaving one place so that you can head to another."

"Oh, brother. Who died and made you the grammar expert?"

"Well, I'm no expert. I'm just a journeyman who cares about these matters. I try to be useful, but my aunt calls me her nauseating nephew."

"I know of only one person fitting your description. Sir, doff thy cloak and show thyself at once," ordered the captain. I complied.

"It's you!" the captain shouted, removing his hood and revealing that he was really a she, and in fact she was none other than Aunt Ruth!

"Aunt Ruth, what are you doing here?" I cried.

"I'm going to defeat this storm, if it doesn't defeat me first. And you?"

"I was expecting a comfortable cruise on the Queen Elizabeth II ocean liner—you know, QE-II. Somehow, I got on the wrong ship."

"Well, this is QE-II also. At least that's what it says on the side of my ship."

"You can't name it QE-II. That moniker is already taken! And this is your ship?"

"First, Mister, this is a fishing trawler, not a cruise ship. How you could have missed that fact, I don't know. Second, if you read the fine print, you'll see that the name of the ship is really Queen of English Grammar II. The name is written in a tiny font except for a 'Q', an 'E', and the 'II.' Now, let me take care of this storm. Back in a moment."

Aunt Ruth—Captain Ruth, that is—began barking out orders: "All hands on deck! Get me the boatswain, coxswain, Mark Twain, cosine, sine, tangent, arc tangent, and cosecant. I need someone to stow the cargo and bury the hatchet; someone to raise the mizzenmast and hoist the mainsail; and someone to moor the rigging and determine the angel—"

"Angle," I interrupted.

"—angle that we need to head in to the wind."

"Head *into* the wind, not *in to* the wind."

"Sigh," sighed Captain Ruth.

"Sigh," sighed all the shipmates in unison, obeying the captain's order.

"See what I have to put up with?" whispered Captain Ruth. She continued issuing orders. "Set the windlasses, find my sunglasses, and see if we have any jars of molasses. Flibber the gibbets. Store the star fruit in the starboard containers and marinate the chicken in the port containers. Lift the anchors, cover your ears for the big boom, and somebody find me some pieces of eight. Oh, and I need cotton swabs for the poop deck. Shiver me timbers! Yo ho ho and a bottle of ... how does that go?"

With that, the flurry of activity began, and Captain Ruth resumed singing, "He is trampling out the vintage where the—hey, has anyone seen my epic Steinbeck novel? I usually store it on the book shelf."

"Is now a good time to talk about *into* versus *in to*?" I asked.

"We're three pages into the story and haven't really addressed it yet, so ... yes, let's do it," said Captain Ruth.

"Okay, it's like this. *Into* is a preposition that can be used in a plethora of ways. Usually, *into* indicates heading or moving toward or to the inside of something. It can mean meeting or encountering something. You could find yourself sailing *into* a storm; you may one day move *into* a dorm. You may bump *into* your good friend Norm. You might sink your teeth right *into* a rich cake; you might tell your boss to jump *into* the lake (but I wouldn't advise it)."

"So," she said, "for example, at night I could dive *into* my bed?"

"You got it. Now, the thing you're heading into doesn't have to be a physical object or location. You could be heading into a circumstance or situation. The touchdown sent the crowd *into* a frenzy. Eating my sister's chocolate pie got me *into* a ton of trouble."

"Okay, so could I say: I hope to someday earn my way *into* the hallowed corridors of the English Grammar Hall of Fame?"

"Fat chance; but yes, you can certainly say that. Note that in many cases, *in* will suffice for *into*. I dropped my keys *in* my soup. The crackers fell *in* her tuba. If something does not indicate movement but is already there, you'll probably just use *in*. I left my sandwich *in* the car. I've had a pain *in* my side for weeks. I found a worm *in* my apple. You wouldn't say, 'I found a worm *into* my apple.' Anyway, that's more or less an overview of *into*."

"Okay, got it. So, what about *in to*?" asked Captain Ruth.

"With *in to*, the most common form is when *in* is part of a verb phrase (e.g., jump in, phone in, walk in, stop in, wander in), and *to* is used with the meaning *in order to*. Think of it like this: *a subject is entering some place in order to do something*, e.g., he jumped *in to* swim; she phoned *in to* ask; he's walking *in to* apply; Stella will stop *in to* chat; and he wanders *in to* shop. In none of those would you use *into* instead of *in to*.

"In another common form, *a subject is giving something to somebody*, e.g., hand the homework *in to* the teacher; turn the evidence *in to* the police, and call your comment *in to* the radio host. The *in* and *to* are not tied together. You could put the object between *in* and *to* and not affect the meaning, e.g., hand *in* the homework *to* the teacher; turn *in* the evidence *to* the police, and call *in* your comment *to* the radio host.

"Could you hand the homework *into* the teacher? Perhaps. Would that mean that you are stuffing the homework in the teacher's mouth or ear? I don't know. That doesn't seem reasonable.

"Look at this example: When Melvin found a mysterious watermelon sitting on the counter, he turned it in to the police. He didn't turn the watermelon *into the police* because that: 1) would be quite a feat of magic, and 2) a watermelon does not make a good law enforcement officer."

"Wow, does it have to be this complicated?"

"It's not that complicated, really. With a little practice, you'll have it down pat."

Captain Ruth smiled and began singing, mostly to herself, "In the beauty of the lilies—"

"Captain! Captain!" shouted the boatswain, appearing immediately on the scene. "Our navigational equipment was just swept overboard!"

"Don't tell me we're lost."

"We're lost! We're lost!"

"I told you not to tell me that. Whatever shall we do? We don't know how many degrees to turn off of true north. Maybe now is the time to panic."

"Now is not the time to panic," said a tall man with dark hair, a beard, and a stovepipe hat, suddenly appearing from out of nowhere. He handed Captain Ruth a sheet of paper. "Use this address, Aunt Ruth," he said. "You'll find it helpful."

At the top of the paper was the word *Gettysburg*.

"Gettysburg? What the … Mister, where did … hey, where did he go?"

The man was gone, just like that.

"How is this going to help?" muttered Captain Ruth. "We ain't anywhere near Pennsylvania."

"Just read it," I suggested. "Maybe there's a relevant clue or something."

"Four score and seven … hey, that's it! Four score and seven is how much … 87? Hey, boatswain, coxswain, Mark Twain, or somebody, turn the ship 87 degrees from true north. I'll bet you anything that's our way to safety."

"Captain, may I give you a quiz on *into* versus *in to* now?" I asked.

"Do I have a choice?"

"No."

"Let's get started then."

"All right, Captain. Fill in the blanks with **into** or **in to** and give me reasons for your choices."

> 1. When Edgar was done, he pushed his Hoover vacuum _____ the closet.
> (He pushed it to or toward the inside of the closet.)
>
> 2. At some point in their lives, Dr. Jekyll and Mr. Hyde entered _____ a period of disagreement.
> (They headed to or toward a circumstance or situation.)
>
> 3. Sidney swooped _____ save Lucy from losing her head.
> (The verb phrase is *swooped in*. Why did Mr. Carton swoop in? To save Miss Manette from *le guillotine*!)
>
> 4. We have stumbled _____ an arrangement whereby we both win.
> (We headed to or toward a circumstance or situation.)
>
> 5. I ran _____ Henry at the store today.
> (I met or encountered Henry.)
>
> 6. I saw the queen's carriage riding _____ town.
> (The queen was heading to or toward the inside of town.)
>
> 7. We have rushed _____ rescue the damsel in distress.
> (The verb phrase is *rushed in*. Why did we rush in? To rescue the damsel in distress!)
>
> 8. We turned the aardvark _____ the Lost and Found room.
> (The verb phrase is *turned in*. To whom was it turned in? To the Lost and Found room.)

"Nicely done, Captain Ruth!"

A short time later, after the ship had righted its course, we could see land, and the coxswain called out, "Captain, where to next?"

"See that light straight ahead? Sailing toward that light will lead us *into* the harbor. Then we can run *in to* eat at Baklava Bell. I'm starving!"

"Very good, Captain," I said. "You used *into* and *in to* correctly. Now, if you'll excuse me, I have to rush to the side of the ship. I don't feel well."

"Land blubber," Captain Ruth sighed.

"That's land lubber," I said, correcting her one last time.

As we parted ways, I could have sworn I heard her softly singing, "Aunt Ruth is marching on!"

Answers to Captain Aunt Ruth's Quiz

1) into   2) into   3) in to   4) into

5) into   6) into   7) in to   8) in to

3

Aunt Ruth and Lou Gerund's Practicing

Ring! Ring! Ring!

I picked up the phone and was instantly greeted by a voice singing, "Take me out to the ballgame, take me out to the crowd, buy me some—"

"Hello, Aunt Ruth," I yawned. I glanced at the clock, blinked my eyes, and looked again. It was 2:15 a.m.

"Top of the mornin' to you," said a cheerful Aunt Ruth.

"Bottom of the night," I sighed in return. "Aunt Ruth, I still have three or four hours of anticipated sleep before I'll be ready to wake up. I like sleeping. In fact, sleeping is one of my favorite gerunds."

"Wait, don't hang up," pleaded the voice on the other end of the line. "I have tickets! And what's a gerund?"

"I'll explain the gerund thing later. You have tickets for what?"

"I have tickets for … are you sitting down?"

"I'm lying here in bed," I moaned.

"Good enough. I have tickets for a Yankees baseball game!"

"A Yankees game? You called me up at two-something in the morning just to tell me that you have tickets to a Yankees game?"

"Not just any Yankees game … a 1927 Yankees game! I'm sure you remember that the 1927 Yankees team is widely considered to be, by far, the best baseball team in the history of the game."

"Yes, indeed!" I exclaimed. "The 1927 Yankees had the most fearsome batting lineup ever, aka Murderers' Row—wow, you have tickets! Really? Aunt Ruth, how did you score tickets for a '27 Yankees game?"

"Remember when I borrowed your time machine last week?"

"Yep. You said you were doing research on the rare tendency toward complete agreement found in nameless sea urchins or something."

"Right. I call it the Anonymous Anemone Unanimity Anomaly Project. Well, I made a side trip to the Bronx that I didn't reveal to you," she said, and I could picture her furtively casting her brow at me over the phone. "Anyway, the game is this afternoon, and I thought maybe you'd want to go see some of the old greats—Babe Ruth, Lou Gerund, and those guys."

Aunt Ruth didn't need to do any arm-twisting. After breakfast, I quickly dressed, picked up Aunt Ruth at her apartment, and then she and I took the time machine to the Big Apple, landing in New York City on a sunny afternoon in June, 1927.

As we walked into Yankee Stadium, we purchased our obligatory stadium brat wursts, and then we found our seats behind the Yankee dugout.

"Wow, these are great seats, Aunt Ruth! How did you get them?" I asked, but she ignored the question.

"Look at him, just look at him," crooned Aunt Ruth. "He's the only guy on the team who is out there warming up before the game."

I glanced up and saw a uniformed ball player with the number "4" on the back of his jersey. "Who's that?" I asked.

"That's Lou. Lou Gerund. *Practicing* is something Lou takes great pride in," said Aunt Ruth. "He works hard on his *batting*, and he diligently practices *fielding*."

"Lou certainly seems like a gerund kind of guy," I said.

The instant I finished uttering those words, a hush fell across the stadium. Not a sound could be heard. All eyes were upon me.

The man wearing number "4" called up to me from the field. "What do you mean that I'm a gerund kind of guy?" It was Lou Gerund.

Someone handed me a microphone. I cleared my throat. "Hello, Lou. My aunt," I explained, "just used three gerunds to describe you."

"Three gerunds? Has your aunt been talking to my wife and kid? The three of us are Gerunds."

"No, I'm talking about the grammatical gerund. You know what I mean, right?"

"Oh, the grammatical gerund," he nodded. "Yep, the good old grammatical … uh … gerund. Yes indeed, grammatical gerunds. Maybe you … uh … want to explain it to the rest of the crowd who may not be in the know."

"Certainly!" I cried with glee.

"Oh, brother," sighed Aunt Ruth.

I overhead a boy sitting behind us whispering to Aunt Ruth, "Is he always like this?"

Aunt Ruth whispered back, "Oh, don't get me started."

"Let me open this discussion," I began, "by explaining that a gerund is a word that started out its life as a present tense verb. Take any present tense verb: *dance, sing, run, give, fall,* and *fire,* to name a few. Then add 'ing' to the end of each of those words, dropping the final 'e' or doubling the final consonant where necessary. This gives you words like *dancing, singing, running, giving, falling,* and *firing.* Now, each of those -ing words is the present participle form of the corresponding verb, but each is also the gerund form of the verb."

I paused to let it sink in, and then I continued. "When we use that -ing word as a noun, we call the word a gerund (to pronounce *gerund,* think of *errand* with a *J-* sound at the beginning).

"So, Lou, my aunt said that practicing was something you take great pride in. Well, *practicing* is the present participle of the verb *practice*—you could say 'I am practicing' or 'I had/have been practicing'—and in those examples, *practicing* is being used as a verb. When Aunt Ruth says that *practicing* is something that you take great pride in, however, then it is being used as a noun. In fact, it (*practicing*) is the subject of the sentence.

"She also said that you diligently work at fielding. Again, *fielding* is the present participle of a verb (*field*), but it is being used as the object of the independent clause (i.e., you diligently work at what? You work at fielding). She also said you work on your batting. The thing you work on is *batting*, so *batting* is a noun and is also the present participle of the verb *bat*."

"Thank you, Nauseating Nephew," said Lou, taking the microphone from me. "I appreciate your explaining this gerund stuff to all of us. That is why … today (*today, today*, his voiced echoed) I consider myself (*self, self*) the luckiest man (*man, man*) on the face of the earth (*earth, earth*)."

Aunt Ruth whispered to me, "I think he used *explaining* as a gerund. Is that correct?"

"Yes, indeed," I whispered back. "He used *explaining* as a noun. He appreciates the *explaining*."

"Shouldn't he have said, 'I appreciate you explaining' instead of 'I appreciate your explaining'?"

"No, he said it correctly. Though he may appreciate me for explaining, it's really the explaining itself that he appreciates. He appreciates my explaining. So he said, 'I appreciate your explaining.' That is correct."

"Wow, I think I have reached an understanding of this gerund stuff. Whoopee!" shouted Aunt Ruth.

Moments later, a rotund figure in a Yankees uniform bearing the number "3" stepped out of the dugout and looked toward us.

"Hi, Babe," shouted Aunt Ruth, waving.

The man waved back. "Hi, Ruth. I just wanted to thank you again for letting us play in your stadium. It's always an honor."

"Why, you're quite welcome!" exclaimed Aunt Ruth. "Could you hit one out of the park for me this afternoon?"

"For you, Ruth, I'll hit two," said the man called Babe before disappearing back into the dugout.

"Wait … Aunt Ruth," I began, "did he say 'your stadium'?"

"Yes, my stadium. They don't call it 'The House That Ruth Built' for nothing!"

I spent the rest of the afternoon watching the 1927 Yankees play. In fact, *watching* the Yankees play was one of the best gerunds I've had in a long, long time.

4

Aunt Ruth's Go-Cart Has Gone

She wasn't following me. I was certain of that. When the light turned green, I eased my car forward. Through the lenses of my dark, incognito-guaranteed sunglasses, I glanced at the side mirrors and then at the rear view, and I saw nothing suspicious.

The goal, of course, was to have a ruthless (well, Aunt Ruth-less) Saturday. All that I really wanted was a couple of hours to myself, and I hoped I could spend those two hours driving a little go-cart around a track. Moments later, I pulled into the parking lot of Grammar World Theme Park. I felt cautiously optimistic.

Within a matter of minutes, I was sputtering around the track in a bright red go-cart, along with a handful of other go-carts. Tossing all caution to the wind, I pressed the proverbial "pedal to the metal," and the vehicle sped up to an exhilarating five m.p.h. If I had hair, I would have almost been able to feel the breeze running through it. No doubt about it—my go-cart was basically a self-propelled lawn mower with a seat and steering wheel attached. As I approached the half-way point of my first lap, I was feeling relaxed.

ZOOM!

A bright blue go-cart passed me like I was standing still. The driver of said vehicle was female and was wearing dark shades similar to mine. Her scarf flapped behind her like a flag in a gale force wind.

ZOOM!

She passed me again! Who was this surreptitious speedster? I was curious. Finally, as I neared the completion of my first lap ...

ZOOM! ZOOM!

She passed me twice more; then, she pulled over onto the shoulder and came to a stop. She motioned for me to do the same. I complied.

"Hello," said the covert car-driver. There was something familiar about her voice. "How many times have you went around the track?" she asked.

Silent grammar alarms were unleashed in my head. "Hi. Um ... I have *gone* around just once," I answered, hoping she would take the hint that she had used the wrong word—*went*—as the past participle of the verb *go*.

"Well," she said, "I have went four times around in the time it took you to go one time."

Somewhere, many miles away, a coyote howled in anguish.

"Excuse me, madam, but this has gone too far," I exclaimed.

"It has went too far?"

"No, it has gone too far!"

"Isn't *went* the past tense form of *go*?"

"Yes, it is. Now you go. Yesterday you went."

"So, I went four times. Is that not correct?"

"That is correct."

"I have went four times. Is that not also correct?"

"No, it's not correct. When you are using the auxiliary helping verbs *has*, *have*, and *had* to express something that happened in the past, you need to use the corresponding past participle. The past participle of *go* is *gone*. I have gone. I have gone one time. By the time I finished my first lap, you had gone four laps. Now, for completeness, you should note that the present participle is *going*. I am going around the lap. I have been going for the past five minutes."

"I knew I should have brung my aspirin … I think I'm coming down with one of my headaches," lamented the mysterious driver.

"Brung? No, ma'am, that's not acceptable. The past tense and past participle forms of *bring* are both *brought*. I brought my aardvark. I have brought my aardvark to the party."

"Now, wait a minute," she demanded. "It's ring / rang / rung, right?"

"Yes, like this: She wants to ring the bell; she rang the bell yesterday; and she has rung the bell more than anyone."

"And it's swing / swang / swung, yes?"

"Well, not exactly. See, it's like this … the past tense of *swing* is *swung*, and the past participle is also *swung*. He swung with all his might. He has swung the bat well all season. I will admit, though, that in some dialects you may hear *swang* used."

"I need some comfort food. I knew I should have boughten some chocolate when I was at the store," she sighed.

"Boughten? Again, you are mistaken," I said. "What's the past tense of *buy*?" I asked her.

"I think it's *buyed*."

"No, it's not. The past tense of *buy* is *bought*, and the past participle is *bought*."

"Really?"

"Really. The verbs *ring*, *swing*, *bring*, and *buy*, just to name a few, are all irregular verbs."

"Irregular? There are off-the-shelf pills that can help with that sort of thing."

"No medicines will help. Learning conjugation just requires old-fashioned, sleeves-rolled-up, hard work and memorization."

"I think I'm going to have to confer with my nauseating nephew to make sure this is right."

"Pardon? Your what kind of nephew?"

"My nauseating nephew is what I said," she replied.

I took off my glasses. "I am he of whom you speak, Aunt Ruth."

She gasped. "It's you! How did you know it was I?" She removed her glasses. "I thought I was incognito," she said. "Anyway, whatever happened to the 'just add –ed' rule for making past tenses of verbs?"

"That works for many past tense verbs, but not for the irregular verbs."

"I know you've gone over this with me before, but could you try it again? It doesn't seem to be sticking. What are some of the commonly used irregular verbs?"

"I'm glad you asked! Ones that I periodically hear and that seem to give people trouble are some of the following:

see / saw / seen

> I see a bald eagle flying over the barbershop.
> I saw a grizzly bear wading in the rapids for Mr. Godot.
> I have seen salmon swimming in streaming video.

drink / drank / drunk

> I think I'll drink lemonade with dinner tonight.
> I drank a lot of water yesterday.
> I have drunk kombucha before and lived to tell about it!

sink / sank / sunk

> I hope our fishing boat doesn't sink again today.
> My canoe sank yesterday.
> His boat has sunk every day this week.

drive / drove / driven

> I can drive my red wagon to your house.
> Aunt Ruth drove to Grammar World Theme Park.
> We have driven to the zoo three or four times.

swim / swam / swum

> Watch me swim across the English Grammar Channel.
> I swam eight laps this morning.
> I have swum for sixteen years (with intermittent breaks).

sing / sang / sung

> When I wake up, I just want to sing.
> I sang the school's fight song all the way to the game.
> I have sung the blues ever since losing my indigo crayon."

At that moment, I heard the dinging of my cell phone alarm.

"That's enough for now," said Aunt Ruth, hopping back into her bright blue car. "It must be time to vamoose."

"Where are you going?"

"Your cell phone's alarm dang."

"What? *Dang* is not a verb. It's not even the past tense of a verb."

"Isn't it ding / dang / dung?"

"No, it's ding / dinged / dinged."

"You're kidding."

"No, I'm not. *Ding* is a regular verb."

"Speaking of which, what are you going to do with your new boat?"

"What new boat?"

"I think you are getting a little dinghy. Anyway, see ya!"

"Aunt Ruth, you can't end on that pun! We need one more example."

"Why? We are about to *run* out of time."

"I think we already *ran* out of time. Yep. We *have run* out of time!"

"I don't know where the time has went."

"Grrr! Aunt Ruth, it's where the time *has gone*!"

5

Aunt Ruth Herself and Henry VIII

Thwump! Thwump! Whirrrr thwump! We came to a sudden stop and silence filled the air. Though the landing was a bit rough, the time machine seemed to be none the worse for the wear. The problem was that I didn't know where we were, nor did I know *when* we were. The goal was London, 1964. Did we succeed? That was the question.

I opened the lid, and Aunt Ruth took a quick peek outside. "Looks like this might be the British Isles," she said with a smile. "Thank you for bringing *myself* to England!"

"Thank you for bringing *me* to England," I said, correcting her.

"I brought you here?" she asked, with an inquisitive look on her face. "No, I don't think so. You brought myself here, I believe."

At that moment, she was interrupted by a booming voice that appeared to be immediately outside our vehicle. The person was singing:

> "I wake up in the morning and I'm glad that I'm the king,
> I am so very happy and it makes me want to sing!
> There is one thing that troubles me—it causes lots of strife—
> I must remove my current spouse and find another—

"Thunder and blazes! What on earth do we have here? What in the royal name of King Henry VIII of England is in this box?"

"Aunt Ruth," I whispered, "I have a sneaking suspicion that things aren't looking so great for us right now. Keep your head about you."

At that moment, I heard the sound of rapping on the outside of the time machine, and a deep voice bellowed, "Out, ye stranger, ye alien, ye wizard!" I stepped out and found a behemoth of a man who held in his hand an enormous roasted turkey leg.

The man cowered the moment he set eyes on me, and his brave facade disappeared faster than you can say Tower of London. "Oh, please don't cast a magical spell on me! I am Henry VIII, King of England, and I'll give you anything you ask," he said, visibly shaken and upset but apparently still hungry as he took a ravenous bite from the turkey leg. "Who might you be, a traveler from another planet?" inquired the king, wiping his mouth on his sleeve. "Where you be headed?"

"Where I be headed? Do you mean to where am I going? Well, I was attempting to go back in time to England—specifically, London in 1964."

The king belched a loud and royal belch. Then, timidly and apologetically, he said, "Excuse me. You wanted to go *back* to 1964? I don't have an inkling what you're talking about. The year is 1543."

"I accidentally took a left turn at the sixteenth century," I sighed.

"What?"

"Never mind."

"You know, you startled the living daylights out of *myself* a few minutes ago," said the king, his timidity fading and his courage rising.

"You startled the living daylights out of *me*," I said, correcting him.

"What? How could I have startled you?" exclaimed the king.

"Oh, he does this to me all the time," sighed an empathetic Aunt Ruth, standing up and climbing out of the time machine.

"Another one!" gasped the king. "This one is a stunningly beautiful lady from the future! It appears that all bodes well for this planet. To whom do I have the honor of extending my welcome? Tell me your name. I at least deserve to know who you are!" He smiled and winked at Aunt Ruth, who blushed.

"I am Aunt Ruth," said Aunt Ruth, "but you may call me Ruth."

"I am pleased to meet *yourself*, Ruth," said the king.

"I am pleased to meet *you*," I said, correcting the king.

"And I am pleased to meet ... wait a minute, I've already met you," replied the king, confused.

"Excuse me again, your royal highness, sir," I tried explaining, "but you should have said, 'I am pleased to meet you.' 'I am pleased to meet yourself' is not correct."

"How many of you are in there?" asked the king, frowning at me and ignoring my correction.

"Just us two chickens," said Aunt Ruth with a coy smile.

Resuming his royal confidence in full stride, Henry VIII asked, "May I call you Ruth VIII?"

"Sure, if I may call you Hank VIII."

"Deal," said the king.

She leaned toward me and whispered a question that was meant only for my ears.

"This guy is wearing tights and I think he's still in his pajamas. Is he really the king?"

"Indeed, I am the king, Madame, and you are to serve *myself*," said the king, apparently overhearing the conversation.

"You are to serve *me*," I said, again correcting the king.

"Are you claiming to be the king?" said Henry VIII, bristling.

"No, but I am attempting to improve your grammar," I responded. There was silence.

"I think your goose is cooked, my non-diplomatic nephew," muttered Aunt Ruth.

"Goose? Where? I'm still hungry," said Henry VIII, looking around. "Anyway, who is this nifty nephew?" he exclaimed.

"Nifty?" Aunt Ruth and I said, in unison.

"Yes, nifty. I love grammar!" said the king. "In fact, grammar is my third favorite hobby, right behind food and wives."

Eager to continue this grammatical discussion, I said, "I'm your grammar consultant and I'm here to help you." I handed him my business card. "If it pleases your highness, allow me to try to explain how to use *myself*, *yourself*, and those other -self words. Remember, if this is too confusing, in a few hundred years you will be able to find further help on my web site."

Turning toward me, Henry VIII said, "Prithee, proclaim my offense."

"What?" I asked.

"That's how we talk. I mean, please tell me what I'm saying incorrectly. Let me ask you this, oh noteworthy nephew. When should *myself* be used, or *yourself*, *himself*, *herself*, and *itself*? In fact, what about *themselves* and *ourselves*? But make it quick, please. I'm very busy. I have a nation to run."

"Well, there are two general cases that will cover most of your needs—reflexive and emphatic."

"Reflexive and emphatic? Okay, good. Thank you for clarifying. This has been utterly helpful to myself. May I go now?" asked the king.

"Nope. You don't get it yet. This will only take a minute, though."

"All right, please continue," said the king.

"Your royal highness, sir, the reflexive case is something like this: I hurt myself, I fed myself, I hit myself in the head with a hammer."

"Or chopped it off with an ax?" asked the king, smiling.

"Yes, chopping it off with an ax would work fine here," I agreed, "assuming it's possible to chop off one's own head. So, do you get it?"

"You mean that's it? I don't get it."

"Okay," I tried again, "it's like this. When the subject is doing something to someone, and that someone is the same person as the subject, then one of the -self words can be used. However, if the subject is different than the person receiving the action, then the regular object pronouns (e.g., me, you, him, her, etc.) are used."

I let that sink in for a moment. Aunt Ruth, sound asleep and snoring, was leaning against the wall, but Henry VIII seemed alert and interested.

"I, and only I, can perform an action on myself," I continued, "but you cannot perform an action on myself. You or anyone else can only perform an action on me. For example:

> I treated myself to an ice cream cone last night (I can treat *myself*.)
> You treated me to an ice cream cone last night (You can treat *me* but not *myself*.)

"Similarly, you and only you can perform an action on yourself. I or anyone else cannot perform an action on yourself; I or anyone else can only perform an action on you.

> You bought yourself a copy of *I Laid an Egg on Aunt Ruth's Head*.
> He bought you a copy of *I Laid an Egg on Aunt Ruth's Head*.

"If 'they' is the subject, they might do something to themselves, but if they do something to anyone else, just use the simple object pronouns.

> They locked themselves out of the house.
> They locked us out of the house.

"Similarly, if 'we' is the subject, then we might do something to ourselves, but if we do it to anyone else, the simple object pronouns apply.

> We made ourselves dinner.
> We made them dinner.

"I might say," I went on, "that something is annoying to me or annoying to you or him or her or it, but I wouldn't say that it was annoying to myself, yourself, himself, herself, or itself, unless the subject and the object are the same. One could say, 'I annoy myself,' or, 'He annoys himself.'"

"Oh, I get it!" exclaimed the king. "It's called reflexive because it is as though the subject looks in the mirror and sees his reflection. When the subject is doing something to himself (or herself, or itself), I'm free to use a -self word."

"Right, and the other case—the emphatic—is when the pronoun is used for emphasis, like this:

> I myself ate a gallon of ice cream last night."

"Wow, that sounds good."

"The grammar explanation?"

"No, the ice cream. But the grammar lesson makes sense. I suppose I could have taught myself, but I'm glad that you came and taught me. I'm a busy guy—you've seen it yourselves. I, myself, am hoping to put a turkey leg onto the tables of every family in my kingdom. Just a turkey leg a day makes the medicine go down, as they themselves say."

"They do say that," I agreed. "Anyway, I think you have the whole thing with myself, yourself, himself, and the other -self words all squared away."

"I believe so. Now, my dear Ruth VIII and her nifty nephew, would you two be my guests on a carriage tour of the estate?"

Aunt Ruth looked at me. I nodded.

"We'd love to, Hank VIII."

At that moment, a woman walked into the courtyard. Henry VIII said, "This is Anne, the lady-in-waiting to my wife. She will accompany us. Everyone stay right here. I'll go get the carriage and I'll be right back."

I asked, "Is the carriage a four-door hatchback from the House of York?"

"No, it's a Tudor," said Anne.

"A two-door sedan?" asked Aunt Ruth. "Are you sure that we'll all fit?"

"Yes," said Anne. "I can climb in back with the king."

"Okay," said Aunt Ruth, "but be careful. With these Tudors you really have to watch your head."

Aunt Ruth Is a Superlative Super Relative

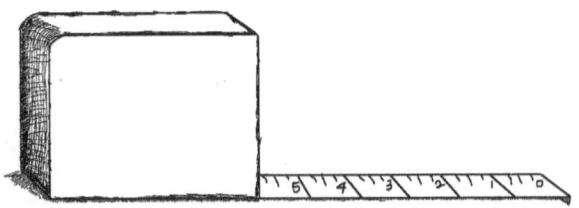

The bright sky—brighter than the previous day's sky and perhaps the brightest in months—greeted me as I stepped outside to tackle some yard work. Rake in hand and deep in thought—deeper than usual and maybe the deepest in a year—as I contemplated the decline of the subjunctive in American writing, I was startled to hear a piercing whistle that reminded me of a bomb falling from a fighter plane in a bad World War II movie. I looked up. Sure enough, I spied a blue and red *something* plummeting from the sky. The colors were stunning—the falling object was definitely bluer and redder than most objects I had noticed zipping through the skies, and possibly it was the bluest and reddest object I had ever seen.

I trained my binoculars on said object. What I saw made my heart jump. A rather fubsy, masked woman wearing a bright red cape and a blue skin-tight outfit—she looked like twenty gallons of blueberry ice cream squeezed into a fifteen-gallon garbage bag—was hurtling downward through the atmosphere, possibly doing more damage to the ozone layer than the 1982 Hair Spray Convention. Her jowls were flapping in the air like a basset hound driving a convertible through a wind tunnel.

As this astronomical enigma was falling through the friendly skies, I kept the binoculars on her out of curiosity. I won't say that she was fat—I'm not sure that's quite politically correct these days—but she was of such girth that she could have had her own moons orbiting about her.

I did some quick back-of-the-napkin calculations as she drew closer. If she did nothing to alter her trajectory, she was on course to land smack dab in the middle of my backyard.

At that moment, a big semi tractor-trailer rig showed up. "Sorry, I'm late," said the driver. "I went to the wrong house. Hope I'm not interrupting your grammar lesson. Anyway, where do you want the stuff?"

"Shhh! We're in the middle of a story that's being written live!"

"What do you mean, 'written live'? Can't I be edited out?"

"No matter. Put the stuff in the middle of the backyard—and hurry!"

He hurried. Moments later, a mountain of bubble-wrap filled the yard.

I found the falling *phenom* again with the binoculars, and the countdown began. Ten ... nine ... eight ... she was coming down so fast there was a trail of sparks behind her ... seven ... six ... five ... four ... I began worrying that the impact might damage the tulip bulbs I had just finished planting ... three ... two ... one ... thwump-pop-pop-pop-thwump-pop-pop-pop! A series of bubble-bursts sounding like a giant bowl of Rice Krispies rattled off, and then all was silent.

Dazed and more than a little confused, she popped her head out of the bubble-wrap pile and yelled, "It's a bird; it's a plane; it's ... it's ... it's the Super Relative! In the name of grammatical correctness, I make my way around our fair city in search of misused, erroneous, and sometimes even felonious occurrences of superlatives and comparatives everywhere. It is I, the Czarina of the Comparative and the Sultana of the Superlative."

She removed her mask. It was Aunt Ruth! "Here I am," she shouted, "in all my glory, much gloriouser than yesterday, and perhaps the gloriousest I've been all—"

"Whoa, Aunt Ruth, wait a second," I interrupted. "*Gloriouser* and *gloriousest*? Those aren't words!"

"Sigh," she sighed. "That's the problem. When I studied to get this job, I researched how to fly—well, the aerodynamics of being blasted out of a cannon—in-depth, but I forgot to learn about superlatives and comparatives. So, my nature-loving nephew, I am here for your help. Could you teach this old, super relative about superlatives and comparatives?"

"Sure," I said. "Teaching you grammar would bring me great joy."

"Really?"

"No, not really, but I wouldn't be able to look at myself in the mirror if I ignored the cries of a distraught soul in grammatical distress. Besides, I figure you would prefer a grammar class over the alternative, the water torture thing."

Aunt Ruth rolled her eyes and said, "That is so benevolent of you."

"Anyway," I continued, "a *comparative* is when we are comparing two things. Which one is the bigger buffoon. Which one has the smaller brain. Which one is more obnoxious. Which one is a better alligator wrestler. Which one is better or worse at whatever. Take height, for example. Let's look at how tall, or short, we are. You are *shorter* than I am. I am *taller* than you. *Taller* and *shorter* are comparatives because we are using them to compare you and me. *Taller* is comparing 'tallness' and *shorter* is comparing 'shortness.' Got it so far?"

"So far so good," she replied.

"I have two chimpanzees. The *younger* chimp likes to throw food at the *older* chimp. Note that it's not *youngest* / *oldest*, but *younger* / *older*, because there are two chimpanzees that we are comparing."

"Really? Wow. Anyway, I see."

"Good! It's the same idea for *superlatives*, but we're comparing three or more things, and we want to show which thing has the most or least of whatever it is that we are comparing. Who is the tallest; who is the shortest. Who is the best at something; who is the worst at something. Take age, for example. I am *younger* than you. Our friend Clovis is *younger* than you also, but Clovis is *older* than I. To compare all three of us at the same time, we need to use superlatives, and we'd say that I am the *youngest* and you are the *oldest*. *Youngest* and *oldest* are superlatives. *Youngest* is comparing 'youngness' and *oldest* is comparing 'oldness.'"

"What are the rules for making comparatives and superlatives?" she asked.

"I don't think I would call them rules, because they're not necessarily hard and fast. There are exceptions."

"Exceptions? In English? Good heavens, who would have thought!" exclaimed Aunt Ruth, breaking into a laugh.

"All right, my dear aunt, let's take a stab at this," I began. "First, let's talk about one-syllable words."

"Some of my favorite words are one-syllable words, like dog, cat, fish, and worm," said Aunt Ruth.

"I guess I should back up a moment," I sighed.

"Why, do I smell bad?"

"No, not at all. I mean there's more to explain before we begin. Comparatives and superlatives come from adjectives, not nouns."

"But what if I have a pet that's a dog, and I have another pet that's even more a dog? Couldn't I say one is *dogger* than the other?" asked Aunt Ruth.

"Dogger? Really? Something is either a dog or it's not a dog. If you have two things that are dogs, one cannot be more of a dog than the other, genetic mutations not withstanding."

"Okay, I guess *dogger* is out."

"Now, Aunt Ruth, if a one-syllable word ends in a single consonant and has a short vowel sound, often the comparative or superlative can be formed by doubling the consonant and adding -er or -est, respectively, at the end. Would you care to try some examples?"

"I do think I know this one. Some of my favorite words of this type are: dim, dimmer, dimmest; thin, thinner, thinnest; fat, fatter, fattest; hot, hotter, and hottest." Aunt Ruth glowed with pride. "So, I could say that I'm hotter than you. That's a comparative. And I could say that between you, me, and Elmer Fudd, I'm the hottest. That's a superlative."

"Okay," I said, "here's another rule. If you have a one-syllable word ending in -e, the comparative can be formed by adding -r to the end, and the superlative can be formed by adding -st to the end. Want to try some examples?"

"Sure. How about: nice, nicer, nicest; fine, finer, finest; and sane, saner, sanest?" offered Aunt Ruth.

"Good! Now," I continued, "for one-syllable words that have more than one vowel or that end in more than one consonant, add -er for the comparative and add -est for the superlative. Examples include light, lighter, and lightest; and great, greater, and greatest."

"So tight, tighter, and tightest are in this category," said Aunt Ruth.

"Very good. Now, the next rule is this: If the word is two syllables and ends in -y, you can change the -y to -i and then for the comparative add -er and for the superlative add -est.

"Examples of this," I continued, "include: funny, funnier, funniest; loony, loonier, looniest; lumpy, lumpier, lumpiest; noisy, noisier, noisiest; sickly, sicklier, sickliest; goofy, goofier, goofiest; and scary, scarier, scariest."

"Are you open to an astute question from the audience?" she asked.

"Of course. Fire away."

"What about one-syllable words that end in -y? I'm thinking specifically of: *dry, shy,* and *sly.*"

"Ah, good question. This is an area where there are exceptions, and you pretty much have to learn these individually (i.e., memorize them).

> dry: drier, driest
> shy: shyer, shyest
> sly: slyer, slyest"

"So it's *drier* and not *dryer*?" she asked.

"Yes. A *dryer* is what you put your clothes in to dry them after washing."

"Well, that doesn't seem too hard," chirped Aunt Ruth.

"Good! Okay, here's the last rule. If the word is two syllables and does not end in -y, or if the word is three or more syllables, then you do not change the form of the adjective. Instead, you can use words such as *more* or *less* for the comparative and *most* or *least* for the superlative."

Aunt Ruth's eyes lit up. "So I think this means: insane, more insane, most insane; anxious, more anxious, most anxious; worried, more worried, and most worried. By jove, I think I've got it! Well Natty Nephew, I must be on my way," she said, putting her arms up in the air.

"Not so fast, superlative super relative! I have one more part to this lesson. Did you know that it is not proper English to say *funner* and *funnest* as the comparative and superlative for *fun*?"

"No, really? Why?"

"The word *fun* is not really an adjective. *Fun* is a noun. I am going to have *fun*. I like *fun*. We would not say—well, we might, but we shouldn't—that we went to a fun party, but rather an enjoyable or amusing party."

"Ugh. I don't like that exception. I use *fun party* all the time."

"I do too. I'm just heightening your awareness. For comparatives, you could say *more fun* or *less fun*; use *most fun* or *least fun* for superlatives."

Aunt Ruth shrugged and said, "Well, at least I picked the most prettiest day to fly."

I sighed. "You said, 'most prettiest.' That's bad."

"Why?"

"That's called a double comparison. *Prettiest* is already a superlative. It's the best. It's at the top. You can't go higher than the highest. So, adding *most* doesn't make sense."

"What if I wanted the opposite of prettiest? Would I say it's the ugliest day?"

"*Ugliest* works, yes, or you could say *least pretty* if you wanted to compare things on a sort of 'prettiness scale' and wanted the least of these."

"All right. Well, I've got to fly now," she said, spreading out her arms and rising into the air.

"Wait, you can't really fly. How are you doing that?"

"I'm not sure, but it's the excitingest thing I've ever done!" she cried.

"Grrr. *Most exciting*," I corrected as she passed over head, barely clearing the roof of the house before sailing out of sight.

Aunt Ruth Is a Historic Anomaly

Dear Donald Wigglethorpe, Sr.,

I read in this morning's Gazette that you are seeking a docent for your living history farm, Dyson Estates. I was an history teacher for years and would love the opportunity.

Yours,
Aunt Ruth

Dear Aunt Ruth,

Thank you for your correspondence, but "an history" teacher? Really? Please learn how to use articles and then try again. Dyson Estates prefers decent, deserving docents. Also, there is no need for the comma between "Wigglethorpe" and "Sr." That has been out of vogue for decades.

Sincerely,
Donald Wigglethorpe Sr.

Dear Donald Wigglethorpe Sr.,

Of course I know it's "a history" and not "an history." That was just a typo on my part. Please forgive me. I still hope you will consider me a decent deserving docent. I've always admired Dyson Estates as an historical locale.

Yours,
Aunt Ruth

Dear Aunt Ruth,

Ahem, far be it from me to be a grammar snob, but we have a couple of items in your recent letter that need to be addressed.

First, you wrote "decent deserving docent" instead of "decent, deserving docent." When you stack adjectives in a list, you should put a comma between them unless the adjective(s) closest to the noun are considered to be part of the noun. For example, at our annual Dyson Days, we sell dunking doughnuts. These are distinct from our other doughnuts, the glazed doughnuts. In fact, we sell dunking doughnuts for a dime less than we sell our glazed doughnuts. So "dunking" here is considered almost part of the name of the item, that is, "dunking doughnuts." Dunking doughnuts are their own "thing," if you will. For example, then, we could call them "dry dunking doughnuts" rather than "dry, dunking doughnuts."

Next, you said "an historical." Technically, it should be "a historical," though some Americans do tend to use "an historical."

Now, please leave me alone. I am much too busy planning this season's Dyson Days to deal with you.

Sincerely,
Donald Wigglethorpe Sr.

p.s. I decided that I need dancing docents. Surely, you don't dance.

Dear Donald Wigglethorpe Sr.,

I stand corrected. I read your letter while sitting on the bench in a herb garden I have. You are right about "a historical." Please accept my apologies. And I do dance.

Yours,
Aunt Ruth

Dear Aunt Ruth,

You are impossible. I can't let a sleeping grammatical error lie uncorrected. You said you were in "a herb garden." I presume that you mean "an herb garden" (unless, of course, you are British, in which case your herb has the aspirated "h" and, therefore, "a herb garden" is perfectly fine).

You do dance?

Well, I'm sorry, but this year at Dyson Days we're going to have only dancing docents from Delaware.

Sincerely,
Donald Wigglethorpe Sr.

Dear Donald Wigglethorpe Sr.,

Dover, Delaware. November 27, 1934. You can verify it with my nauseating nephew. He's a heir of mine.

Sincerely,
Aunt Ruth

Dear Aunt Ruth,

You're over 80? And you still dance? Oh, it's "an heir," not "a heir." Please pay attention to your aspirations. If your "h" is aspirated—that is, if pronouncing the "h" makes the flame of a candle waver or go out (think My Fair Lady)—then the "h" is aspirated. No flicker, no aspiration.

Sincerely,
Donald Wigglethorpe Sr.

Dear Donald Wigglethorpe Sr.,

Yes, it's true that I'm over 80 and that I don't have an hair on my head that's not gray, but what of it? I can still dance.

Yours,
Aunt Ruth

Dear Aunt Ruth,

We really must stop corresponding like this. Would you cease and desist including grammar errors in your letters?

It's "a hair," not "an hair." Sigh.

In addition, I'll have you know that I need a dozen dancing docents, and I want them to all come from the same environment so that they know each other and can practice learning the required dancing moves. I guess that leaves you out of the picture. I'll be recruiting twelve students at a nearby university.

Sincerely,
Donald Wigglethorpe Sr.

Dear Donald Wigglethorpe Sr.,

You need a dozen? I recruited and found eleven others this morning who will join me in being your dozen, dancing docents. We are all from Delaware. We all live in the same block of the neighborhood and all are members of the local community center. We have a dancing class together. In addition, all of us are former history teachers and have all researched the history of Dyson Estates.

So ... are we in, or should I contact my attorney, Mr. J.S. Elderberry, III?

Yours,
Aunt Ruth

Dear Aunt Ruth,

Wow, you're good. Yes, you get the position. If you accept the offer, then I need you and your friends to show up on Thursday morning next week, seven o'clock sharp.

It's J.S. Elderberry III with no comma.

Warm regards,
Donald Wigglethorpe Sr.

Dear Donald Wigglethorpe Sr.,

It'll be a honor! I'll tell the girls, and we'll be there on time next week. See you then!

Cheers,
Aunt Ruth

Dear Aunt Ruth,

One thing that I need to address before your arrival is your horrific usage of articles when used before words that begin with the letter "h." The whole key to success with this particular rule hinges around the question: Is the "h" pronounced or is it not?

If the "h" is pronounced, as in words like history, historical, hope, hair, head, his, hymn, Hawaii, hotel, hero, and howdy, use "a" as the article. As I've said before, this pronounced "h" is what we call aspirated.

You have a hope, a habit, a hobbit, or a hammer.

If the "h" is not pronounced, i.e., not aspirated, as in words like herb, heir, and honor, use "an" as the article.

You have an herb or an heir. It would be an honor.

I should point out that the word humble, though usually pronounced with the aspirated "h", is not pronounced with an aspirated "h" in some places in the South. So, you could say "a humble" if aspirated and "an humble" if not.

Now, I should tell you that it's been a privilege for me to work with you on your grammar these past few weeks. It has definitely helped me refresh and hone my fine grammar skills, and I hope that it has been helpful to you as well.

See you Thursday.

I'm looking forward to having you try our delicious, dry dunking doughnuts. They're delectable!

Fond regards,
Donald

Dear Aunt Ruth,

Congrats to you and your retinue for the brilliant performances during Dyson Days last week! The reviews and comments from the spectators indicated that the Dancing Delaware Docents were by far the most popular item in the festival. Your reputation grew so quickly around town that our attendance was up over 500% from last year's attendance.

Now, I do have a question for you. Though our net revenue exceeded all expectations, our budget sheets are indicating that you and your girls consumed an enormous number of the complimentary dry dunking doughnuts.

If you did, that's fine. After all, you were our big money-maker. I just need to verify for future accounting and planning purposes.

Anyway, thanks again and I look forward to doing this again next year.

Respectfully yours,
Donald

Dear Donald,

Well, I tried one glazed doughnut. It was too soggy, but ... a dozen decent, deserving, daring, demanding, dancing Delaware docents don't deny devouring desirable, delicious, dry dunking doughnuts daily during Dyson Days.

Maybe we could limit our consumption next year, perhaps setting the max at two doughnuts a hour per person.

Thanks and see you next year!

Regards,
Aunt Ruth

Dear Aunt Ruth,

Great, thanks!

It's an hour, not a hour.

(Sorry to have to have the last word …)

Anyway, thank you again for giving such an heroic effort. You wowed all of us!

I apologize for the brevity of this note. I have to catch a flight to our other living history farm—on the French Riviera—so that I can interview candidates for the employment opportunities there.

Say, you don't know anyone who speaks French, do you?

As Always,

Donald

Dear Donald,

I think you meant "a heroic effort," n'est-ce pas?

Au revoir,

Aunt Ruth

8

Aunt Ruth Brings It

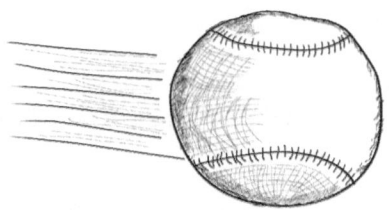

We were up by a run, but the other team had runners on second and third with no outs in the bottom of the ninth inning in the last game of the regular season. Our playoff hopes were dependent on the outcome of this game, and the situation was looking precarious. Our starting pitcher was in trouble.

Coach, head down, walked to the mound, where I was standing with our pitcher. "One more inning in that arm?" he asked.

I shook my head. "I don't think so, Coach. We need a fresh arm." I was the catcher, and it was my job to know how well our pitchers were throwing.

Coach took the ball from the pitcher's hand and signaled to the bullpen. Normally, two pitchers—one right-handed and one left-handed—would already be warming up, and Coach would raise his right hand if he wanted the right-handed pitcher and his left hand if he wanted the southpaw. This time, though, Coach put his hands on his belly, swung his hips in a big circle as if he were trying to keep a hula hoop going, and then he waddled like a penguin. He looked like an overweight Charlie Chaplin doing a poor imitation of a constipated hula dancer demonstrating the Macarena.

"What are you doing, Coach?" I asked.

"It's time for her," he said mysteriously.

"Her?"

"The indomitable one, she who banters fearlessly with pirates and emperors, artists and great composers. I'm calling in Aunt Ruth, our secret weapon. She's going to pitch us to the championship."

"Whatever you say, Coach." Aunt Ruth had spent the whole season on the bench, but with our top four relievers all out with the flu, I guess Coach figured it was time to give her a chance.

Aunt Ruth jogged out to the mound. "Aunt Ruth, whatcha got?" I asked, expecting her to say the usual arsenal of pitches—fastball, curve, sinker, and slider.

"Mmm Hmph, Phmph Hmph, buh ththhmph, mmnn nmph."

"Aunt Ruth, take that wad of gum out of your mouth. I can't understand a word."

She yanked a mass of gum, a glob as big as my fist, from her mouth and tossed it over to the first base line, where it landed with a plop.

"You want to know what pitches I took with me?" she asked.

"No," I said, "I want to know what pitches you *brought* with you."

"Wait a moment," she said. "I was in the bullpen. Coach called me in. I *took* some pitches with me, right?"

"Sure. But—from my perspective, at least—you *brought* some pitches with you. That is, Coach signaled for you because he hoped you would *bring* your pitches to the mound. So, you *brought* your pitches, or at least I hope you did."

"Now," began Aunt Ruth with a puzzled expression, "what if I were still in the bullpen. Would I be figuring out which pitches to *take* with me or which pitches to *bring* with—"

"Hey," I interrupted, "we've got a game to play. There are fans, people sitting in the stands, waiting for us to play baseball."

"Don't forget, Noun-nerd Nephew, that there are readers behind the pages of this book who are waiting for a grammar lesson," she retorted.

"Whom do you think you are trying to kid? The readers only want people to think they are studying grammar. In reality, the readers are captivated by the stories, by the effervescent creativity of the writing, by the ebullient brilliance of the—"

"Warm up!" shouted the impatient umpire behind home plate.

"Okay. So, Aunt Ruth, back to my original question: Whatcha got?"

"Slowball, Slowball, Slowball, and Slowball," she replied.

"You wanna tell me about them?" I asked.

"No, not really," she smiled. "They're just slow, and that's all you need to know. Come on, let's warm up."

We began warming up. She threw a few pitches to me that we clocked with the speed gun. She was coming in at about 18 mph (miles per hour). Her fastest pitch was 20 mph.

The first batter up was Rabbit Speedville, a fearsome hitter and a terror on the base paths. We had to keep him off base because he could pretty much steal any base at will.

I ran back out to the mound. I was going to tell her about Speedville.

She spoke first, saying, "Okay, Speedville is fast. With the runner on third, we've got to watch for the bunt. If you pick up the bunt, hold the runner on third. We can't let them score."

"Wow, Aunt Ruth. That's exactly what I was going to say."

"I'm ready, Catcher Nephew. Let's play ball," she said.

"You realize the importance of this game, right?" I reminded her.

"Of course I do. If we win, we go to the playoffs. If we lose, we're just another team that spent the summer playing ball so that we could eat fried chicken and watermelon after the games and maybe hear our names on the radio once or twice."

"Right. Let's do it."

"No fears, Nephew."

Aunt Ruth's first pitch sizzled across home plate at about 15 mph, and

Speedville laid down a beautiful bunt. The ball stopped dead in the grass halfway between Aunt Ruth and me. I raced forward and picked it up; looked toward third and held the runner so that he wouldn't try to score; and then I turned and fired the ball to first base, where I was not expecting to beat the runner. I figured Speedville was too fast for that. However, Speedville stepped on the piece of gum that Aunt Ruth had tossed aside, and it stopped him dead in his tracks. He couldn't get closer than about 10 feet from first base. The umpire called him out at first. One down, two to go.

The next batter, Moe Flimaggio, was full to the brim with confidence, and he was trying to rattle Aunt Ruth a bit. "Come on, Ruthy, old lady, bring it. Bring it right here. Show me what you got."

Aunt Ruth looked confused and she signaled me to come out to the mound. I ran out. "What's up, Aunt Ruth?"

"He wants me to bring it. Now, I know that if I carry the ball to home plate, that would be bringing it. But what if I throw it? Does that count as bringing it?"

"Um, Aunt Ruth, *bring it* is just an expression. It means, basically, give me your best shot, and it better be good because otherwise I'm going to walk all over you."

"It means that?"

"More or less, that's what it means."

Aunt Ruth went into her windup, her right arm going way behind her and her left leg going way up in the air, and she fired the ball toward home with everything she had. This time the ball was clocked at 19 mph. Flimaggio let it go by—ball one.

"We want a pitcher, not a belly itcher," yelled Flimaggio.

Aunt Ruth's face turned beet red. The coach ran out from the dugout. Aunt Ruth began handing him the ball, thinking her turn was done.

"Ruth, keep it. You'll get us out of this. When I signed you onto the team, I did so because I knew that in particular situations you have an incomparable tenacity. All I need from you is two more outs. Get us this win, and you'll be a hero. Come on, Baby, you can do it."

Aunt Ruth blushed. "Yes sir," she said quietly, as the coach ran back to the dugout.

"Aunt Ruth," I began.

"Did you hear that?" she asked.

"Hear what?"

"He called me Baby."

"Is that good or bad?"

"It's not bad, that's for sure. I like it. I think Coach is kind of cute."

I rolled my eyes. Whatever. But if this motivated her, great.

"Get ready for some heat," said Aunt Ruth with confidence.

I walked back to home plate, smiling. I knew she could do it.

Flimaggio stared at me. "Why are you smiling? You're going down."

"Guess again, Flimaggio," I said quietly.

"Come on, Ruthy, bring it. Bring it right here."

"Mr. Flimaggio, I can bring it all right. You better be ready."

"Oooo," said Flimaggio, "she's talking tough now. I can hit her pitches blind-folded."

Flimaggio took his stance. Aunt Ruth began her windup, and the ball whistled over the plate at 95 mph. Flimaggio watched it go by. Strike one.

The next pitch came at 102 mph. Flimaggio swung and missed it by a mile. Strike two.

Without hesitating, she threw yet another pitch that screamed across the plate at 110 mph. Flimaggio, swinging and missing, was out of there.

The next batter, Bucky Jackson, stepped in. He wasn't messing around—he saw what Aunt Ruth had done to Flimaggio.

I ran back out to the mound. "Aunt Ruth, this guy is tough."

"I know. He hits a fastball like it's nobody's business."

"What should we do?"

"I won't throw him a fastball."

"Okay, let's go."

I ran back behind the plate. Aunt Ruth began her windup, and her pitch went way up in the air. It went up; it went further up; and eventually it reached its peak. Bucky Jackson stared at it; he stared at it some more; and then he stared at it again. Finally, the ball started coming down, and it looked like it was going to be right over home plate. Jackson decided to swing at it, and he ended up hitting a slow roller right back at Aunt Ruth. She picked up the ball, flipped it to first, and Jackson was out. Game over.

"Aunt Ruth," one reporter asked after the game, "how does it feel to bring this team to the playoffs?"

"So, did I bring us or did I take us to the playoffs?" she asked.

"Well," I said, "someone at the destination would say something was brought, while someone at the embarking point would say something was taken. The person doing the bringing (or taking) could see it as either bringing or taking. Not only that, but the team being brought or taken could also see it either way also. So, the team could say that Aunt Ruth brought us to the playoffs or that Aunt Ruth took us to the playoffs. Would more examples help at all?"

The crowd nodded.

"I guess I think of bring and take as being analogous to come and go. When you bring, you come, and when you take, you go. The one who is coming is also the one who is going. Suppose my children are packing for a trip. My wife is going on the trip and I am not. My daughter comes in and asks whether she should bring her pillow.

"Now, from my wife's perspective, since my wife is going on the trip, she could say, 'Yes, bring it with you.' Well, that is, of course, unless there are too many pillows already at the destination or perhaps there's not enough room in the car for an extra pillow.

"From my perspective, since I am not going on the trip, I could say, 'Yes, take it with you,' again with the same caveats. Make sense?"

"Caveats?" asked Aunt Ruth. "Aren't caveats those fish eggs that you eat on crackers?"

"Uh, no. You're thinking of caviar."

"And Cracker-Jacks. Take me out to the ball game," Aunt Ruth began singing. "What about that? Should it be 'Bring Me out to the Ball Game'?"

"From the perspective of the person going to the game, it could go either way."

"So Aunt Ruth," asked the reporter, "what was going through your mind when Flimaggio kept egging you on, telling you to bring it."

"I knew I could bring it. I didn't know if he could take it," she said with a smile. "He's a nice boy, though."

"You know him?"

"Oh, yes. I used to play hopscotch with his grandmother, back when we were little girls. I watched him grow up, and I even taught him everything he knows about baseball."

"You're responsible for bringing him fame?"

"Well, yes," said Aunt Ruth with a blush.

"Aunt Ruth, I have one more question for you as we wrap up our interview. If you taught Flimaggio everything he knows about baseball, how come he couldn't hit you tonight?"

"I said I taught him everything he knows. I didn't say I taught him everything I know."

9

Aunt Ruth and the Okay Chorale

The time machine skidded to a halt, waking me up. There was a bang that sounded like backfire. I made a mental note to have my mechanic look into this. Einstein's Garage was the only place in town that knew how to do carburetors and exhaust pipes on time travel machines.

I yawned and popped the lid on the time machine, and Aunt Ruth stuck her head out and announced, "I'm here for my singing audition." I had let Aunt Ruth drive the time machine while I napped, and I had no idea where we were.

BANG!

A gunshot rang out from somewhere in the distance, and Aunt Ruth's flowery hat was blown into smithereens.

"Well, that's disappointing," she lamented. "Someone appears not to like purple lupines. Let me try my yellow rose hat." As she put on her new hat, she was humming "Yellow Rose of Texas."

"Did you know, Aunt Ruth, that nearly every poem written by Emily Dickinson can be sung to the tune 'Yellow Rose of Texas'?" I cleared my throat and began singing, "I never saw a moor, I never saw the sea; yet know I how the heather looks, and what a wave must—"

"Uh, no, I did not. Thanks, Nostalgic Nephew, I am a better person for knowing it. Now, let's try this again." She stuck her head up through the port hole.

BANG!

The hat with the yellow roses exploded like a canary over a cornfield.

"What on earth does that mean?" she asked. "Like a canary over a cornfield … is that a metaphor?"

"Well, it would be a simile because it's using *like*, but I don't know what it means. I can easily picture it though. It's quite visual, and—"

BANG!

"Aunt Ruth, why is someone shooting at us? Where are we, anyway?"

"Oh, we are in Tombstone, Arizona. I brought us here so I could audition for the famous Okay Chorale and thus fulfill my dream of singing in a choir. I've always loved choral music, you know, and—"

"The … Okay … Chorale?" I choked.

"Yes. One of my favorite pieces of music is the Great Symphony—I think it's the ninth—by Sherbet. Anyway, I figured if the Great Symphony is so great, the Okay Chorale at least will be okay, and that's good enough for me to enjoy."

I sighed. "Aunt Ruth, I think you brought us to the OK Corral—you know, the place where they had the famous shoot-out with all the bad guys—Wyatt Burp, Doc Holiday Inn, Bart Maverick, Mr. Rogers, and that whole crowd. And it's Schubert, not Sherbet. Sherbet is like ice cream. Schubert is the composer."

"How is corral different of chorale?"

Grammar sirens went off; lights were flashing everywhere.

"What in tarnation?" a confused voice in the distance exclaimed. Somewhere, a coyote howled. A tumbleweed rolled from left to right in the background. A cow's skull baked in the hot sun at the base of a cactus.

"Aunt Ruth, it's not *different of*. You should be using *different from*, or *different than*, or possibly even (though rarely) *different to*; definitely, it's not *different of*."

"Drat. I hate it when that happens," she said. "All right, how do I know which to use and when to use it?"

"If you were British, you would use *different from* almost exclusively. If you were American (and you are), you would find some people using *different than*, though in formal writing *different from* still wins. *Different to* used to be the choice in older English literature, but it's out of fashion now. Stick with *different from* or *different than*, and you will be safe."

"Okay, now answer my original question, please. How is corral different from chorale?"

"Well, a corral has a group of gunslingers, maybe a guy who sings 'Git Along Little Dogie,' and a cook who makes a pot of beans with whatever scraps of meat that he can find before the next cattle drive. A chorale, on the other hand, has a group of singers, maybe a guy who sings 'O Sole Mio,' and a chef who makes *hors d'oeuvres* stuffed with whatever shellfish, fresh cheeses, and exotic herbs that he can find before the next opera performance."

"What?"

"Never mind."

"Sigh. What do we do now? Any ideas?"

"Put up a white flag," I suggested. Aunt Ruth held up a white flag; we heard a barrage of gunfire; and by the time she pulled the flag back in, it had been riddled with more holes than a pork tenderloin at a Piranha Over-eaters Anonymous meeting.

Suddenly, I had a lightbulb moment.

"Aunt Ruth, hold up a cowboy hat."

"A cowboy hat?"

"A cowboy hat."

She held up a cowboy hat. The hat was met with ... silence.

"Now, stick up your head."

"My head?"

"Your head."

"You've got to be kidding. They'll shoot it clean off."

"No, they won't," I said.

"How can you be so sure?"

"I spoke to the author this morning, and he promised."

"Okay, here goes."

Aunt Ruth bravely stuck her head up, out of the time machine.

"Well, lo and behold, and boil my britches, it's Aunt Ruth!" shouted a gunslinger standing nearby.

"And who might you be?" asked Aunt Ruth.

The man belched. "Excuse me," he apologized. "My name is Burp, Wyatt Burp. You might remember me from grade school as Wyatt Belch. That was back before they gave me my Hollywood name."

"Belch, yes, I remember you. You sat behind me in Mrs. Carnivore's class. What are you doing in Arizona?"

"I borrowed a neighbor's time machine, took a wrong turn in Tucson, and ended up here."

"Fascinating. You know, Wyatt, I always use to think your name should have been Wyatt Burp," said Aunt Ruth, "and now it really is!"

I quickly covered my ears with my hands. The grammar sirens and flashing lights began again.

"What did I say wrong now?" sighed Aunt Ruth.

"You said, 'use to.' You should have said, 'used to.' When you're talking about an event from the past, you should use the past tense of *use*, which is *used*, e.g., I *used* to swim with sharks; I *used* to wrestle alligators; and I *used* to go to movies with Aunt Ruth."

"Is that all?" asked Aunt Ruth, her eyes looking a bit glassy.

"No, there are examples worth considering. Let's examine your fondness for pizza. You might say:

> I used to like armadillo cactus pizza.

"That's straight-forward. Finding the appropriate negative case, however, can be a bit awkward:

>I *used not* to like sausage and mushroom pizza.

"That's almost too stuffy and formal-sounding to our modern ears, as is this example:

>I *used* to like *not* sausage and mushroom pizza.

"Regardless of our concerns about the evils of the dreaded split infinitive, an accepted way of saying this in today's American vernacular is:

>I *used* to *not* like sausage and mushroom pizza.

"Any of those ways of expressing the negative case is valid."

"Are we done?" asked Aunt Ruth, her eyes perking up a bit.

"Nope, there's more! Suppose of your pet elephant you said:

>Binky *used* to perform at the circus.
>Stinky *did not use* to perform at the circus.

"Did you notice what we did there, Aunt Ruth? When we used the auxiliary *did* (or *did not*), we then used the present tense *use*. See, when the verb phrase contains an auxiliary, the tense of the auxiliary determines the tense of the phrase. Does this make sense?"

"Not exactly," said Aunt Ruth. "Explain *did not use* versus *used not*. Those two phrases mean the same thing, don't they?"

"Yes, that's true. It's mainly a matter of word choice. The verbs *use* / *used* are no different than other verbs, e.g., *run* / *ran*.

I *ran* to the park.	I *used* to like pizza.
I *ran not* to the park.	I *used not* to like pizza.
I *did run* to the park.	I *did use* to like pizza.
I *did not run* to the park.	I *did not use* to like pizza.

"So, *I ran not to the park* negates the statement *I ran to the park*, but admittedly it feels clunky and archaic. The more conventional way to say it nowadays is *I did not run to the park*. Because we added the auxiliary *did*, we change the verb form from past tense *ran* to present tense *run*.

Similarly, with the *used* example, when we add auxiliary *did,* we change the verb form from past tense *used* to present tense *use*. Got it?"

"Not really," said Aunt Ruth. "Can someone find me a comfy chair? I think I'm getting one of my grammar headaches."

At that moment, a stage coach turned the corner and came straight at us. The horses skidded to a halt, creating a cloud of dust. The stage coach driver barked, "Package for Aunt Ruth at the Okay Chorale."

"That would be for me," said Aunt Ruth, and within seconds she was sitting in a comfy chair. "Now, where were we? Oh, yes. We were talking about liking pizza and running to the park and names and stuff. Anyway, you know, Wyatt, if I were to adopt a new name, I don't think it would be Burp. Ha, Aunt Burp. Imagine that."

"Listen," said the gunslinger, "you have your name and I have mine. I don't like my name any more than a canary flying over a cornfield."

"That's the second time today I've heard that expression. What's it mean?"

"I don't know. Boy, I sure could use something cold and refreshing now."

At that moment, an ice cream stage coach zipped around the corner and screeched to a halt right in front of us. A man opened the window and said, "Hi. My name is Bert. I sell delicious frozen desserts. Would you like something to eat?"

"I love sherbert!" cried Aunt Ruth. "Can I have an orange sherbert?"

"No, you can't," said Bert.

"Could I have lime sherbert?"

"No, you couldn't," said Bert.

"How about blueberry?"

"No."

"Watermelon?"

"No."

"Lemon?"

"No."

"Do you have any sherbert at all?"

"There is no such thing as sherbert," said Bert with a smile.

"What's it called then?" asked an exasperated Aunt Ruth.

"Well, I think you mean sherbet, not sherbert," said Bert. "But listen. If you tell me your favorite composer, I'll give you a free sherbet."

Aunt Ruth smiled and said, "Sherbet? Sure, Bert. Schubert!"

10

Aunt Ruth Is Only in a Quandary

"I'm in a query," she said, mystifying me. Phone conversations with Aunt Ruth were often difficult.

"So," I began, "someone is asking a question about you?"

"No, wait … I don't mean query. I mean quarry."

"Ah, that's better. You're in a quarry. You are digging up rocks and gems and things. Pretty cool. Hey, if you find any pieces of obsidian, I'm trying to build up my collection."

"Okay, I guess I don't mean quarry either. Oh, maybe I'm in a quarrel."

"Are not."

"Are too."

"Are … listen, we're arguing. You are in a quarrel indeed, and I guess I'm part of it."

"Hmm. I think now that I'm not in a quarrel either. What am I in?"

"Are you in that yellow polyester pant suit that is five sizes too small, and when you walk it looks like there's a bunch of bobcats in there trying to escape?"

"Uh, no."

"Are you in a pickle, a jam, a tough spot, or a quagmire?"

"Something like that. It begins with Q, but it's not quagmire. It's something like quadrilateral or quarter or quatrain or quesadilla. That's it. I'm in a quesadilla."

"Ever been the CEO of a company?" I asked.

"Nope," she admitted.

"Then you've never been the 'Big Cheese.' You can't be in a quesadilla."

"How about a quaff or a quell or a quaint question?"

"You are in a quandary, perhaps," I suggested.

"That's it! Yes, precisely. I am in a quandary."

"What is your quandary?"

"If only I knew."

"If only you knew?"

"Yes, precisely."

"Aunt Ruth, if only you knew, then no one else would know. You would be the only person to know."

"Know what?"

"Whatever it is that you want me to know."

"Well, I do want you to know. That's why I mentioned it."

"Right, but then you said, 'If only I knew,' meaning what it says … if only you knew, not if someone else knew."

"Dear me, I'm getting confused."

"I am too. Let's sort through this and lay it out in a way that makes sense. I think what you meant was 'if I only knew.'"

"But doesn't '*if I only*' mean the same thing as '*if only I*'?" asked Aunt Ruth.

"No, not quite. The word *only* generally modifies the word directly after it."

"Oh great. I think I need some examples."

"Suppose I go to hear your chorale of forty or fifty singers perform a concert. If *only you* sang, it would be a solo for you, and depending how you did, I would either sit up proudly or slink into my seat in shame. Now, if *you only* sang, instead of also doing back flips and grunting and making faces at the conductor, then I would possibly enjoy the show."

"Are there any other nephews or nieces around I can talk to?" she sighed, her eyes rolling back in her head.

"I'm the only one," I smiled. "Relax. It gets better. Now, while you have to be cautious with *only* placement, you are given some grace because of common-sense context awareness. Suppose you said, 'I *only have* a dog.' That is, you only possess the dog. You don't love the dog, you don't feed the dog, you don't walk the dog, and you don't train your dog to stay, jump, shake hands, mow the yard, or pay the bills."

"I don't?"

"You don't, literally. But of course, that's silly. We know what you meant. Now, if you *have only* a dog, then you have a dog but not a cat, nor do you have an elephant, a hippo, or a purebred Guernsey cow."

"What if I have a dog and a cow?"

"Then you say that you have a dog and a cow," I said.

"Wow, I might be able to handle that. But, I have a question. If I say I have only a dog, then does that imply that I have nothing else at all? I have a dog, but I don't have an alarm clock; I don't have a pair of gym shorts; I don't even have an umbrella."

"Well, it needs to be in context, doesn't it?" I explained. "I mean, if you say you have only a dog, perhaps you are in the middle of a conversation about pets or companions. If you have only a dog, that doesn't mean you don't have a nose."

"Well, unless I'm in a conversation about pets, companions, and my body parts," said Aunt Ruth.

"Uh, I suppose that's true. You and I have conversations about pets, companions, and body parts all the time. Everybody knows you have a nose, though."

"How does everybody know I have a nose?" asked Aunt Ruth.

"Everybody knows you have a nose because you smell."

"How do I smell?"

"Quite well, I presume."

"If my nose were cut off, would I still smell?"

"Of course."

"How would I smell?"

"If you only knew."

11

Frankly, My Dear Aunt Ruth

"I ... don't ... know ... if ... I ... can ... do ... it," she managed to stammer between her gasps of Tibetan air. Tangled in a web of rope, cords, and carabiners, Aunt Ruth dangled fifty-feet below me like a yo-yo that had come to a dead standstill. The fulfillment of our quest to climb Mount Everest seemed to be at risk.

"Remember the little engine? I think you can; I think you can," I said, trying to encourage her.

"Honestly, we should turn back," she opined.

"Hold your horses, Aunt Ruth! I don't think that turning back has anything to do with honesty."

"What do you mean?" she asked.

"You said *honestly*, which means in an honest manner. How do we turn back in an honest manner? For that matter, how do we turn back in a dishonest manner?"

"I'm suspended here like bait on a fishing line, waiting for the Jaws of Fate to seal my doom, and you're worried about my adverb usage?"

"Well, if you put it that way, then yes. Here's the problem. If Bob was honest when he filled out the corporate accounting books every night, we could say:

Bob honestly kept the financial records.

"You could also say it like this:

> Honestly, Bob kept the financial records.

"That means the same thing.

"The issue arises," I continued, "because people also use that phrase to mean, 'Hey, I'm not kidding (i.e., I'm being honest when I tell you this), Bob kept the financial books.' The adverb used this way—intended to modify the tone or intent of the entire sentence—is known as a *sentence adverb*. The integrity of our language is crumbling; the foundation of our Grammar Castle is being undermined by giant serpents of ignorance."

"Seriously, Nepalese-like Nephew, you're being goofy," she admonished.

"I'm being goofy in a serious manner? What does that mean?"

Aunt Ruth sighed. "We discussed all this in the last book, right? Hopefully, you'll get past this sentence adverb thing soon enough."

"Now, what would I be hopeful about?" I mused.

"Say what?"

"You said I would get past this sentence adverb thing in a hopeful manner."

She rolled her eyes. "I said *hopefully*, meaning *it is my hope that*."

"Perhaps that is what you intended," I explained, "but what your sentence really meant was that I would get past this in a hopeful manner."

"Maybe you'd be hopeful that you won't have to talk about it again," she muttered. "Anyway, while we're here—that is, assuming your reader hasn't abandoned the story by this point and gone on to more pleasant things like ramming bamboo chutes underneath his or her toe nails—can you give me a quick refresher on *hopefully*?"

"Certainly!" I cried with delight. "Suppose we said:

> Hopefully, the arsenic will arrive on Friday.

"Now, how in the world can an inanimate object, e.g., arsenic, be hopeful about anything?"

"Okay, I get it. If I really wanted to say, 'I hope that the arsenic will arrive on Friday,' then I should say it that way. Now, um, can you get me down from here? Or up from here? Or something?"

"You're changing the subject. Here I am, trying to cure you of this serious grammatical malady—or, if not a malady, it's carelessness at the very least—and you are avoiding the issue. Frankly, isn't this adverb stuff kind of fun?" I suggested.

"There! Aha! You did it yourself! You used a sentence adverb—*frankly*!" she shouted, triumphantly.

"Oops, you're right," I admitted. "These sentence adverbs are pervasive."

"They're being used all over the place," agreed Aunt Ruth.

"Regrettably, they are," I sighed. "And yes, I know, I just used another sentence adverb."

"Right. I doubt that sentence adverbs themselves are used in a regrettable manner. Well, actually, I'll bet people do regret how sentence adverbs are sometimes used."

"Well, actually, Aunt Ruth, *actually* is one of those sentence adverbs."

"Oh! So it is. Tell me, Neon Nephew, what other sentence adverbs are lurking out there, seeking to steal our grammarian skills out from underneath us?"

"Oh, we have such traps as *fortunately*, *basically*, *strictly*, and *thankfully*. The biggest culprit is *hopefully*, though."

"You said 'culprit'—does that mean you think that sentence adverbs are at fault ... offspring from the Evil Empire of English Errors, the Mordor of Mediocrity and Misunderstanding, the Sinful Slope of Sloppy Semantics?"

"Actually, I don't," I confessed. "I understand the need for sentence adverbs, of course. If I want to indicate that I am hopeful that something will occur, it's rather awkward for me to have to say, 'I am hopeful that something will occur.' Having a word like *hopefully* available to use would be helpful. I'd prefer, though, that there were some other distinct word that we know is being used as a sentence adverb—no proposals here, just something to think about."

"I'm surprised that you are not going to ride this horse all the way into battle, charging up the hill, pillaging and plundering every village you find that is using -LY words as sentence adverbs, and then falling on your sword in a final, dramatic … uh … something."

"Finale? Well," I conceded, "you've got to pick your fights, as they say. I know that language evolves—and our language is blessed to have such a diverse community of international backgrounds to contribute to the evolution of the language. That doesn't mean, though, that we should be lax in our understanding of sentence adverbs."

"And why is that?" asked Aunt Ruth.

"In formal writing, if you want to be taken seriously, I think you need to be cognisant of the fact that there are people who will consider usage of sentence adverbs as a display of grammatical ignorance. That's just the way it goes."

"I guess so," agreed Aunt Ruth.

"And now, dear aunt, I have a riddle for you."

"Oh, I love riddles," she cackled.

"What did the grammar author do when it was time to end the story, but his great aunt was still suspended by rope over a precipice on the side of Mount Everest?"

"I don't know. Please tell me," she said.

Deviously, I left her hanging.

12

Aunt Ruth and Metaphors

When I woke up, it took me a while to get my bearings. I looked all around me and saw nothing but ocean—well, ocean and a little inflatable, rubber life boat in which Aunt Ruth and I were floating.

"Wh—what happened?" I stammered.

"Don't you remember? We were on a cruise ship heading to Bora Bora, and like a thunderbolt in the sky, a meteor hurled down and squashed our ship like a bug."

"Wow, Aunt Ruth," I said, "you used two similes in one sentence: *like a thunderbolt in the sky* and *like a bug*. I'm impressed."

"Quick as lightning, the ship sank. I put on a life jacket and also strapped one on you, and there we were, just large bobbers floating in the great fish pond of life."

"Aunt Ruth, you're amazing. That was a simile AND a metaphor in the same sentence: *quick as lightning* and *large bobbers*."

She beamed.

"I knew that our dangling legs were giant earthworms for the fish, and I realized that if we didn't find a raft our goose was cooked. Then I spotted a lifeboat."

"Hail to the Queen of Metaphor! You just reeled off two more metaphors: *our legs were giant earthworms* and *our goose was cooked*."

"Aw, shucks," she blushed. "It's nothing, really."

"Okay, you're right. Any news on what the weather's supposed to be today?"

"Wait—it is something, isn't it?"

"What?"

"You know, the metaphor queen thing. I said it's nothing, but it's really something, right?"

"Oh, I was just very impressed with your usage of similes and metaphors."

"Oh, okay. Thanks. Well, you know how it is. Either you can do similes and metaphors, or you can't."

"Yep. That's the truth."

We sat there, bouncing in the gentle waves. After perhaps ten minutes had passed, Aunt Ruth cleared her throat and said, "Nautical Nephew, I have two questions."

"Sure, Aunt Ruth."

"What's a metaphor? And what's a simile?"

"I was wondering when you were going to ask," I said with a smile. "Do you have a minute?"

"Uh huh. I've canceled my morning hair appointment."

"All right then. Let's begin. A metaphor is a word or word phrase that is used as a vehicle to vividly describe something. The metaphor is not to be taken literally but as a parallel or analogous depiction. For example:

> With no physics, math, or engineering background, Aunt Ruth was a fish out of water at the National Thermodynamics Conference.

You aren't really a fish, Aunt Ruth."

"Well, some of my ancestors were Fins," she chuckled.

"Here, the phrase *a fish out of water* is a metaphor acting as a noun, and it means *one who is out of place.*

> Aunt Ruth, a lion on the prowl, opened the refrigerator door.

"Here, a *lion on the prowl* is a metaphor for Aunt Ruth raiding the icebox looking for food.

> Throughout the meeting, Aunt Ruth tried hard not to laugh, but when Chairman Buxley's toupee finally slid off of his head, she exploded.

"Here, *exploded* is the metaphor. Aunt Ruth didn't literally explode. She didn't break apart into thousands of pieces, but the word *explode* brings to mind an image of something being blown apart.

"Where you need to be careful is with mixed or confusing combinations of metaphors. A mixed metaphor is when you take parts of unrelated metaphors and end up with a metaphor that doesn't really make sense.

"We have seen *a fish out of water* as a metaphor. *A bull in a china shop* is another metaphor. It's used to depict someone or something (the bull) who is likely to cause damage in some particular situation or circumstance (the china shop). Mixing the metaphors could give you: *a fish in a china shop*, or *a bull out of water.* Neither of those really makes a whole lot of sense."

"Unless the fish is really big, perhaps," suggested Aunt Ruth.

"Right."

"Speaking of fish, what about the phrase *fishing for a compliment*? Is that a metaphor?"

"Yes, it is. When you fish for a compliment, you aren't really fishing. You are putting a *line* out there—that's another metaphor, symbolizing a thought or idea—that you are trying to get someone to acknowledge and use as the basis for a compliment."

"So, it has nothing to do with real fishing?"

"Right, unless, I suppose, you are fishing for a compliment on a salmon-colored sweater or your shrimpy IQ or crabby disposition."

"Or the way you flounder when you're trying to write grammar books," she chuckled. "So ... what's a simile?"

"A simile is a metaphor that uses *like*, *as*, or *than* to make a comparison that helps describe or illustrate a point.

> Like a speeding bullet, Aunt Ruth shot past the salad bar.
> As quick as lightning, Aunt Ruth bolted past the entrees.
> Faster than the naked eye could detect, Aunt Ruth made a beeline straight to the dessert table."

"Oh, I think I can handle that," said Aunt Ruth. "May I try some?"

"Be my guest!"

"He is sly like a fox. She is sweeter than candy. He is happy as a clam. How's that so far?"

"Good, Aunt Ruth. Want to try more?"

"Sure ... how about: hotter than a blast furnace; colder than a snow-cone at the North Pole; smooth as silk; like taking candy from a baby."

"Those work. Because those examples are commonly used, you may want to save them for very informal writing or daily conversation. In good writing, you want to avoid the tired, over-used similes and metaphors because they become cliche."

"Well," said Aunt Ruth, clearing her throat, "I would ask you to give more examples of similes and metaphors that aren't cliche, but you said that was in good writing and so it probably shouldn't appear here."

"Ouch, Aunt Ruth! That stung like the first stroke of a cat-o-nine-tails!"

"Question. You said a simile is a metaphor. Does that mean a metaphor is a simile?"

"Good question, and the answer is no. Something that is a metaphor isn't necessarily a simile."

"How can that be? If Jack is a dog, isn't a dog Jack?"

"No, it's like this. A chihuahua is a dog. In fact, all chihuahuas are dogs. A dog, though, isn't necessarily a chihuahua. A dog could be a pit bull instead. Similarly, all similes are metaphors, but a metaphor isn't necessarily a simile."

"Wow, that's deep."

| All similes are metaphors. | Not all metaphors are similes. |
| All chihuahuas are dogs. | Not all dogs are chihuahuas. |

"You think that's deep, Aunt Ruth? Listen to this: Because I used a chihuahua and dogs to illustrate similes and metaphors, we could say that … a chihuahua is a metaphor for a simile!"

"Wow!" gasped Aunt Ruth. "So that means … that … dogs are metaphors for metaphors?"

SPLASH!

Something had come hurtling out of the sky, plummeting into the ocean right next to us. Moments later, a head bobbed up out of the water.

"Bill the Grammar Fairy, what are you doing here?" cried Aunt Ruth.

"I'm here to rescue you," he said.

"Hooray! We're saved! Um, do you have a motorboat and a plan for getting us out of here?" I asked.

"It's not 'We're saved,'" he retorted, "it's 'She's saved.' I'm here only to save Aunt Ruth."

"Only to save her? That's not fair! I'm stuck in the water too."

"Water schmater! I'm not saving her from the water, I'm saving her from your statement that a chihuahua is a metaphor for a simile. That's just plain silly. Now, hop on my back, Aunt Ruth, and I'll take you home with my jet pack. Sorry, I can only take one passenger."

"But … but … what about me?" I felt as lonely and wilted as the last flower of autumn.

"Here is an oar," said Bill, pulling it out of his backpack. "You can paddle to safety. Just head north. Bye."

Moments later, Bill and Aunt Ruth were out of sight.

It would have been easy to give up hope and be discouraged at that point in time, but I would have none of it. I decided to encourage myself with metaphors.

"I am the captain of this navy," I shouted. "I am Ulysses, the master of this sea! Like Lewis and Clark, I am setting off on great adventures!"

Well, that was about as helpful as getting a foot bitten off by sharks. Over the next couple of days, I sweated bullets, I worked like a well-oiled machine, and I did more paddling than a junior high school principal in a room full of misbehaving monkeys. Finally, just as my arms were falling off, I reached Paradise.

Metaphorically speaking, that is.

13

Queen Ruth Borrows Your Ear

In a far away land in a far away time, there lived a lovely royal highness by the name of Queen Aunt Ruth. Now, Queen Aunt Ruth ruled the kingdom with a firm but fair heart and with pragmatic and just decisions. Queen Aunt Ruth was the great-great-great-something-grandmother of the Aunt Ruth (on her mother's side) whom you know and love. Her kingdom was called Ruthlandia, a place that has long since been forgotten.

It came to pass that her nitwit nephew, the official court jester (and the great-great-great-something-grandfather of the nephew (on his father's side) whom you adore and admire today), was busily awaiting Queen Aunt Ruth's next command on a sunny Monday afternoon.

"Nitwit Nephew, my court jester, it would please Her Royal Highness to hear a joke from you."

"Queen Aunt Ruth," proclaimed the nitwit nephew, "I for you have a joke to tell."

"Proceed at once, Nitwit Nephew," announced Queen Aunt Ruth.

"The invisible man went to the doctor for a checkup," began the nitwit nephew, "and he asked the nurse to announce his arrival to the doctor. The nurse did so, saying, 'Doctor, the invisible man is here for his appointment.' The doctor said, 'Tell him I can't see him now.'"

Queen Aunt Ruth laughed and laughed until her side hurt, finally wiping the tears from her eyes and saying, "Imagine that, he asked the nurse to announce his arrival. Is that the funniest thing or what?"

It was often the case that Queen Aunt Ruth would not quite comprehend the nephew's jokes, and she would end up laughing for the wrong reasons. That suited the nonstop-joke-telling nephew just fine: as long as Queen Aunt Ruth was laughing, his job was secure.

"Oh my," said the queen, still reeling with laughter. "Could you borrow Her Royal Highness a tissue so we could dry her royal countenance?"

"Could you *lend* me a tissue," corrected the non-diplomatic nephew jester.

"No, we asked you first," scolded the queen.

"I mean, Her Royal Highness should say *lend* instead of *borrow*."

"Really?"

"Really."

"What about *loan*?" asked the queen.

"Well, actually, in American English, it is acceptable in casual writing and conversation to use *loan* as a verb; in British English, *loan* is used more as a noun. Formal writing should probably still err on the conservative side and use *loan* as a noun and *lend* as a verb (with *lent* as the past tense)."

"That's interesting," said the queen, "but it doesn't answer the question of why we cannot borrow a tissue from you."

"You can borrow one from me," the nephew replied.

"So we may borrow a tissue?"

"Yes, you may borrow one."

"Then please borrow one to Her Royal Highness."

"Nope."

"Grrrrr," replied the queen. "You are displeasing her royal countenance."

"I realize I may be putting my life in jeopardy, dear Queenie, but—"

WHAM!

"Wow, where did that royal umbrella come from?" remarked the nephew jester, still reeling from being hit on the top of his head by Her Royal Highness.

"Never mind. Now, borrow Her Royal Highness a tissue or we will have to dispose of you."

"You may borrow one, but I cannot borrow you one."

"What?"

"The person doing the borrowing is the person who receives it."

"Wait, say that again."

"The person doing the borrowing is the one who gets what is being borrowed. The person who is giving it to the person receiving it is the person who lends it. So, I may lend her royal highness a tissue. In fact, I'll give Her Royal Highness a tissue. If I have a tissue and Her Royal Highness wants one, I cannot borrow it to Her Royal Highness. All I can do is lend or give it to Her Royal Highness. But Her Royal Highness may borrow it from me."

"Wow, we almost got that," remarked the queen.

"I'm relieved," commented the nephew. "Look, Queen Aunt Ruth, we need to delve into more practical matters. The editor just whispered to me and said that if we don't put more meat in this story, he's going to pull it."

"I could care less what the editor says," said Queen Aunt Ruth with a glare of defiance.

"I think you mean *couldn't care less*, right? Saying you *could care less* means that it's possible for you to care less than you do."

"Do not put words in our mouth, Jester Nephew. I say what I mean and I mean what I say. It is true that I could care less, because I DO care about this. We don't want to give up our job as Queen Aunt Ruth of Ruthlandia—doing so may mean that we get stuck playing some dreadful character like Lady Macbeth or Little Orphan Annie in some other story."

"Wow, okay, I understand. Do you have any topics in mind, oh Princess of Pragmatism?"

"Well, actually, yes we do. We have always had this mental block with linking verbs and need you to clarify them for Her Royal Highness. How do they work?"

"Linking verbs are my favorites! Sure, I'd be happy to expound upon them."

"Proceed at once," she gently but firmly commanded.

"I think of linking verbs as being from one of two categories: one category includes forms of *to be*; the second category includes what I call *Feels / Appears / Seems / Tastes (or F.A.S.T)* non-action words used to connect nouns with descriptive phrases."

"We require some examples."

"Certainly. I'm assuming you are familiar with the forms of *to be*: *is, am, are, was, were,* etc. Now, Queen Aunt Ruth, let me ask you a question. What does the word *linking* mean?"

"Well, we would say that it means to join, to connect two things, to bind two things together."

"Very good. Suppose we have the simple sentence:

    He is Mortimer.

"This is a very efficient sentence because it tells us a lot in very few words."

"It does?"

"Certainly it does. It tells us that the name—the identity—of the person in question, i.e., the 'he' in this sentence, is Mortimer. It links this person—this 'he'—to Mortimer. It puts Mortimer and the 'he' person together. They are one and the same. That means that you could use 'he' in places where you use 'Mortimer,' and you could use 'Mortimer' in places where you use 'he.'"

"Okay, we are with you so far."

"Good. Now that we have established that he is Mortimer, I think you would agree it is reasonable to flip the sentence around so that we can say:

>   Mortimer is he.

"That makes sense; you replaced 'he' with 'Mortimer' and 'Mortimer' with 'he.'"

"Precisely. Incidentally, this is why saying 'Mortimer is him' is bad. You would never say 'Him is Mortimer,' because *him* is an object pronoun. You need to use the subject pronoun form (in this case, *he*)."

"What are the subject pronoun forms?" asked Queen Aunt Ruth.

"I, we, you, he, she, it, and they. Those are pronouns that can be the subject in a sentence."

"What are the object pronoun forms?"

"Me, us, you, him, her, it, and them. Those are pronouns that can be the object in a sentence."

"Okay, so I have another question. The word *is* is a verb, right?"

"Yes."

"And verbs need subjects, right?"

"Yes."

"And *is* identifies the subject as basically being equal to the thing on the other side of the *is*, right?"

"Well, sort of. That 'thing on the other side of the *is*'—i.e., the thing opposite the subject—can be a noun, an adjective, or another verb."

"When it's a pronoun, is it always the case that we will use the subject pronoun form with the *to be* linking verbs?"

"Yes, it is."

"Then why do we hear so many people say 'This is him' or 'This is her'? Isn't that wrong? Shouldn't it be 'This is he' or 'This is she'?"

"Yes, you are right. Informally, the trend these days is to use *him* / *her* in those situations. That doesn't make it right, though. Using *he* / *she* is still correct. Now, moving on, I want to show you that general nouns can be linked to other general nouns. Quite simply:

> She *is* a golfer.
> They *are* my grandparents.
> We *were* the last to arrive at the party.
> The chicken *is* my pet.
> That tennis player *was* her psychology professor.

"In all those examples, the linking verb says that the thing on the left is identified as being the thing on the right."

"We think we've got that straight."

"Good. Now let me show you how the *to be* linking verbs can be used with adjectival phrases. Consider the following:

> The goose is small.

"We know," I continued, "that *small* is not a noun here. It's not a thing. *Small* is an adjective."

"What about the subject and object pronouns when using adjectives?"

"Good question. The same rules apply. Since this is a linking verb, use the subject pronouns:

> He is tall. (you would never say, 'Him is tall')
> Tall is he. (not conventional but certainly legal)
> We were victorious.
> Victorious were we.
> She is tired.
> Tired is she.

"Does that make sense?"

"We believe so. Now, what about the other category of linking verbs?"

"Yes, allow me to tell you about the F.A.S.T. (*Feels / Appears / Seems / Tastes*) non-action words. These are words like *feels*, *appears*, *seems*, *tastes*, *smells*, *sounds*, and *looks*. These words have multiple uses, so they won't always be used as linking verbs."

"Really? Doesn't that make it hard to determine whether it's a linking verb or not?"

"Not usually. Just ask the question: Is this verb an action or is it like a taste/feel/seem kind of word? Let's look at some examples:

> The soup *tasted* funny. (linking verb)
> The dinosaur *tasted* the tree. (action verb)

"The dinosaur took a bite out of the tree to see if it was good. The soup didn't take a bite out of anybody; in fact, the soup had an odd (funny) taste to the person who tasted it. In the soup example, the soup (or the soup's taste, rather) is linked to *funny*. Thus, *tasted* here is a linking verb. Another way to look at it is that the soup's taste *was* funny (notice the linking verb *was*).

> I *feel* nauseated. (linking verb)
> Most people *feel* with their fingers. (action verb)
>
> Something *smells* funny about this. (linking verb)
> Dogs can *smell* with uncanny ability. (action verb)
>
> It *looks* like things will be fine. (linking verb)
> She *looks* through her glasses. (action verb)

"Does that make sense?"

"I think I understand. Back to the *to be* verbs for a question."

"Sure."

"Aren't there times when the *to be* is linked to another verb, like:

> The knight is riding through the forest.

"How does that work?"

"Okay, it's time for a quick side-lesson. Every verb can be conjugated into a present participle and a past participle, and these participles are used in many of the verb tenses. For a participle to be a main verb, it needs a helper (such as *to be*, or *to have*).

"In this example, *riding* is the present participle of the verb *ride*. (The past participle is *ridden*.) So, the verb phrase here is *is riding*. This is the present continuous (or progressive) tense. We'll learn more about verb tenses in other adventures. In your example, what is the knight doing? The knight *is riding*."

The queen asked, "What if we were a fan of horses and we said:

Our favorite hobby *is riding* through the forest.

"Is *is* a linking verb or a helper verb in that case?"

"Well, *is riding* certainly sounds active … except that it implies that the subject ("hobby") is actually doing the riding; however, the 'is riding' in *a hobby is riding* is different than the 'is riding' in *a knight is riding*. A hobby cannot ride like a knight can ride. *Riding*—the present participle, remember—is being used here (in the hobby example) as a noun. When that happens, we call the word a *gerund*."

"Wait—so, if *hobby* is a noun and *riding* is a noun, then that means that *is* is a linking verb in this example."

"You are correct!"

"Whew. This linking verb stuff is kind of fun! Her Royal Highness will have to ponder these words of grammar, probably revisiting the royal transcript as recorded by her royal scribes."

"I know that linking verbs can seem scary at the first encounter, but with a little practice you will be able to tell them apart from action verbs. Oh, and here is the tissue that you wanted to borrow from me."

"Thank you for borrowing me the tissue."

"I didn't borrow it to you. You borrowed it from me. I lent it to you."

"We *are* not amused, but … we do *feel* we like using linking verbs!"

14

Aunt Ruth Fishes Tight, Fishes Deep

"Now remember, Aunt Ruth, the weather has been really hot the past few weeks, so the fish are down deep. You've got to fish deep if you're going to catch them. You've also got to fish tight—that is, keep your line tight at all times. Any slack in the line will make it easier for a fish to get away. Got it? Fish deep and fish tight."

"Got it, Nephew. No worries here," she said, as she pulled out her lawn chair and plopped down into it, with her fishing rod at her side. "I'm going to take a short nap first, and then I'll do some fishing."

"Fine, Aunt Ruth. Clovis and I are going to the other side of the lake. We'll stop back in a couple of hours."

"Have fun, boys," said Aunt Ruth with a smile as she nodded off to sleep.

For the next two hours, Clovis and I fished hard. We used every lure in our tackle boxes; we had two poles each; and we tried all the tricks we knew. We fished deep; we fished shallow; we reeled in the lures fast; we reeled in the lures slowly. After two hours, all we had to show for our efforts was a small bluegill, so we ended up throwing him back.

"Slow day, I guess," muttered Clovis. "Well, maybe Aunt Ruth caught something," he said, smiling.

"Aunt Ruth? Yeah, right," I laughed. "She wouldn't know a fish if it bit her in the nose. I probably should have stayed with her a while to help her get started."

"Oh, she's okay," said Clovis. "She probably just did her own thing. I don't see her getting too worked up over fishing anyway."

"You're right. I hope it was a relaxing afternoon for her."

We picked up our stuff and headed back to where we had left Aunt Ruth. From a distance, I could see three people—two guys were fishing, and Aunt Ruth was slumped over in her lawn chair nearby, apparently sound asleep.

"Aunt Ruth!" I called out as we approached, waking her up.

She yawned. "Oh my, is it time to go already? I feel like I'm just getting started."

"Yes, we should be getting back. Those dark clouds look ominous," Clovis said, pointing to some thunderheads that had moved into the area. Aunt Ruth grabbed her pole, tackle box, and net, and we started walking toward home.

"Oh, I almost forgot!" she exclaimed. "Just a moment." She ran back to the pier, leaned over the side, and pulled up a stringer of fish. She had an assortment of eight or ten fish—bass and catfish—each weighing at least three pounds.

"Wow! Aunt Ruth, where did you get those?"

She gave me a blank look. "What do you mean? We went fishing, right? You said to fish deep, so I fished deep. You said to pull the line tight, so I pulled the line tight. My only question was why I wasn't fishing *deeply* and why wasn't I pulling the line *tightly*. *Deep* and *tight* are adjectives, and (to) *fish* is a verb, so I thought I needed adverbs. This whole adjective and adverb thing has been troubling me this afternoon."

"Well, Aunt Ruth, you've happened upon one of the mysteries and great inconsistencies of the English language," I said.

"Inconsistencies? In English? I find that hard to believe," snorted Aunt Ruth.

"Well, yes, believe it or not. So get this: *deep* is an adjective, it's true; however, *deep* can also function as an adverb."

"Why?"

"I don't know why. It's just used that way and it's been used that way for a long, long time. Now, in some sense, there may be a subtle difference between fishing deep and fishing deeply, depending how you look at it. Fishing deep, of course, means to fish in the deep areas, to fish somewhere other than shallow water. Fishing deeply, if you take deeply to mean something other than fishing in the deep, might also mean to fish profoundly, to fish with an inner intensity, to ..."

"To fish profoundly? To fish with an inner intensity? You've got to be kidding. Don't most people just say fish deep?"

"Yep, that's right. Keep in mind, though, that some people take their fishing very seriously."

"I guess so. Well, I'm a novice at all this, and I suppose that you and Clovis caught a bunch yourselves."

"We, uh, well, um, no, we didn't exactly catch much."

"One bluegill," added Clovis.

"Right, a bluegill, a nice bluegill," I hastily agreed.

"Where is it?" asked Aunt Ruth.

"We had to throw it back," said Clovis.

"Why?" asked Aunt Ruth.

"We threw it back because it was, um, too small," I admitted.

"Hey, tell me about *tight* and *tightly*," said Aunt Ruth.

"Well, *tight* as an adverb often accompanies verbs that have to do with closing or sealing something shut, e.g., close tight the windows or shut tight the door. This tends to apply to something that becomes tight and then remains tight for a while. You could almost think of close tight as meaning close, make it tight, and keep it tight."

"And what about *tightly*?"

"You can think of the adverb *tightly* as being more about the application of the verb and not the end result. You might put on a lid tightly, and it will be tight; you might glue two blocks of wood together, and not glue tightly (i.e., you're not pressing the blocks together hard), but the end result is something that is tight. You glued the blocks tight, but you didn't glue them tightly. Make sense?"

"I guess so. Do you have a list of adjectives that are also adverbs?"

"There are a few that come to mind: deep, easy, fast, hard, late, long, quick, silent, slow, and tight. Easy, silent, slow, quick, deep, and tight also have adverb forms ending in -ly: easily, silently, slowly, quickly, deeply, and tightly."

"Well, I'm sure you boys would have caught some fish if you really wanted to," said Aunt Ruth softly. "You guys are the expert fishermen, after all. You just wanted to make me look good. Every aunt should have a nephew and a nephew's friend as considerate as you two."

"You're too kind, Aunt Ruth. Anyway, I'm impressed with your fish," I said.

"I am too," said Clovis.

"Now, will you clean them for me, Nephew? I don't have a clue how to do that."

"Sure thing, Aunt Ruth."

"Would the two of you like to come over for dinner tonight? I will make you a deep-dish apple pie. It's from a recipe that I love deeply," said Aunt Ruth with a smile.

"Oh, Aunt Ruth, we don't want you to go through too much trouble on our account."

"Oh, it's no trouble at all. I'll be baking a couple of other pies anyway for some new friends I've made recently and to whom I am deeply indebted."

She turned and winked at the two guys who were fishing nearby, and they waved back at her as the three of us headed toward home.

15

Aunt Ruth Burned or Burnt the Toast

Normally I wouldn't have thought much of it, but this was in a public library after all. The man in the beige trench coat was a bit conspicuous with his five gallon bucket of white-out—that's a seriously hefty amount of the "nectar of the editors"—and an orange wheelbarrow full of books, but it was the name emblazoned on his coat that was the big clue for me: Mr. Ed.

I watched Mr. Ed out of the corner of my eye as he removed a book from the wheelbarrow. Sitting at a table, he perused the book one a page at a time, frequently using the white-out and then carefully writing in black ink. When he finished the book, he put it on the table, and he selected another book from the wheelbarrow and began paging through it. I observed him as he did this to all the books in the whole wheelbarrow. When he finished, he loaded the books back into the wheel barrow and then wheeled the books to their proper locations on the shelves. Fascinated, I watched him do three rounds of this.

I picked up the walkie-talkie. "Mongoose 7, Mongoose 7, do you read me? Over."

There was a pause, and then I heard the telltale hiss of the walkie-talkie. "Cobra 6, Cobra 6, I read you loud and clear. Over."

"Mongoose 7, the perpetrator is a guy named Mr. Ed. His MO fits the description that Marian, Madame Librarian, gave us. Over."

"Cobra 6, MO? What's an MO besides an abbreviation for Missouri? Over."

"Mongoose 7, MO is *Modus Operandi*, his mode of operation, or how he does things. They use MO in all the big detective shows—Dragnet, Hawaii Five-O, the Andy Griffith Show, all of the great ones. Over."

"Cobra 6, is this case that big? If we break it open, could we become famous? Over."

"Mongoose 7, maybe, but that doesn't matter. We're doing this for the preservation of literature, remember? Over."

"Cobra 6, do we know what he's changing in the books? Over."

"Mongoose 7, not yet. Over."

"Cobra 6, well, have you looked? Over."

"Mongoose 7, no. Over."

"Cobra 6, well look! Over."

"Mongoose 7, Roger. Are you coming over? Over."

"Cobra 6, I've got a suspect over here I am investigating as well. Will keep you posted. Over."

This spy stuff was invigorating. I stealthily sneaked up behind Mr. Ed—he was in deep concentration, oblivious to my clandestine presence—and removed one of the newly-modified books from the table. There were three other books just like it, still in the wheelbarrow, unmodified. I quietly lifted one of them as well.

I began comparing the pages of the modified and unmodified books. On page 679 of the book, I found a difference. Aha! I knew what Mr. Ed was doing.

"Mongoose 7, Mongoose 7, I've got it! I know Mr. Ed's game. Come here, pronto. Over."

"Cobra 6, I'll be right over. Over."

A moment later, a tap on my shoulder startled the daylights out of me.

"Jumpy, aren't we?" asked Aunt Ruth, standing there.

"Mongoose 7—I mean Aunt Ruth—you won't believe this," I whispered. "Mr. Ed is finding all occurrences of the word *burnt* and is changing them to *burned*."

"The horror! The sacrilege!" said a stunned Aunt Ruth.

"Well, I wouldn't exactly proclaim it to be *that* serious," I said, unwilling to say that Ed's actions were a total abomination.

"Okay, how about this then: The injustice! The misdemeanor! The not-a-really-great idea!" said Aunt Ruth.

"That's probably more like it," I agreed, "but actually this word-ending issue can go either way. Folks in the UK typically use the '-t' ending, while Americans tend to use the '-ed' ending."

"So, he's not really modifying the language as such, though he is defacing books. We've got to stop him."

"Oh, yeah?" said Mr. Ed, suddenly standing up and confronting us. "Who's going to make me?"

"So tell me, Mr. Ed, for the love of language, what have you got against the word *burnt*?" asked Aunt Ruth.

"*Burnt*? You think I'm doing this all solely for the word *burnt*? Guess again, lady. This is big, really big. It boggles the mind."

"How big is it?"

"Have a seat," said Mr. Ed. We complied. Mr. Ed looked left and then right. He leaned forward and whispered, "Here's the list I care about: *burnt, dreamt, clapt, knelt, leant, leapt, slept, smelt, spelt, spilt, spoilt, stript, sunburnt,* and *vext*. Now, don't tell me this isn't the most serious problem in the western hemisphere."

"Mr. Ed, this isn't the most serious problem in the western hemisphere."

"I told you not to tell me that."

"Mr. Ed, you are aware, aren't you, that people in the United Kingdom tend to use the '-t' endings, while we here in the good old U.S. of A. tend to use the 'ed' endings?"

"They do? I thought they just talked funny over there."

"No, they write funny too, but that's the way it is. Those words you listed are valid words for ending in '-t,' and I think we need to avoid more language wars. Besides, there are places in the U.S. where the '-t' endings are frequently used, such as New England."

"Well, I tell you," said Mr. Ed, "out on the plains of western Nebraska, where men are men and words ending in '-t' are rare, we tend to use the '-ed' ending. The sun *burned* down in a fury, and soon the *spoiled* carcass *smelled* bad. We wouldn't say the sun *burnt* down in a fury, and soon the *spoilt* carcass *smelt* bad."

"That's all fine and good, Mr. Ed, but in the name of polite and acceptable behavior, we shouldn't go around changing the books in the library system like this. I want so badly to lock you up, but I figure if you go and undo all of your changes, that will suffice. However, if I ever catch you doing this again, you'll be behind bars faster than you can say, 'Dewey Decimal System.'"

"Well, I suppose you're right," admitted Mr. Ed.

"Hey, I've got to go back to my post in Fiction and check out this other suspect," said Aunt Ruth. With that, she stepped around the corner and was gone.

Mr. Ed and I shook hands, and all seemed happy in the western hemisphere once again. Case closed.

It was then that I heard the voice over the walkie-talkie, "Cobra 6, Cobra 6, do you read me? Over."

"Mongoose 7, what's up? Over."

"Cobra 6, my suspect just pulled a five gallon bucket of white-out from underneath his trench coat. Over."

"Mongoose 7, oh no, not another guy named 'Mr. Ed,' I hope. Over."

"Cobra 6, no, the name on this guy's shirt is simply 'Mr. T.' Over."

"Mongoose 7, I'll be right over. Over."

Aunt Ruth and Double Negatives

Aunt Ruth stared at herself in the shoe store mirror, turning her ankle this way and then that, trying to gain an appreciation for the shoes that had looked so good in the store window.

"Is it not the case that these are the most darling shoes you've ever seen?" she remarked.

I had to think long and hard before answering her question. The shoes were absolutely hideous.

"Yes," I answered.

She was satisfied with that answer, though I don't think she should have been.

She continued trying on shoes, and she actually found a pair that I liked.

"Do you not like these?" she asked.

"Nope."

"Why don't you like them?"

"I do like them."

"Then why did you just say nope?"

"Because you asked if I do not like them. If, instead, you had asked if I like them, I would have said yes."

"Why are you being so difficult?"

"I'm trying to drive home a grammar point. One of the things that confuses people about English is the subtle distinction between negative and positive sentences."

"Actually, I think you're correct, but sometimes the misuse of negative and positive sentences ends up in results that aren't subtle at all," said Aunt Ruth.

"I'm afraid you're right, Aunt Ruth," I agreed. "What's more, depending on who is speaking, you will find different ways of approaching negative questions."

"For instance?"

"For instance, suppose you are in a fancy restaurant. You've eaten your fill of some delectable morsels—"

"I don't care for seafood," interrupted Aunt Ruth.

"I didn't say anything about seafood," I said, confused.

"You said delectable morsels. Aren't morsels kind of like clams? I see people eating steamed morsels all the time at Joe's You Catch 'Em, We Clean 'Em, Cook 'Em, and Charge You through the Nose for 'Em Pier."

"No, those are steamed mussels."

"Oh, that's right."

"Okay, so you've filled up at a restaurant, and the waiter brings a plate of delicious-looking desserts. You decline, but the waiter persists, asking, 'Don't you want to try one?'"

"What's wrong with that?" asked Aunt Ruth.

"Nothing, technically. Semantically, though, *don't you want* is not really the same as *you don't want*. In *don't you want*, the question is really meant to ask if the listener wants. That is, even though *don't you want* is literally the same as *you don't want*, colloquially it asks if you do want. In *you don't want*, the question (or statement) is really meant to ask if the listener does not want. If you answer yes to *don't you want*, people will think you are saying that you do want. If you answer yes to *you don't want*, people will think you are agreeing that you do not want something."

"When you think about it, no matter how much you rationalize what *don't you want* means, if the waiter were to ask, 'Do you want,' it's clear what he means. It seems obvious that *don't you want* and *do you want* do not mean the same thing, but in context, people will answer *don't you want* in the affirmative, meaning they do want. However, if you are Asian, you likely will take this literally. It's best to answer so that there is no ambiguity. Answering yes to *don't you want* will tell an Asian no while telling an American yes."

"So what's the point?" muttered Aunt Ruth.

"The point is that whether I am asking the question or answering the question, I should strive for clarity."

"I need to sit down. I feel one of my headaches arriving," moaned Aunt Ruth.

"Don't you want to go bowling?" I asked.

"No," she replied.

"So ... you don't *not* want to," I teased. "But, saying you don't not want to is not quite the same as saying you want to. You may not be opposed to the idea (don't not want to) but you're not necessarily supportive of the idea. Don't I have that right?"

"Yes," said Aunt Ruth. "I mean, uh, no. I'm not sure what I mean. Can't you repeat the question please, but leave out all the negatives?"

"Yes," I smiled.

Aunt Ruth looked at me with glazed eyes and her mouth agape. "Do you mean yes you can't or yes you can?"

Then she shook her head violently, as a dog shakes water off its coat, and she laughed. "Don't you think that maybe it's time to invent a new language?"

17

Aunt Ruth Passes the Pasta Pesto Test

"Aunt Ruth, wouldst thou please pass the pesto pasta, pronto?"

"Nauseating Nephew, why talkest thou like this? In fact, why talkest I like this? I think we're in the middle of a silly word story. Anyway, be that as it may, I proclaim that the pesto pasta has been past!"

"The pesto pasta has been past what? Past its prime? Past its heyday, its glory years, its existence, its—"

"What do you mean, past what? I past it to you a few minutes ago. It's sitting there on the table, right next to you."

"You cannot have past it to me. That makes no sense, English-wise."

"Certainly it does. Is not the past tense of *pass past*?"

"Past what? Past the end of its life? Do you mean that the existence of the past tense of *pass* is now a thing of the past?"

"There you go with the 'past what' thing again. Listen, at one point I told myself that I will pass you the pesto pasta. Then, presto, I past you the pesto pasta. Now you're asking for the pesto pasta, pronto."

"No, you did nothing of the sort, my dear feminine avuncular one. You *passed* me the pesto pasta. You cannot say that you *past* it to me."

"How can you tell the difference? Past and passed sound the same."

"Homonymically, they—"

"Wait, that's not a word. Caught you."

"Oh, right. Okay, those words—past and passed—do indeed sound the same—words that sound similar are homophones—but they look remarkably different."

"But you and I are having a conversation. Who possibly can tell the difference in how the words look?"

"The audience can. This dialog is being written down for all to see."

"Oh, I knew I should have washed and combed my hare."

"You mean your hair, naturally."

"No, I mean Bruno, my rabbit-like pet."

"You have a rabbit named Bruno?"

"Yep, he's Binky's third cousin, but that's another story. Now listen, before this gets too silly, tell me about *past* and *passed*. I find this topic quite fascinating."

"Really?" I asked, excited that Aunt Ruth was interested in this admittedly wonderful topic.

"No, not really. You may as well keep going, though. Even on union hours, I have to be here for another one or two pages."

"All right. It's simple. Looking at *past* first, I will show you how it can be used as a noun, adjective, or adverb. First, here is *past* as a noun:

> Floyd had recurring nightmares from his *past*, usually with vivid images of monsters, phantoms, and sentence diagrams.

"*Past* as an adjective is shown here:

> After fifty years, the trauma incurred from Mrs. Walker's first grade class is past.

"The adverb *past* looks like this:

> Aunt Ruth zoomed *past* the guards stationed in the bakery and launched herself into a head-first dive, landing in the triple deluxe chocolate mousse torte.

"*Passed* is the past tense form of the verb *pass*. Common ways *passed* is used include: She passed the football; he passed the test; she passed the spaghetti; he passed the car in the right lane; she passed the note across the aisle; he passed on the invitation to go to the circus.

"Today you pass something. Yesterday you passed it. Today is in the present. Yesterday was in the past."

"Okay, Nefarious Nephew, let me try. The proposed bill was passed by the Senate. The era of trying to get the United States to go with the metric system is past. I passed my final exam. That doesn't mean that I wadded it up and threw it as I would a football; nor does it mean that it was on the highway and I drove my car around it. It means, in this case, that I succeeded. The past passed quickly. My pastor passed me in the pasture. Finally, this past week, I passed around a pastoral print, produced with pastels, of pistachio-flavored pasteurized milk in a pristine palace. The print was produced sometime in the recent past."

"Wow, I think you've got it. You passed the test! Your confusion of passed and past is now a thing of the past."

"Whew, I sure am glad about that. Now, on to the next problem."

"What problem is that?"

"My eye doctor says I'm having a problem with colors, specifically my two favorites."

"What are your two favorite colors, Aunt Ruth?"

"My two favorite colors are blew and read."

"Aunt Ruth, we need to talk."

18

Aunt Ruth by the Numbers

Ring! Ring! Ring!

I opened one eye. My world was blurry. I opened the other eye, making a total of two eyes that were open. I blinked twice. Everything was less blurry, and I could see that it was 3:00 a.m.

"Hello, Mildred's Mattresses," I said, answering the phone. "I'm sorry, but the mattress is being used at the moment. If you'd like to purchase it, you will have to wait until morning. I can have the fumigation done by nine o'clock but I cannot promise that the mattress will be lice-free. May I ask who is calling?"

There was a deafening pause on the other end of the phone.

"Hi, Aunt Ruth, how are you doing at this early hour of the morning?" I said, making an educated guess as to the identity of the telephonic intruder.

"Hi, uh, Nighttime Nephew," said a weary female voice. "What's up?"

"What's up? I am, Aunt Ruth. It's three o'clock in the morning and you called me, and now you are asking me what's up? At the moment, I think you are about a bubble short of being level ... you're paddling upstream with one oar out of the water ... your lights are on but nobody's home ... or you are three bricks shy of a load. Take your pick."

"Well, it's like this," she began. "1st, I am writing a letter to my constituency and am struggling with the rules on how to write numbers. It's terribly distracting. Bill the Grammar Fairy and I need to rehearse our next story together, but I haven't been able to concentrate. I haven't been able to give him my undivided attention. Anyway, for some numbers, I think I am supposed to spell out the word, but for others I think I am supposed to use the numeric figures. Isn't it something like 'when in doubt, leave it out'?"

"Short answer: No. Long answer: No, not really. First of all, you should use 'first' and not '1st' when writing sequence numbers—"

"Sequence numbers? You mean numbers that are decorated with those little shiny reflective things that they put on dresses in the early 1970's?"

"No, no, and no—it's 1970s (with no apostrophe), not 1970's. Second, I said *sequence*, not *sequins*. Sequence numbers are also called ordinal numbers—think of numbers in a series."

"Okay, how about 7."

"Seven what?"

"7 games."

"What?"

"You told me to think of numbers in a series. In the 2016 World Series—the baseball championship in North America (why it's called 'World Series,' I don't know)—the Chicago Cubs beat the Cleveland Indians in 7 games."

"Seven games."

"That's what I said."

"Maybe it's what you said. It's not what he typed."

"What do you mean?"

"He typed it as a 7, not as a seven."

"Why did he do that, Numerically Nauseating Nephew?"

"He needed to supply an example with you doing it incorrectly. It was one of those editorial demands."

"So, he should have had me say that the series went seven games, not 7 games."

"Right, yes."

"Anyway, so what about the 1st versus first?"

"When you are writing a ranking or place or order in a series, e.g., first, second, and third, write out the number. When you are giving a list of numbers, be consistent—either write them all as words (e.g., seven, two, ten) or all as numeric figures (e.g., 7, 2, 10) but not both (e.g., seven, 2, 10)."

"Those are weird lists."

"Just examples, Aunt Ruth."

"I feel better."

"Me too. Now, the basic rule is that if the number can be written in one or two words, spell it out; otherwise, use the numeric figures."

"Figures? I've got a figure."

"Yes, you do. You've got a short, round figure. It looks kind of like a '0' with legs and arms. Actually, now that I think about it, you look a little bit like Humpty Dumpty."

WHAM!

"I deserved that," I muttered, ruefully rubbing the lump on my head. "How did you strike me with your umbrella over the phone?"

"Never mind. Now," Aunt Ruth said, "please go over this again, would you?"

"Surely, I will."

"I'm Aunt Ruth."

"Yes, I know."

"You called me Shirley."

"I did not. I said, 'Surely.'"

"If I've told you 1^{nc}, I've told you a 1,000,000 times. I am Aunt Ruth."

"Listen, my arithmetically annoying aunt, here's how it goes: In general, you want to use numeric figures when the number is more than one or two words long; when putting the number directly before a unit (e.g., 5 feet); when comparing a number with another number that needs to be written numerically (e.g., between 4 and 128); when listing four or more numbers in a row (e.g., 1, 3, 8, 9); when writing a number as a date, time, size, or part of a formula (e.g., May 18, 3 o'clock, size 42, 6 ÷ 17); and when writing about statistics (e.g., 8%). Got it?"

"Nope."

"It's okay. Look at the examples in the back of the book. I'm going back to bed now, Aunt Ruth."

"Wait, Number-knowledgeable Nephew, I have a question. What's a prime number?"

"Eleven."

"Eleven? Is that the only one?"

"No, of course not. You asked for a prime number, and I gave you one. If what you're really asking for is the definition of a prime number, it is a number that is divisible ONLY by one and by itself. The first prime number is two. Why do you ask?"

"I'm setting up your punch line for the end of this story. Now, Nighttime Nephew, could you tell me a little story first before running off to bed?"

"A story? Aunt Ruth, do you know what time it is?"

"Is it 'Once upon a time'?"

"No."

"Oh, then I don't know the time."

"It was a dark and stormy night," I began, "and I was walking down the sidewalk and I saw this cute little number walk by."

"Cute little number?" asked Aunt Ruth. "Like seven?"

"Like seven," I agreed.

"What's so special about seven?"

"It's a cute little number," I replied.

"Oh, right. Please go on."

"So, there I was, and a fourteen walks up. The fourteen said, 'I need your undivided attention,' but the seven divided it—in other words, we divided fourteen by seven—and ended up with two."

"Sounds serious."

"It is, indeed," I confessed. "Now, do you want to talk about when to write out the numbers?"

"No, I don't, but the writer is keeping me awake at this point."

"Oh, that nauseating writer," I suggested.

"What do you do about numbers in self-referential articles?"

"Hey, this is getting weird."

"Tell me about it. He did this three or four times in the first book and it drove me crazy."

"At least this story doesn't have Bill the Grammar Fairy."

Plop!

"Who's that?"

"Hi, I'm Bill. You rang?"

"Uh, not really. Wrong number or something. Hey, while you're here, can you help us with numbers?"

"Sure, I guess. Do I have a choice?"

"No. Now, we've already talked about when to use figures, and now we're going to talk about when to write out the—"

"I know, I know, yadda, yadda, yadda. Listen, you got any pastrami in the fridge? I haven't eaten for almost 2 days."

"Two days. Remember that if the number can be written in one or two words, you want to write it out."

"Uh, right."

"No, pastrami, sorry."

"Ham?"

"I'll be buying ham at the market tomorrow."

"Salami?"

"Let me check ... uh, nope. No salami."

"What do you have?"

"Oh, I'll bet I have three or four different things you can eat."

"3 or 4 you say?"

"No, three or four."

"Not 3 to 1471?"

"Nope, but you wrote the numbers correctly."

"I get lucky sometimes."

"Write out the number when using common fractions."

"Are fractions common?"

"Well, things like one-half, a third, a fifth, etc."

"Oh, I see. How about 7/23?"

"That's fine as it is. It's not a common fraction. Now, when using very large, round numbers, you probably will want to write them out. (e.g., one million instead of 1,000,000). Also, if using a number to begin a sentence or a title, always write it out."

"Oh, that's good to know. If I were going to begin a sentence with 783,390,220,394,448,291,333, then I probably would want to make sure I moved the number somewhere else, right?"

"Right—or you could use a different number."

Can you provide an example here?"

"Surely."

"Bill. My name is Bill."

"Right, I meant Bill. Here's an example: 783,390,220,394,448,291,333 is what the psychologist thought Bill's IQ happened to be. Subsequent testing revealed that the number was indeed 7, not 7 followed by a whole lot of other numbers."

"So is that sentence correct or incorrect?"

"It's incorrect, Bill, because it begins with a numeric figure. If the number is the beginning of the sentence, the words representing the number need to be written out. I'd put the number somewhere else in the sentence so that you can use the figures and not have to write out the words."

"Such as?"

"Such as this: The psychologist mistakenly thought that Grammar Bill's IQ was 783,390,220,394,448,291,333, but it really was just 7."

"I see. Now I feel better," sighed Bill.

"I thought you might."

"Hey," said Bill, "I haven't seen Aunt Ruth for a while in this story. Is she okay?"

"Oh, I think she's fine. She's not here though. Pick up the phone. She's on the other end of the line."

"Mind if I speak with her for a bit? I'm trying to figure out when she and I can get together to rehearse for our next story."

"No problem; go ahead. She's in prime form right now."

"Prime form? What do you mean by that?"

"Bill, you'd make a great straight-man for a stand-up comedy act."

"Thanks, Mister."

"I said she's in prime form because now she can give you her undivided attention."

Aunt Ruth Fragments

Dear Aunt Ruthie,

Need advice. This morning. I woke up. Put on something. Crushed velour bathrobe. Purple, thick. On sale at the Susan B. Anthony Coin Preservation and Burrito Shop. I sashayed into the kitchen and saw a piece of paper on the table. A note. From my dog. He said, "Bark. Bark bark bark, bark. Sincerely, Bark." Then he said, "p.s. Bark, bark, barkety bark." Of all the things that have ever happened to me, this is. The worst. What. Should. I. Do?

Sincerely,

Mrs. Pieces

Dear Mrs. Pieces,

I can see you're all broken up over your dog leaving. Your sentences are more fragmented than a mosaic wall knocked over by a bulldozer. Get over the dog, honey. You can get a new dog at your local rescue society. What you've got to work on is fixing your sordid tendency to fragment your sentences. It's disgusting.

Now, think back to your basic education. Sentences have what? They have a subject and a predicate. Think simple, like: Subject Verb Object.

Jimmy walked his dog.

That is a complete sentence. You wrote, "Need advice." If "need" is the verb, then what is the subject? I need advice? You need advice? They need advice? Who needs advice? Allow me to share this vignette with you:

> When he was in Little Big Horn, Montana, General Custer sent an urgent memo to his supply officer: Need horses. Well, the supply officer knew that this was not a well-formed sentence because it lacked a subject. So, he assumed that Custer had misspelled the word and actually meant *knead horses*, which could be a command. The supply officer then hired a dozen masseurs who happened to be vacationing locally and paid them to give massages to the horses. This made the horses happy, but Custer never sold lemonade in Montana again (i.e., that was his Last Stand).

You then wrote, "This morning." What is that? Is that the subject or the object? Where's the verb? Shall I continue, or do you want to try this again? This letter of yours gets an "F" in my book, but thanks for trying and have a nice day,

Aunt Ruthie

Dear Aunt Ruthie,

Thank you for your quick response. I am working on eliminating my fragmented sentences. You can see that it's not quite foolproof. Yet. It will get there. I hope. Appreciate your masterful handling of my situation. You are truly ingenuous.

Hopefully,

Mrs. Pieces

Dear Mrs. Pieces,

You have made considerable progress on your fragmentation removal, and I am suitably impressed. It's not clear to me whether you are fully aware of which sentences in your most recent letter are fragments. Let me enumerate:

1. Yet.

Yet can be a conjunction or an adverb, but a sentence does not live by conjunctions or adverbs alone.

2. Appreciate your masterful handling of my situation.

Now, this may be nit-picky, and maybe I should assume that the subject is the personal pronoun "I." Since we're working on eliminating fragmentation, let's be pure about this. Having a subject in one sentence does not mean you can go subject-free in the next sentence. You need a subject in this sentence. Are we all clear on that?

Now, on to other—new—problems.

The word *masterful* is dangerous to use. It's like allowing a room full of monkeys to play with a loaded shotgun. It just isn't done in polite circles. Now, I know that you intended to use it as a compliment, and I thank you for that. However, for the past several hundreds of years (back before even I was born), *masterful* was used to mean domineering, self-willed, or even imperious. *Masterly* has changed meanings once or twice along the way, but suffice it to say that in today's linguistic economy, *masterly* will be safe to use in a complimentary manner; *masterful* … well, it depends on the reader / listener background and preference. It may be safer simply to choose another word. How about *exquisite*?

Now, regarding your choice of the word *ingenuous*, I have a minor qualm. First, note that *ingenuous* and *ingenious* are separate, distinct words. *Ingenious* means brilliantly clever, intellectually skillful, or gifted. *Ingenuous* means artless, guileless, and openly frank. *Ingenuous* is not a bad thing. It means one is open, honest, and not deceitful. *Disingenuous* is the rough one. That is the opposite of *ingenuous* and it means deceitful, not honest or sincere, or hypocritically pretending to be ingenuous.

Aunt Ruthie

p.s. Nice use of the word "hopefully," by the way. You used it correctly! Indeed, your letter was written in a hopeful manner.

Dear Aunt Ruthie,

Thank you again for your quick, timely response. My goodness. While I ate breakfast and waited for my sister to come back from the grocery store. I read some grocery ads and I called her. She came back with a surprise for me. A goose! Prepared and dressed. What she didn't realize was that I already had one in the fridge, also prepared and dressed. Two geese for dinner on Christmas! It's understandable, though. Because my sister and I are so alike. We often do duplicitous things. Duplicity just can't be avoided sometimes. Also, we had an imminent guest for dinner—the town mayor joined us! A good time was had by all.

Sincerely,

Mrs. Pieces

Dear Mrs. Pieces,

First, allow me to point out the sentence fragments from your most recent letter:

> My goodness.

Personal possessive with a noun ... where is the verb?

> While I ate breakfast and waited for my sister to come back from the grocery store.

If you remove the first word, "While," the rest of the sentence is a nice independent clause. That is a complete sentence. Adding the adverb "While," though, turns the independent clause into a dependent clause. A dependent clause can't be a sentence by itself. It depends on something else to make it independent. Since this isn't independent, it's a fragment.

> A goose!

No verb!

> Prepared and dressed.

Are these verbs or adjectives? They could be either. You at least need a subject here.

Two geese for dinner on Christmas.

Two geese for dinner on Christmas … what? Will sing? Will dance? Will do the Charleston, Fox Trot, or Tango? Would that thou used a verb!

Because my sister and I are so alike.

Get rid of "Because" and this turns into a sentence.

Now, are you sitting down? I have a surprise for you. The word *duplicity* does not mean the ability to make doubles or duplicates of something. *Duplicity* means being dishonest with an intent of trying to trick someone. The phrase "double-dealing" comes to mind.

You had an *imminent* guest? *Imminent* refers to something that is going to happen soon or that is just over the horizon. I think the word you wanted to use there was *eminent*, which means esteemed or revered.

You seem to have had a reversal in your progress on eliminating fragmentation. Don't give up—keep at it! Note that some popular authors frequently use fragments. Once you get to the point where you absolutely know how to avoid fragments, come see me about getting permission to use them. Until then, keep on truckin'.

Aunt Ruthie

Dear Aunt Ruthie,

I'm not sure how to end this story. I'm searching for a way.

Respectfully,

Nauseating Nephew

Dear Nauseating Nephew,

Ironically, with a fragment.

Aunt Ruthie

Aunt Ruth Loves Her Transitive Radio

I pushed Aunt Ruth. I pulled Aunt Ruth. I pressed Aunt Ruth, and I squeezed Aunt Ruth, and I greased Aunt Ruth. I even tickled Aunt Ruth. I tried everything *transitive* that I could think of doing to Aunt Ruth—short of detonating her, which wouldn't be very nice—but it didn't work.

So, I grunted; I strained; I heaved; and I hoed. I even tried hopping, skipping, and jumping, but no *intransitive* action by me succeeded either. I simply couldn't get Aunt Ruth through her front door. Blocking the door frame with her feet and clinging to it with her hands, she refused to be removed from her house.

"I will not go!" she defiantly asserted.

"Why not?" I finally sighed in exasperation.

"I don't want to learn about verbs, especially the insensitive ones."

"Intransitive."

"Intransitive," she echoed.

"Aunt Ruth, our dinner date at the National Verb Day Gala Event isn't until next week. I'm here today to take you to the oral surgeon to get your wisdom teeth out."

"My wisdom teeth?"

"Yes."

"We're not attending a verb convention today?"

"Nope. We're having your teeth yanked."

"Well, let's get going then," she huffed. "We mustn't be late."

An hour later, Aunt Ruth was in the dentist chair and I was sitting next to her.

"Now, Narrating Nephew, you promised you would read to me while I'm under the knife. Have you brought a book?"

"Yes! I brought *The Habbit*."

"Oh, goody! I love hearing about the nuns in Middle Earth."

The dentist chuckled and said, "Okay, Aunt Ruth, we're going to knock you senseless with a little laughing gas."

"Don't bother with that, Doc," I said. "She's been senseless for years."

"Oh, please, no laughing gas," pleaded Aunt Ruth. "I want to remain in charge of my faculties." She turned to me, took a deep breath, and asked, "So, Gnarly Nephew, will you begin reading?"

I reached into my satchel and pulled out the book. Oops, I must have grabbed the wrong bag on my way out the door.

"Aunt Ruth, through no fault of your own, it appears that today we will be reading from *Growing Your Verb Garden*."

"Verbs? Horrors! Doc," blurted Aunt Ruth, "give me the gas, and hurry!"

On went the mask. Aware of the great educational opportunity in front of me, and with no time to lose, I cleared my throat and began. "Let's start with a simple question: what kinds of verbs are out there?"

"I'd rather walk on a bed of hot coals," muttered Aunt Ruth, not yet exhibiting the raving enthusiasm for which I was hoping.

"Well," I continued, ignoring her dissenting opinion, "there are two kinds of verbs—**transitive** and **intransitive** verbs. A **transitive** verb is an action performed by a subject that affects a direct object. An **intransitive** verb is one with which there is no direct object to affect."

Aunt Ruth blinked her eyes. "So, let me get this right. If the verb is something that a subject does to a direct object, it's transitive; otherwise—abracadabra—it is intransitive, right?"

"Yep, you nailed it, Aunt Ruth," I exclaimed. "Brilliant."

"Think she's Nobel Peace Prize material?" asked the doctor.

"No doubt about it, Doc. Her reasoning is impeccable," I replied.

"This is going to be fun," she giggled through the gas mask. The sedative was already having an effect. "I would love to hear some grammar examples, my nice nephew."

So I began. "Let's look at examples of transitive verbs first:

> The princess **rode** her unicorn.
> The knight **slew** the dragon.
> Edna **ate** the cole slaw.

"In each of these examples, Aunt Ruth, there is a subject (the princess, the knight, or Edna) who performed an action (rode, slew, or ate) that affected—or somehow had an impact on—a direct object (unicorn, dragon, or cole slaw). Got it, so far?"

"I think so. The unicorn was affected because the princess rode on it; the dragon was affected because the knight slew it; and the cole slaw was affected because Edna ate it."

"Very good."

"You know," began Aunt Ruth, "I used to have a transitive radio. I loved my transitive radio. I listened to my transitive radio all the time. Do you know my favorite song?" She closed her eyes and began singing, "I've got a brand new pair of roller skates, you've got a brand new key—"

"Aunt Ruth, hello, Aunt Ruth!" I said, taking her by the shoulders and shaking her.

"Oh, hi, Natty Nephew. Sorry, I got distracted thinking about my transitive radio."

"I think you mean transistor radio, Aunt Ruth, not transitive."

"Well, let me ask you this. My radio played music, right?"

"Yes, it did, but—"

"And *music* in that sentence—*My radio played music*—is a direct object, right?"

"Yes, it is, but—"

"Then I had a transitive radio!"

I closed my eyes and counted to ten with the hopes that my annoyance would disappear, but when I opened my eyes she was still there.

"Now," I continued, "things get a little more complicated when you include indirect objects and/or prepositional objects."

"Bring it to me, brother," sang Aunt Ruth.

I continued. "Look at this example.

Uncle Tunnard gave Aunt Lillian a frog.

"So, Uncle Tunnard gave a frog to Aunt Lillian. The direct object is frog—frog was the thing he gave; it was the thing that was bearing the action of being given. *Gave* has a direct object, so it is transitive. Aunt Lillian is the indirect object—she is the person to whom the frog was given.

"Another way of looking at this example is like this:

Uncle Tunnard gave a frog to Aunt Lillian.

"Here, frog is the direct object and Aunt Lillian is the object of the preposition *to*. Here's another example with a prepositional object.

The nurse laid the blanket on you.

"*Laid*, the past tense of *lay*, is a transitive verb," I explained. "The subject is *nurse*, and the direct object is *blanket*."

"Wait a minute—question from the audience," responded Aunt Ruth. "Suppose the blanket was laid on me; how could I not be affected? Wouldn't I—or in this sentence, *you*—be the direct object?"

"Well, even though the blanket was laid on *you*, it was the blanket itself that was laid, so the blanket is the direct object. *You* is the object of the preposition *on*, and objects of prepositions cannot be direct objects."

"You know, this is really quite thrilling," she said gleefully. "I feel quite, um, thrilled."

"Okay, I'm happy for you. Now let's talk about intransitive verbs:

You are sitting on a squirrel.

"*Sitting* is an intransitive verb here," I said. "It describes what the subject is doing, and there is no direct object (*squirrel* is the object of the preposition *on*)."

"Ah, got it," she replied.

"Ahem," I coughed. "Are you ready for possibly my favorite intransitive word of all time?" I shook with excitement; I felt almost giddy; and I could feel tears welling up behind my eyes. "Here it is:

The dead flower **smells**."

"That's it?" asked Aunt Ruth, emotions hidden behind a blank stare.

Undaunted with her not-as-excited-as-I-had-hoped-she-would-be reaction, I pushed forward. "Yes, the dead flower smells. Now, flowers don't have noses. A flower cannot detect the smell of another flower. It doesn't smell, say, a unicorn. It doesn't smell a slain dragon. It doesn't even smell cole slaw that has been sitting in the fridge for weeks. A flower—live or dead—can't smell anything! The flower just smells, with no direct object. Therefore, *smell* here is intransitive."

"Wait—can't some verbs be both transitive and intransitive? Isn't it true that I can smell—because I have a nose—without needing necessarily to smell a direct object? I can walk into the kitchen and smell (e.g., sniff) to determine if someone is baking chocolate chip cookies. The flowers smell—that is, they give off an aroma; I can smell—that is, I sniff to find an aroma. They're both intransitive, right?" asked Aunt Ruth.

"Very perceptive, my dear aunt!" I exclaimed. "Yes, you are absolutely correct. *Smell* is an interesting verb. Other examples are:

She tastes the soup. (transitive)
The soup tastes funny. (intransitive)
Uncle Voyle sang his favorite song. (transitive)
Uncle Voyle sang in the shower today. (intransitive)"

"Wait—now I'm confused. The transitive taste means 'eat a small sample of.' The intransitive taste is more about what the food does to the tongue, kind of like what a dead possum does to the nose when we say, 'The dead possum smells funny.' Right so far?"

"Yep. That's another good observation. It's subtle, but the *smell* in *The dead possum smells bad* means to give off a foul odor; that *smell* is all about associating—or linking—the quality of the odor with the possum. In this instance, *smell* is a linking verb. *Taste* in *The soup tastes funny* is also a linking verb. It tells us that a funny taste is associated, or linked to, the soup. I will tell you more about linking verbs in another adventure, Aunt Ruth, but for now be content to know that linking verbs are considered intransitive."

"Okay, I get that. The transitive *taste* has a different meaning than the intransitive *taste*. Now, when the uncle sang a song, that's transitive because he sang something—that is, he sang a song. But when we simply say he sang, and we don't specify what he sang, he still sang something, didn't he? Like, he could have sung 'New York, New York,' yes? Or he could have sung 'Hocus Pocus' by Focus, right?"

"Naturally."

"So ... the transitive *sang* and the intransitive *sang* have the exact same meaning?"

"Yep."

"Therefore, you're telling me that the reporting of the event—at least in this case—determines whether *sang* is transitive or intransitive?"

"That's a good way of putting it. Because we don't know what he's singing—no direct object was provided in the sentence with the intransitive *sang*—we have to say that the verb *sang* in this example is intransitive."

"Even though it's the same kind of singing, like through the larnyx and all that?"

"Larynx. Yes."

"Wow, I'll have to chew on that a while."

"I know it can be confusing. Just remember: If there is no direct object, we're talking intransitive. If there is a direct object, it's transitive."

"Whew. Thanks, Noble Nephew. Are we done yet?"

"Not quite. There's one more thing I want you to think about. Consider the sentence:

> Listen to me.

"Is *Listen* transitive or intransitive?" I asked.

"Well," said Aunt Ruth, clearing her throat, "it doesn't have a direct object (since *me* is a prepositional object), so it's intransitive, right?"

"There are many grammarians who would say that you are technically correct. But what if we replaced *Listen to* with a verb that means the same thing? Look at these examples that are very similar in meaning to the original sentence:

> Mark me.
> Mind me.
> Hear me.
> Heed me."

"Wow, so in these examples ... is *me* a direct object?"

"Yes, indeed."

"So, all those verbs are transitive?" she asked.

"Yep. Notice that replacing *Listen to* with a transitive verb shows us that *Listen to* is itself a verb phrase—that is, *Listen to* is a phrase that can be used as a verb, also called a phrasal verb. So, while *Listen* itself is intransitive, the phrasal verb *Listen to* in this example is transitive."

"Wait, I think my brain just had a meltdown," sighed Aunt Ruth.

"Don't worry if you didn't get the phrasal verb stuff. That's really more for people who like to spend their time arguing about grammar rules. I just wanted to make you aware of its existence."

"Um, thanks, I guess."

"Welcome. Now, one more example. Suppose you have:

> The vulture feasted on the unidentifiable remains.

"Tell me, Aunt Ruth. The verb *feasted*—is it transitive or intransitive?"

"Ew! Well, Nimble Nephew, I think *feasted* is intransitive because it has no direct object. The thing the vulture ate is inside a prepositional phrase—it's the object of the preposition *on*—so it's not a direct object."

"Very good! Technically, that's right. Now, some grammar experts will say that *on* in that sentence is not prepositional at all, that it's just part of the verb phrase *feasted on*. Like, what did the vulture do to the unidentifiable remains? He (or she) *feasted on* them! *Feasting on unidentifiable remains* does not mean the vulture was sitting or standing *on* his food, feasting. That's just the way it is, and I think it's certainly reasonable. Now suppose we changed that to:

> The vulture *devoured* the unidentifiable remains.

"Is *devoured* transitive or intransitive?"

"Well, the preposition *on* has disappeared. It looks like *remains* is a direct object. Therefore, I claim that *devoured* is transitive."

"Bingo. You got it."

"I do have one question before I fall asleep."

"Yes?"

"Did the vulture put the unidentifiable remains in his small travel suitcase so that he could take it with him on a plane?"

"His small travel suitcase?"

"Yes, his carrion luggage."

I heard a "ba-dum ching" and Aunt Ruth was out like a light.

21

The Ripcord Was Pulled by Aunt Ruth

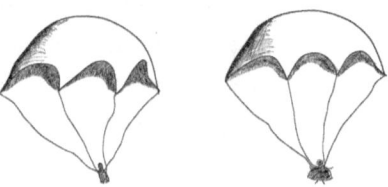

"Whee!" yelled Aunt Ruth as she leaped out of the plane and began the descent of her very first sky dive. Unlike Aunt Ruth's bucket list, mine never included jumping out of a perfectly working plane. Not to be outdone by my great-aunt, however, I followed suit and moments later I found myself in a free-fall.

"Okay, Aunt Ruth," I yelled after somehow catching up with her, "the next thing to learn about verbs is the voice they can have."

"Oh, brother!" grumbled Aunt Ruth.

"Nephew," I said. "I'm not your brother. I'm your nephew."

"No, I meant 'Oh, brother' in the 'I am in a severely agitated and incomprehensibly befuddled state right now' sense."

"Why, Aunt Ruth? Are you feeling conspicuous and self-conscious because a person down on the ground who is observing us may mistake you for the Goodyear blimp?"

WHAM! Ouch. I wasn't expecting her to be carrying her umbrella on this gravity-prone adventure through the friendly skies.

"You have no clue, do you, Dandruff-laden Dunderhead," she barked.

"What do you—"

"Look, Noodle-brained Nephew, your vociferous, vehement, and vexing propensity for shoving volumes of voluptuous verbs into my cerebral cortex is in vain. I don't like verbs. I don't like them, Sam I am."

I resisted the urge to ask her if she liked verbs on a train or in the rain. "Aunt Ruth, I—"

"Neurotic Nephew, you'll chase me to my grave, jumping in the coffin with me before it's nailed shut just so you can tell me the latest news from Verbs Illustrated, the hottest stock in the Verbs 500 from The Verb Street Journal, and the most scandalous gossip from Cosmo-Verbs."

"That's ridic—"

"And then, at the Pearly Gates, Saint Peter will be shocked when he sees me and he'll say, 'Aunt Ruth, you're about ten years too early. How did you get here?' And you know what I'll tell him?"

I swallowed in suspense. "What?"

"I'll tell him that my pin-headed nephew drove me to my ultimate demise with his obsessive love of verbs." She took a deep breath.

I waited a moment and then asked, "Are you done?"

"Oh, I'm just getting started," she retorted. She was in rare form.

"Aunt Ruth, hear me out. Verbs aren't that complicated. I just want to teach you one new thing today."

"I don't want to learn about Stinking Verbs!"

"You mean Linking Verbs? Don't worry. That's not today. All I want to do today is to tell you about the *voice* that verbs have."

"Verbs have a voice? Wow, this sounds complicated," said Aunt Ruth. "I didn't know verbs could talk. Do they have like a southern drawl, a Brooklyn accent, a Valley Girl kind of—"

"It's simple, really. We've learned the two types of verbs—transitive and intransitive—and now we'll learn the two kinds of voice—active or passive."

"Active or passive," she echoed.

"Simple examples of transitive verbs in the active voice are:

> Lenny *ate* the gerbil.
> Sally *smashed* a mosquito.
> Jacquelyn *caught* a firefly.

"This is called the active voice because the subject in each sentence is active—each subject is an actor performing some verb. Lenny, Sally, and Jacquelyn are the subjects / actors, and *ate*, *smashed*, and *caught* are the verbs. Good so far?"

"So far, so good," she answered.

"Now, look at the passive voice in the rewrites of those sentences:

> The gerbil *was eaten* by Lenny.
> The mosquito *was smashed* by Sally.
> The firefly *was caught* by Jacquelyn.

"In the passive voice, the subject is having some verb performed on it by some actor. In '*The gerbil was eaten by Lenny*,' the subject is *gerbil* and the actor or agent is *Lenny*."

"Is Lenny really an actor?" asked Aunt Ruth. "Would I recognize him in any movies, like *Lenny Meets Gerbilzilla*?"

"I didn't mean like a Hollywood actor, Aunt Ruth. I meant someone or something who performs an action."

"So, *was eaten* is passive?"

"Yep, but note that *was eaten* is still considered transitive in this example. It is the passive form of the verb *ate* (from '*Lenny ate the gerbil*')."

"Okay, got it. *Ate* is in the active voice; *was eaten* is in the passive voice; Lenny is not a Hollywood actor; and gerbils apparently are edible. Can we be done now?" asked Aunt Ruth.

"Wait a minute. I never said gerbils are edible. You're going to get me in trouble with the animal rights activists."

"But you said Lenny ate a gerbil. That implies—"

"Lenny was my cat. My cat ate my gerbil."

"Oh, then never mind. Can we be done now?"

"Not yet. Here are more transitive verbs in active voice.

> Mike Trout hit the baseball over the fence.
> Wynton Marsalis played a beautiful trumpet solo.
> Jake Arrieta pitched a no-hitter.
> Grandma executed a perfect pirouette.
> Grandpa ate the corn flakes.
> The bright light temporarily blinded me.

Subject	Verb	Direct Object
Mike Trout	hit	baseball
Wynton Marsalis	played	solo
Jake Arrieta	pitched	no-hitter
Grandma	executed	pirouette
Grandpa	ate	corn flakes
light	blinded	me

"See how each of those sentences has a direct object? Let's convert each sentence to passive voice.

> The baseball was hit over the fence by Mike Trout.
> A beautiful trumpet solo was played by Wynton Marsalis.
> A no-hitter was pitched by Jake Arrieta.
> A perfect pirouette was executed by Grandma.
> The corn flakes were eaten by Grandpa.
> I was temporarily blinded by the bright light.

Subject	Verb	Direct Object	Agent
baseball	was hit		Mike Trout
solo	was played		Wynton Marsalis
no-hitter	was pitched		Jake Arrieta
pirouette	was executed		Grandma
corn flakes	were eaten		Grandpa
I	was blinded		light

"When we transformed each active voice sentence to passive voice, the object in the active voice became the subject in the passive voice. The subject in the active voice became the actor in the passive voice."

"So … the passive voice is saying the same thing but in a different way?"

"Sure. You could write this a number of ways, e.g., 'The baseball was hit by Mike Trout over the fence.'"

"Is it possible for an intransitive verb to have an active voice?"

"Yes, absolutely. Think about verbs that have action without requiring a direct object."

"Um, I can't think of any."

"Let me help you:

>   My ice melted.
>   My skin burned.
>   My trombone exploded.
>   The salmon swam.
>   The elephant roared.
>   Bill the Grammar Fairy vanished.
>   The drummer spontaneously combusted.
>   We all sang.

"These are intransitive—each sentence has no direct object. They are in the active voice—the subject of each is performing an action. Notice also that each of those sentences CANNOT be transformed to a passive sentence."

"They can't?"

"Nope. How would you transform 'The elephant roared' to a passive sentence? Would you say, 'Was roared by the elephant'? It doesn't make sense. Would you say, 'Roar did the elephant' or 'Did roar the elephant'? No, not unless your name is Yoda or you are a poet with a lot of poetic license. Even in those examples, the subject is *elephant*."

"Poetic license? I didn't know there was a hunting season on them."

"Ha ha," I chuckled. "Anyway, an intransitive active voice sentence has no object that it can use as the subject of a passive voice sentence."

"Wow, that almost makes sense. Question for you."

"Sure."

"Is there a preference for one voice over the other? I mean, is it better to use the active or the passive voice?"

"Good question. It depends on the situation. Usually, in public speaking or writing, the preference is for the active voice. It feels more energetic, which (I guess) in our "go go go" society we tend to favor. We like proactive more than reactive. Active voice is more urgent, more direct, and more attention-getting."

"Why would someone ever use the passive voice then?"

"Variety is one reason. Readers (and writers) get tired of reading (and writing) in the same voice all the time. But there's a better reason."

"What's that?"

"The voice can subtly change the emphasis of the sentence. *'Grandma ate the gallon of ice cream'* has a different tone than *'The gallon of ice cream was eaten by Grandma.'* They mean the same thing, but the former answers the question *'Why is Grandma smiling?'* The latter answers the question *'What happened to the dessert we were going to eat tonight?'*"

"So, *'Your parachute's ripcord must be pulled immediately'* is not as effective as *'You must pull your ripcord immediately'*?"

"Correct. In fact, to make the latter even more effective, get rid of the *you must*. That will turn it into a more imperative command to the listener."

"Okay," said Aunt Ruth, "then ... PULL YOUR RIPCORD!"

22

Intransitive Verbs Rock

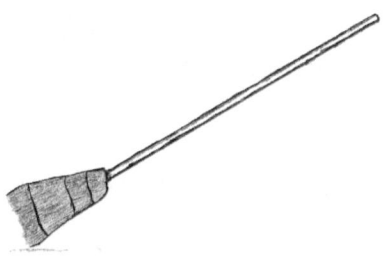

The day began.

I sneezed. That was my first clue. I shivered. That was my second clue. Finally, I fatigued. That was my third and final clue. I was in the midst of an intransitive verb kind of day.

The doorbell rang. The door opened. Aunt Ruth appeared.

"Aunt Ruth, please come in."

She smiled. "Intransitive Verb Day rocks!"

I nodded. "Indeed, the day is so inspiring."

I motioned and I pointed. "Have you eaten?"

She declined. "I ate this morning."

I sighed. "I haven't eaten today."

She waved. "Go ahead. You should eat."

So, I ate.

The pancakes tasted delicious.

Aunt Ruth glared.

"Linking verbs are intransitive, too."

"Are they?"

"Yes, they are."

A shocked Aunt Ruth sauntered into the living room and sat in the comfy chair. She sighed. She slept. She snored. She awoke.

I shuffled into the room.

We talked for a while. She queried. I responded. She asked. I replied. We chatted. We debated. We pontificated. We adjourned.

We walked into the kitchen and we cleaned.

One of my dishes broke, shattering on the floor in thousands of tiny shards.

She wept. I swept.

"You sweeped."

"No, I swept."

I argued. She argued. We argued.

I apologized. She apologized.

She laughed and then I laughed. We laughed together.

Lightning flashed.

Thunder clapped.

The ferociously brisk wind blew.

The weather vane spun.

The house creaked.

The house shook.

The weather precipitated.

Rain fell.

Actually, rain poured down.

I cheered.

She howled.

We watched.

We waited.

We anticipated.

"I'm hungry."

"Me too."

We voted.

I lost.

I cooked.

We ate.

We participated.

We drank.

We sang.

We danced.

We prayed.

We rejoiced.

We played.

We fished and then we hunted.

We worked and then we relaxed.

Then we napped.

Bill the Grammar Fairy arrived.

"Intransitive Verb Day rocks!"

We agreed. "It certainly does."

Bill shouted.

Bill whistled.

Bill hummed.

Intransitive Verbs Rock

Bill whined.

Bill surmised and sermonized and summarized and hypothesized.

Bill privatized and Bill generalized.

Bill winked.

Bill blinked.

Bill spoke.

"These sentences don't have to be so short."

Bill cheered with the enthusiasm of a small bear sitting next to a very large jar of honey.

Bill croaked louder than a bullfrog in the backyard pond at midnight on the Fourth of July.

Bill disappeared, only to startlingly reappear later that night in the bathroom mirror.

Bill vanished into the twilight faster than the speed of sound.

Not one person in the crowd comprising famous authors, political figures, and chihuahuas objected.

The day ended most victoriously as the golden orb that floats across our sky settled into its western nest for the evening.

We had succeeded.

We had won.

We had conquered.

Intransitive verbs rock!

23

Aunt Ruth and Verbs Ala Mode

"Welcome to Clovis's," said a familiar voice as we entered the door of the downtown dessert shop. "Our ice cream will freeze your—"

"Hi, Clovis," I said.

"—lips off," he said as he looked up from the counter he had been cleaning.

"Dude! And Aunt Dude! How are you doin' today?"

"Pretty well, Clovis, thanks," said Aunt Ruth.

"What can I get you, Aunt Ruth?"

"I would like your brownie fudge sundae with extra whipped cream and a macaroni cherry on top."

"I think you mean a maraschino cherry," said Clovis.

"Oh, right. One of those," she said.

I pulled out a school bell and rang it as quickly and loudly as I could.

Aunt Ruth was so surprised she fell flat on the floor. "What was that for, oh Ding-dong Nephew?"

"I want you to have the apple pie ala mode," I said, discreetly signaling to Clovis with a clandestine wink that went unobserved by my aunt.

"But I want a brownie fudge sundae—"

"Three monumental-sized scoops of ice cream, Aunt Ruth," I whispered, "each scoop a different flavor, all piled high on a huge slice of fresh-baked apple pie."

"Deal!" she quickly agreed.

Aunt Ruth sat down in her usual chair at her usual table, and Clovis set a large slab of pie, buried under a three-flavored ice cream mountain, right in front of her.

"Wow, Clovis, this is amazing," she cried with glee.

"Welcome to your next lesson on verbs, Aunt Ruth!" I exclaimed cheerfully.

"My next ... oh brother," she sighed, rolling her eyes. "Listen, Napoleonic Nephew, I'm not in the mood for verbs."

"Well, I am in the mood. In fact, I'm in an *In the Mood* mood." I looked over to my left and yelled, "A one and a two and a three!"

Bright lights flashed on, and a big band orchestra, previously hidden in the shadows on a makeshift stage in the far back corner of Clovis's restaurant, broke into a stirring rendition of Glenn Miller's 1930s jazz hit.

"Wow, they're pretty good," admitted Aunt Ruth. "Okay, maybe I'm in the mood now."

"Here is a spoon, Aunt Ruth. You eat, I'll talk. Now, dive in!" She needed no further convincing.

I began the lesson. "Just as your ala mode dessert has three flavors of ice cream, English verbs have three modes, also called moods. A mode or mood gives us a hint of how the verb should be understood or interpreted.

"There are many moods found in the world's various languages, and in English the three that we need to care about are **indicative**, **imperative**, and **subjunctive**.

"The **indicative** mode states a fact or asks a question. This is the most common mode. It's like the vanilla ice cream after a meal of meat and potatoes. It's the faded blue jeans and sneakers of the linguistic world—nothin' fancy, but popular with everyone.

"Examples of the indicative mode are:

> The invisible man **went** to his doctor appointment.
> The doctor **said** that he couldn't see him.
> **Have** you **seen** Aunt Ruth's broom?
> Why, **does** she **need** to fly somewhere?

"The **imperative** mode is a command or request. It hints of the *I'm in charge* mind-set, the *take no prisoners* philosophy. It is the chocolate ice cream after a dinner of blackened salmon and jalapeno corn fritters. Everyone likes it, but if you eat too much of it, too late at night, it may keep you awake longer than usual.

"Examples of the imperative mode are:

> **Keep** your boa constrictor away from Mr. Martin's cat.
> **Go** to the store, and **buy** another cat for Mr. Martin.
> **Apologize** to Mr. Martin, and **tell** him we didn't think the boa constrictor would do that to Mrs. Martin too.

"The **subjunctive** mode states an idea that is not a fact but is more like a *suppose this happened* or *what if that happened* speculation. Because this mode, with its hypothetical statements, reminds me of Sherlock Holmes, and with a nod to Britain's general fondness for strawberries and cream, I say that strawberry ice cream following a hardy plate of fish and chips suits this mode quite well.

"Usually the subjunctive mode begins with a subordinate conjunction such as *if, that, unless, though,* or *except,* etc. Note that using a conjunction does not always make it subjunctive.

"You might use the subjunctive mode to describe a wish, doubt, demand, suggestion, or a future, unknown situation. For example:

> If Jupiter **were** (instead of **was**) someday to crash into Earth, all literature containing grammar errors would be destroyed.
> I suggest that she **bake** (instead of **bakes**) the cake in the morning.

"Something that is conditional is not automatically subjunctive. If the conditional is true, then the verb is not subjunctive.

If a marble **is** round, it can easily roll on the floor.

"This is indicative, not subjunctive, because we know that marbles are indeed round. However, we could change the conditional to make it subjunctive:

If a marble **were** square, it would not easily roll."

"Not to be disrespectful, Neapolitan Nephew, but hasn't the subjunctive gone the way of the dinosaur? I mean, isn't the subjunctive distinct?"

"I think you mean extinct, and no, the subjunctive is not extinct. We just don't realize we're using it and getting it right. In English, most of the time, the subjunctive form of a verb is the same as the indicative."

"This subjunctive stuff is confusing me, Nasturtium Nephew," sighed Aunt Ruth. "I'm not used to it."

"You can do it, Aunt Ruth. Let me give you a couple of hints that may be of use to you.

"First of all, in modern English the subjunctive will (for the most part) only appear in subordinate clauses—*If* and *that* being the most common.

I suggest *that* she **take** the train on Saturday. (**take**, not **takes**)
Andy recommended *that* Aunt Bea **fly** to Wahoo for the wedding. (**fly**, not **flies**)
If he **were** there, he would have eaten both iguanas. (**were**, not **was**)
If she **were** queen, we would have chocolate pudding at every meal. (**were**, not **was**)"

"So," asked Aunt Ruth, "if the verb is not in a subordinate clause, that means I don't have to worry about it being subjunctive?"

"Right. Of course, if you're reading some older English literature, your mileage may vary."

"Got it. What's the second hint for subjunctives?"

"Are you ready for this? Hold on to your dentures, Aunt Ruth. In English, the subjunctive form of the verb will be the same as the indicative form of the verb except in cases where: 1) the verb is third person singular in the present tense, or 2) the verb is a form of *to be*, past or present tense."

"Boy, that's a mouthful," cried Aunt Ruth.

"What, the ice cream?"

"No, this subjunctive garbage," she grumbled.

"Look, it's not that hard, really. I'll show you a couple of examples. Give me a verb, any verb."

"Okay, how about *run*."

"Good. Now, for the indicative mood, we say *I run, we run, you run, they run, and he / she / it runs*. Note how the third person singular (he / she / it) is *runs* but all the others are *run*.

"Now, for the subjunctive mood, we say: *I run, we run, you run, they run, and he / she / it run*. They're all the same now. They are all the simple verb form. When would we say 'he run'? I'm glad you asked.

> Doctors recommend that he **run** five times each week.
> I insisted that she **run** to the beach.
> It's been suggested that he **run** to the museum and back."

"So," said Aunt Ruth, "I would say: My vet recommends that my pet yak Yolanda **eat** five times each day?"

"Yes. It would be incorrect to say your vet recommends that your pet yak Yolanda **eats** five times per day."

"I have a problem with that, though," said Aunt Ruth.

"What's that?"

"You said third person singular. Yolanda is not a person; she's a yak."

"Well, 'person' here doesn't mean a human being. It just means it's not first person (I or me); it's not second person (you); but it's third person (he, she, or it). And remember, it's only for the singular."

"Right. Yolanda is not married. She's single."

"Sigh. Aunt Ruth, you're impossible. Now, let's talk about *to be*."

"How about *not to be*? I understand that that is the question."

I ignored her Hamletian reference and continued. "When we are talking about the subjunctive forms of *to be*, tense matters. That is, are we talking about past tense or present tense? It would behoove us to talk about past and present forms of *to be* and their subjunctive counterparts.

Person	Past	Present	Past Subjunctive	Present Subjunctive
1st	was	am	**were**	**be**
(Indicative) Last week, I was king for a day. Now I am president.			
(Subjunctive) If I **were** king for a day, I would eat only ice cream. They insisted that now I **be** president.			
1st plural	were	are	**were**	**be**
(Indicative) We were at the zoo when it rained. We are there now.			
(Subjunctive) If we **were** at the zoo, we would have gotten wet. Aunt Ruth insists that we **be** there by five o'clock today.			
2nd	were	are	**were**	**be**
(Indicative) You were in the garden. You are my scarecrow today.			
(Subjunctive) If you **were** in the garden, the crows would have gone. Aunt Ruth commands that you **be** the scarecrow again.			
3rd	was	is	**were**	**be**
(Indicative) She was the fastest and won the race.			
(Subjunctive) If she **were** the fastest, she would have won. For her to advance, it is required that she **be** the fastest next week.			
3rd plural	were	are	**were**	**be**
(Indicative) They were goofy and ate dessert first.			
(Subjunctive) If they **were** goofy, they'd have eaten dessert first. It's important that we **be** quiet now!			

"For the past subjunctive, use *were* in all cases. If I **were** dead; if you **were** in the garage; if she **were** absolutely livid; if they **were** asleep.

"Finally, in the present subjunctive, the form of *to be* is simply *be*.

"*I am contemplative* in the indicative becomes (*It is important that*) *I* **be** *contemplative* in the subjunctive.

"*You are grateful* in the indicative becomes (*He insists that*) *you* **be** *grateful* in the subjunctive.

"*She is on time* in the indicative becomes (*The boss demands that*) *she* **be** *on time* in the subjunctive.

"*We are happy* in the indicative becomes (*She recommends that*) *we* **be** *happy* in the subjunctive.

"*They are Cubs fans* in the indicative becomes *(The security guard requires that) they* **be** *Cubs fans* in the subjunctive.

"Thus ends the saga of the subjunctive, and thus ends the lesson on verb moods. Now you can creatively write and speak, unleashing the magnanimous ideas that flood your soul."

I heard a snore. I looked up and noticed that Aunt Ruth had fallen asleep, her head face-down on her plate. Fortunately, she had finished most of her pie and ice cream.

"Ahem, Aunt Ruth," I said rather loudly, clearing my throat.

Her head snapped up. She had a small blotch of vanilla ice cream on her forehead. "Yes, Nitwit Nephew?"

"There you have it—the three moods of verbs in the English language."

"This is hard stuff, you know."

"Well, you don't need to be an expert in this stuff, but it's good to be aware of its existence. Actually, English has it easier than many other languages. Some languages rely heavily on the subjunctive and have many other moods."

"I'm glad we only have three moods," said Aunt Ruth.

"Why is that?"

"Three scoops is my limit of ice cream, and if I were to exceed my limit, I'd shout, 'Look at me; I'm going to pop!'"

CRASH!

"What was that?" I asked, wiping dust off my glasses.

"It's I, Bill the Grammar Fairy. I am here to give Aunt Ruth an award."

"An award? Why?"

"You may have missed it, Mr. Nephew, but your aunt just used all three English moods in one sentence. She's got the indicative (*Three scoops is my limit of ice cream*); she's got the subjunctive (*if I were to exceed my limit*); and she's got the imperative (*Look at me*).

"Congratulations, Aunt Ruth! Let me present you with this award," said Bill the Grammar Fairy.

"I love awards," said a glowing Aunt Ruth. "What's the award?"

"For you, my dear," said Bill the Grammar Fairy as he reached into his backpack and pulled out a large bowl, "I have three scoops of ice cream—vanilla, chocolate, and strawberry—all piled on top of a queen-sized slice of apple pie. Enjoy!" He placed the bowl on the table in front of Aunt Ruth.

Aunt Ruth sighed and fainted. Her face landed in the bowl of ice cream.

Bill looked at her for a moment and then said, "Clovis, could you fix me a sandwich, perhaps a nice, thick reuben with sauerkraut and—"

"Well, Bill" he said, "if this **weren't** the end of the story, I would make one for you. I've already turned the grill off and it's time to close up for the night. Maybe you can, uh, get Aunt Ruth to share her bowl with you."

"Um, never mind," sighed Bill. "If only I **were** in the mood for ice cream!"

24

Aunt Ruth and the Tense Predicament, Part I

The roar of the engines added to the excitement in the air. Thumping, my heart pounded wildly, each beat firing like a cannon. I climbed into the cockpit of the F-14, aka Tomcat, fighter plane.

It had always been a dream of mine to fly a Tomcat, and for my birthday I received an official "Fly By Numbers: Learn to Fly the F-14 and Earn a Free Flight" coloring book from an anonymous benefactor.

I read the book forward and backward, memorizing every little nuance that seemed even remotely relevant. When I was confident that I had mastered the knowledge required, I called the 1-800 number and set up a reservation for my free flight. And now the day had finally come.

"Okay, Bub," I heard someone shout over the headset, the voice apparently that of the instructor who was already seated behind me in the other cockpit seat. "Let's get this baby off the ground. We is to fly!"

We is to fly? What? Argh. I could tell that this was going to be a grammar-challenged event. I decided to ignore it for the moment and focus on taking off. "Roger," I replied. "Let's go." We zipped smoothly down the runway, and before you could say "Top Gun," we were high in the friendly skies.

Though part of me was giddy with excitement, I couldn't keep the grammar episode from grating on my nerves. I knew the infraction would gnaw at my soul and that I had to defuse the situation or I wouldn't be able to concentrate.

"Listen," I shouted into the headset microphone, "you should be using the first person plural form of *to be* with the first person plural pronoun. You should say something like, 'We are to fly.' Remind me to give you—for free—a lesson on verb tense when we reach the ground."

I glanced at the instructor in the mirror. I wasn't really expecting a thank you, but what did I get? Nothing but a blank stare. Even with the instructor wearing dark goggles, I would recognize that stare anywhere.

"Aunt Ruth! What are you doing up here?"

"I am flying. And you?"

"I'm flying too, I suppose."

"I hope you like your birthday present!" she said.

"It's from you? Wow, I do like it! Thank you so much! Now tell me, when did you learn to fly one of these?"

"Oh, I don't know how to fly a Tomcat. I convinced the boys back at the base to let me fly with you though."

"But … um … Aunt Ruth, do you know how to land this thing?"

"No sir, I don't," she replied.

"Well, neither do I," I sighed.

"What? You didn't read the manual?"

"I devoured every word, but the manual only covered takeoff and cruising. Landing is taught in Volume Two."

Aunt Ruth instantly radioed to the air traffic control folks. "May day! May day! We have a tense predicament up here!"

"Roger, Aunt Ruth," said a voice from the other end. "I've got my three tense experts here: Captain Past, Captain Present, and Captain Future. They'll walk—or fly—your nauseating nephew through this."

"Okay," I choked. "This is Nonplussed Nephew. What do I do first?"

"Captain Present here. First, look at the control panel and check your

Verb meter. Tell me what it says."

"It says *fly*."

"Good, that's excellent. Looks like *fly* is the verb you will be conjugating as we attempt to bring you safely to ground. Now, *fly* is one of many irregular verbs in the English language. To be able to conjugate the irregular verbs, there are some things you need to know. I hope you know them. Fill out the chart on the computer screen in front of you."

This didn't look overly daunting. First person singular, I remembered, is for the personal pronoun "I." I would say, "I fly." First person plural is "We," and I would say, "We fly." Second person is always treated as plural, and it's "You fly." For some odd reason—I don't know why—the third person singular is treated differently. "He flies" or "She flies" or "It flies" is correct. Then, for third person plural, it's "They fly." I completed the chart:

Simple Present Tense		
	Subject Pronoun	**Verb**
1st person singular	I	fly
1st person plural	We	fly
2nd person	You	fly
3rd person singular	He / She / It	flies
3rd person plural	They	fly

"Very good," said Captain Present. "Now, find your Present Participle control. Set that to the -ing form of *fly*."

I found the control and set it to *flying*. "Present participle … *flying* … got it," I said, my heart still racing.

"As an aside, your present participles will always end in *-ing*. There are a lot of things that you can do with the present participle—dicing, slicing, making julienne fries, and using it as a fishing lure, ha ha ha."

I remained silent.

"Uh, sorry," said Captain Present. "Just trying a little 1970s television advertising humor to add some levity to the situation. I'll limit my focus today on how the present participle is useful in verb conjugation."

"Okay, thanks," I said, not sure what else to say.

A new voice appeared in the headset with a Southern drawl so thick I could almost smell the hot barbecue sauce dripping off the tongue.

"Captain Past *hay-yer*. Son, first *tay-yell* me what your Simple Past *Tay-yent*s button *say-yez*." That's what it sounded like. What he actually said was, "Captain Past here. Son, first tell me what your Simple Past Tense button says."

"The Simple Past Tense button says *flew*."

"Good. Just to make sure we're on the same page, let me point out that *flew* is the Simple Past *Tay-yents* verb *foe-orm* for all persons and number, e.g., I flew; we flew; you flew; he / she / it flew; and they flew."

"Got it."

"*Nay-ow, say-yet* your Past Participle control. Be *cay-yer-ful* because *fly* is an irregular verb, and the past participle of irregular verbs is something *thay-yet may-yen-nee* people *gay-yet* wrong."

He was right. I needed to exercise caution. My mind flashed back to many of the "present/past/past participle" verb families I learned as a kid. Of course, there were regular verbs like jump/jumped/jumped or slice/sliced/sliced, where the past participle is the same as the simple past tense and is formed by adding -ed or -d to the end of the simple verb.

Then there were the irregular verbs, where—as the old adage goes (or would go, if indeed there were an old adage)—"ya just gotta learn 'em." Some of my favorite verb families included drink/drank/drunk, sing/sang/sung, lie/lay/lain, swim/swam/swum, and ... fly/flew/flown!

"Past participle ... *flown* ... got it."

"Great job!" said Captain Past.

A different voice then came in via the headset.

"Captain Future here. Okay. Tell me what you would say if you were talking about doing this again tomorrow. Use WILL[1] plus your base verb."

"I will fly," I said. Under my breath, I whispered to Aunt Ruth, "This is easy."

"Not so fast, cupcake," said Captain Future, apparently overhearing my words. "*I will fly* is correct, but you can also say this another way, using a form of BE plus 'going to' with the verb."

"You mean ... *I am going to fly?*"

"Bravo! Yes. They have roughly the same meaning, but *will* tends to be used more as a promise, and '*form of BE + going to*' is used more as a plan.

    I will fly to LaCrosse on Wednesday.
    It's a beautiful day. I am going to fly this afternoon.

"This is your Simple Future Tense."

Simple Future Tense	
Subject	Verb
I, We, You, He / She / It, They	will fly
I	am going to fly
We, You, They	are going to fly
He / She / It	is going to fly

"Set your Future Participle button." His voice was robot-like, not varying in pitch or rate. The pronunciation he used for "button" was amusing but not enough to relieve the situation of its gravity.

"I ... uh ... I don't have a Future Participle button!" I said, panicking.

"Good! You shouldn't. Ha ha, there's no such thing," he replied in his stiff, mechanical tone.

"Very funny," I sighed. "What's next?"

"Captain Present, back again. Let's quickly make sure we're talking

---

[1]   Alternatively, "*shall*" can be used in place of "*will*." See the exquisite book *I Laid an Egg on Aunt Ruth's Head* for the rules on *shall / will* usage.

about the same participles."

Present Participle	flying
Past Participle	flown
Future Participle	(just kidding)

"Yes, those are my participles," I agreed.

"Just so you know, those participles, *flown* and *flying*—past and present—are the building blocks for your conjugation of *fly*. Are you ready to continue?"

"You bet. Keep going."

A new voice—a rich baritone with a slightly vague Mediterranean accent—appeared on the radio: "Will the nephew save the day with correct conjugation? Will he be the victorious hero? Or will he become just another victim of the irregular but quite practical verbs? Stay tuned for the next episode, same grammar time, same grammar channel."

Suddenly, a rousing rendition of a song (pick your favorite movie theme song with the words "gonna," "fly," and "now" in the title) began playing somewhere in the background.

I heard the author yell over the radio, "That's a wrap for Part I. Nauseating Nephew, I need you to circle the plane around in a holding pattern a bunch of times. Back to you in five minutes."

Past Participle Guilt (Intermission)

"What is going on?" I bellowed. "What is the author thinking? Has he gone mad? This is annoying!"

"I haven't seen you this upset since they canceled reruns of your favorite show, 'Lost in Adverbs.' I guess I forgot to tell you," said Aunt Ruth, "that the author wants to have an intermission in the middle of this story."

"In the middle of a chapter? It just isn't done. I was making great progress on conjugating *fly*. I was entering my participial groove, as they say."

"The author said it will be too long of a story otherwise; the reader may not be able to finish the chapter before having to move on to another activity and may lose his or her place upon returning to finish reading."

"What, like the reader is afraid of using a bookmark or something?"

CRASH!

From out of nowhere appeared none other than Bill the Grammar Fairy. He sprang to his feet, shrugged, and said, "Someone's got to teach the grammar lesson while you're taking an intermission break. Got any prosciutto, maybe wrapped around a crisp stalk of fresh asparagus? Back in the old country, my grandma used to make—"

"Bill, uh, no. I have no prosciutto. And please call it a grammar story, not a grammar lesson. We don't want the reader suspecting that he or she may be both enjoying the story and learning grammar concurrently. Anyway, thanks for volunteering."

"Oh, you think I wanted to do this? I drew straws with Binky the elephant and that Medici guy from your first book."

"Peachy?"

"Yeah, Peachy Medici. Anyway, I lost, so here I am. Mind if I get started?"

"Be my guest."

"You really don't have any food I can eat first: a veggie tray, some liver pate, a deviled egg with a hint of paprika sprinkled on top, or stalks of celery and a little hummus? You know, back in the old country, Grandma could make this amazing—"

"Here Bill, take this. It's all I've got," I said, handing him a gray, rock-hard glob that I just happened to be carrying with me (call it one of those coincidental *deus ex machina* moments).

"What's this?"

"It's gum."

"What is its origin?"

"I found it under my chair. I think the gum was my grandmother's, from back in the old country."

"How do you know that?"

"Her teeth were still in it. Now, Bill, please continue with your performance. The intermission will be over before we know it."

"All right then," said Bill as he stepped in front of a camera.

"Ahem. Today, I am going to sing for you a little (mostly) iambic ditty that I wrote on the back of a napkin on my way here. I call it 'Get Past Your Past Participle Guilt.'

"Okay, boys and girls, moms and dads, grandmas and grandpas, aunts, uncles, cousins, friends, neighbors, dogs, and cats, follow along with me in your book or on your screen while I sing this little number for you. When I present the verbs to you, the simple present tense will be <u>underlined</u>, the past tense will be in *italics*, and the past participle will be **bold**. Also, note that with the past participle I will use some sort of helper word like 'had, has, or have' in the conjunction form (you'd, he's, we've, etc.).

"To keep this interesting—riveting, even—I am going to focus solely on irregular verbs. With regular verbs, you typically make the past tense by adding -ed, and the past participle is the same as the past tense (e.g., the regular verb hunt has past tense *hunted* and past participle **hunted**).

"In addition—this is worth at least fifty cents of the price of the book alone—I am going to concentrate only on past participles. Figuring out the present participle of a verb is easy-peasy. You simply append your verb with -ing.[1]

"So, with all those caveats, disclaimers, excuses, and sufficient erudite language to obfuscate any possibility of liability that could lead to legal action, let's proceed." Bill cleared his throat and began:

> The bells that ring, they *rang*, they've **rung**.
> The birds that sing, they *sang*, they've **sung**.
> The yard I mow, I *mowed*, I've **mown**.
> That grass can grow, it *grew*, it's **grown**.
>
> The boats that sink, they *sank*, they've **sunk**.
> The sailors drink, they *drank*, they've **drunk**.
> The piggies stink, they *stank*, they've **stunk**.
> You just might shrink, you *shrank*, you've **shrunk**!
>
> The kids we bear, we *bore*, we've **born**.
> The clothes we wear, we *wore*, we've **worn**.
> We have to choose, we *chose*, we've **chosen**.
> It's cold. We'll freeze, we *froze*, we've **frozen**.
>
> The dogs may bite, they *bit*, they've **bitten**.
> The authors write, they *wrote*, they've **written**.
> Our foe we smite, we *smote*, we've **smitten**.
> We like to ride, we *rode*, we've **ridden**.

---

[1] It's not quite as simple as that, really (but almost). If a verb ends in -e, you will generally need to drop the -e before adding the -ing. Thus, the present participle of *practice* is *practicing*. If the last two letters are a vowel followed by a consonant, you will typically double the consonant and then add -ing. The present participle of *refer* is *referring*.

We like to eat, we *ate*, we've **eaten**.
They can't be beat, we *beat*, we've **beaten**.
I mistake, *mistook*, and have **mistaken**.
The sun does rise, it *rose*, it's **risen**.

We tip, we fall, we *fell*, we've **fallen**.
In cars we drive, we *drove*, we've **driven**.
Friends we forgive, we *forgave*, we've **forgiven**.
Sometimes we hide, we *hid*, we've **hidden**.

We like to run, we *ran*, we've **run**.
And then we swim, we *swam*, we've **swum**.
The ball we throw, we *threw*, we've **thrown**.
In planes we fly, we *flew*, we've **flown**.

The beans to grind, we *ground*, we've **ground**.
Something to find, we *found*, we've **found**.
A book to bind, we *bound*, we've **bound**.
Sorrows to drown, we *drowned*, we've **drowned**.

A snake will slink, he *slunk*, he's **slunk**.
Guitars we string, we *strung*, we've **strung**.
A game to win, we *won*, we've **won**.
A neck to wring, we *wrung*, we've **wrung**.

Now when we teach, we *taught*, we've **taught**.
And when we bring, we *brought*, we've **brought**.
And when we buy, we *bought*; we've **bought**.
It's what we think, we *thought*, we've **thought**.

The monkeys swing, they *swung*, they've **swung**.
The babies cling, they *clung*, they've **clung**.
The art we'll hang, we *hung*, we've **hung**.
Arrows I sling, I *slung*, I've **slung**.

Fishing rods cast, we *cast*, we've **cast**.
The products cost, they *cost*, they've **cost**.
Our bubbles burst, they *burst*, they've **burst**.
Something to lose, we *lost*, we've **lost**.

The toughest yet is lie, *lay*, **lain**—
Don't let it muddle up your brain.
You lie right now; last night you *lay*;
And when you're done you say you've **lain**."

"Psst!" I heard someone say. I looked over my shoulder. It was Aunt Ruth. "We have to get back to the story. Bill's going out of control. How do we make him stop?"

Quick-thinking as always, I grabbed a microphone and said, with as official a voice as I could muster, "Free pastrami in the deli across the street!"

ZOOM! Just like that, Bill was gone. Intermission was over.

We resumed our positions; some people touched up our make-up; and somebody said, "Three, two, one, ACTION!"

Aunt Ruth and the Tense Predicament, Part II

[In our previous episode, Aunt Ruth and her nephew found themselves somehow flying a jet fighter plane but with no knowledge of how to land said vehicle. The story continues. They are in a tense predicament indeed, and only by correctly conjugating the verb *fly* can they safely land.]

"Stay calm. I know you can do this," exclaimed Captain Present. "Okay, tell me exactly what you are doing right now—in the present—using a form of TO BE and your Present Participle."

"I am flying."

"Good. That's your **Present Progressive.** I repeat, it says what you are doing right now, in the present.

Present Progressive	
Subject	Verb
I	am flying
We, You, They	are flying
He / She / It	is flying

"The Present Progressive can also be used to talk about something that will be happening soon—'I am *flying* to Lincoln later tonight'—or something that happens regularly—'I am *flying* to Montreal on Thursdays this year.'"

"Got it," I said, still feeling a bit apprehensive.

"All right," said Captain Present, taking a deep breath. "Now, tell me what you will say, once you reach the ground, when you describe what you have just finished. Use HAVE and the past participle."

"I have flown."

"Excellent. That is called the **Present Perfect** because it is something that, here in the present, you can say you have completed or accomplished. Now you can say you've done it!"

Present Perfect Tense	
Subject	Verb
I, We, You, They	have flown
He / She / It	has flown

"So far so good?" he asked.

"Hanging in there."

"Last one from me," said Captain Present. "Tell me what you would say if someone called you and asked what you have been doing this morning. Use HAVE BEEN and the present participle."

"I have been flying."

"Good job. That's the **Present Perfect Progressive**."

"So ... I could use that in sentences like:

> I have been flying dozens of times.
> I have been flying for the past three hours.

"I have a question, though. Suppose some asks me what I've been doing this morning. Can I use *have been flying* even if I haven't actually completed a flight yet?"

"Good question, Nosy Nephew. Yes, you may say that. Flying is a continuous kind of event, so if you're up in the air for a minute, you have flown for that minute. You have been flying for a minute. And you are still flying. So, yes, *have been flying* can apply to previous events or it can apply to the current event in progress."

Present Perfect Progressive	
Subject	Verb
I, We, You, They	have been flying
He / She / It	has been flying

"All right," said Captain Perfect. "One down, two to go."

"Howdy, Nauseating Nephew. Captain Past here (*hay-yer*)."

"Howdy, Captain Past."

"Now (*nay-ow*), tomorrow, what words will describe (*day-yes-scribe*) what you are doing this moment? Use a form (*foe-orm*) of TO BE (*bay-ee*) and your present (*pray-yez-ent*) participle.

"I … was flying?"

"Good! That is your Past Progressive tense (*tay-yents*)."

"Could you explain?"

"Sure (*shoo-er*). Right now (*nay-ow*), you say *I am flying*. Tomorrow, when (*whay-yen*) you think back on today, change the form (*foe-orm*) of TO BE (*bay-ee*) from present tense (*tay-yents*) to past tense (*tay-yents*): *am flying* becomes *was flying*."

Past Progressive Tense	
Subject	Verb
I, He / She / It	was flying
We, You, They	were flying

"Got it."

"Now (*nay-ow*)," said Captain Past, "in a week or a month, when (*whay-yen*) you think about this as a completed event (*ee-vay-yent*), how would you describe (*day-yes-scribe*) it? Use HAD (*hay-yad*) plus your past participle."

"I had flown before breakfast that morning."

"Excellent (*ay-yexcellent*). That's your Past Perfect tense (*tay-yents*)."

Past Perfect Tense	
Subject	Verb
I, We, You, He / She / It, They	had flown

"Now, finally," said Captain Past, "if tomorrow you were to describe (*day-yes-scribe*) to someone the 'formerly-in-progress-but-now-completed' action of what you are doing right now, what would you say? Use HAD (*hay-yad*) BEEN (*bay-yen*) and your present (*pray-yez-ent*) participle."

"I had been flying."

"Great job. That's your Past Perfect Progressive tense (*tay-yents*)."

"Thanks (*thay-yanks*)," I said. Oops. "So, I use this when I'm talking about having flown some time in the past.

> I had been flying for three years before I knew what that lever on the control panel did.
> I had been flying peacefully until I discovered Aunt Ruth was sitting right behind me."

"Yep (*yay-yep*), you got it, son."

Past Perfect Progressive Tense	
Subject	Verb
I, We, You, He / She / It, They	had been flying

"Got enough in you for one more round (*ray-ound*)?"

"I hope so," I said. I was sweating bullets.

"Don't blow it. Our lives depend on you," whispered an encouraging Aunt Ruth.

"All right Bucko, this is Captain Future. Let's do it. Ready?"

"I'm ready, Captain."

"Okay. If yesterday you described what you are doing right now, how would you have done it? Use WILL BE plus your present participle."

"I will be flying."

"Right! Good. Again, you can also use *form of BE + going to be*. That's your Future Progressive."

Future Progressive Tense	
Subject	Verb
I, We, You, He / She / It, They	will be flying
I	am going to be flying
We, You, They	are going to be flying
He / She / It	is going to be flying

"Bring it on, Captain."

"Okay, Nephew. Tell me … if yesterday you described what you would be able to say after having finished this mission today, how would you have said it? Use WILL HAVE and your past participle."

"I will have flown."

"Good. That's the Future Perfect tense."

"Wait—why am I using the past participle for the Future Perfect tense?"

"The past participle tells us that the action has been completed. The words before the participle tell us whether we're talking about something in the past (*had flown*), the present (*have flown*), or the future (*will have flown*)."

"Ah! I get it. So I can use this in sentences like:

> By the time I retire, I will have flown to Omaha fifty times.
> I'm going to have flown there before Aunt Ruth wakes."

Future Perfect Tense	
Subject	Verb
I, We, You, He / She / It, They	will have flown
I	am going to have flown
We, You, They	are going to have flown
He / She / It	is going to have flown

"Excellent! Finally, if yesterday you were to describe what you will have completed and will still be doing at some point in the future, how would you say it? Use WILL HAVE BEEN and your present participle."

"I … uh … I will have been flying?"

"Yes! That's the Future Perfect Progressive tense. Can you come up with some examples?"

"I think examples of Future Perfect Progressive would look like:

In June, I will have been flying for seventeen years.
Aunt Ruth is going to have been flying with the same broom for over forty years."

Future Perfect Progressive Tense	
Subject	Verb
I, We, You, He / She / It, They	will have been flying
I	am going to have been flying
We, You, They	are going to have been flying
He / She / It	is going to have been flying

Before I knew it, we had landed to a hero's welcome.

"I had confidence in you, Nauseating Nephew," smiled Aunt Ruth.

"It was a little scary up there," I admitted, "but when I realized there were patterns, it all kind of made sense."

"Patterns? What patterns?" asked Aunt Ruth.

"All of the progressive tenses use the present participle (the -*ing* word). The only things that change are the words in front of the participle: *am flying; have been flying; had been flying; will be flying;* and *will have been flying.*

"The perfect tenses—those showing completion—use the past participle. For us, today, the past participle was *flown*, and we saw it used in the present perfect *have flown;* the past perfect *had flown;* and the future perfect *will have flown*. When perfect and progressive come together (e.g., past perfect progressive), the progressive wins (i.e., the present participle is used). That's why the past perfect progressive is *had been flying*.

Conjugation of the verb *fly*

Tense	Person	Verb Form
Simple Present	1st Sing, 1st Pl, 2nd, 3rd Pl	fly
	3rd Sing	flies
Simple Past	all	flew
Simple Future	all	will fly
Present Progressive	1st Sing	am flying
	1st Pl, 2nd, 3rd Pl	are flying
	3rd Sing	is flying
Past Progressive	1st Sing, 3rd Sing	was flying
	1st Pl, 2nd, 3rd Pl	were flying
Future Progressive	all	will be flying
Present Perfect	1st Sing, 1st Pl, 2nd, 3rd Pl	have flown
	3rd Sing	has flown
Past Perfect	all	had flown
Future Perfect	all	will have flown
Present Perfect Progressive	1st Sing, 1st Pl, 2nd, 3rd Pl	have been flying
	3rd Sing	has been flying

Tense	Person	Verb Form
Past Perfect Progressive	all	had been flying
Future Perfect Progressive	all	will have been flying

"For the Future-related tenses (Simple Future, Future Progressive, Future Perfect, and Future Perfect Progressive), *will* can be replaced with the phrase TO BE *going to*, where TO BE is the appropriate form of *to be*, based on the person.

"For example, above we see that the Future Perfect Progressive conjugation of *fly* is *will have been flying*. If we choose to use TO BE *going to* instead, we have:

Tense	Person	Verb Form
Future Perfect Progressive	1st Sing	am going to have been flying
	1st Pl, 2nd, 3rd Pl	are going to have been flying
	3rd Sing	is going to have been flying

"I'm thankful," I said, "that you three are captains and not ghosts of Christmas," as Captains Past, Present, and Future walked up to me and shook my hand.

"Ghosts of Christmas? Why?" they asked in unison.

"Glad you asked. Flying—and landing—with Aunt Ruth was frightening enough, but a story with the ghosts of Christmas Past, Present, and Future would have scared the 'dickens' out of me!"

27

Aunt Ruth Hunts the Subjunctive Beast

Would that I were to have another two hours of sleep.

Baxter, my butler for the weekend, recommended that Aunt Ruth cook breakfast for us before the big hunt. I proposed that she also eat breakfast with us. I knew that if I were she, I would want as much energy as possible for the day I was about to have.

I had requested that Clovis be here no later than 7:00 a.m. If I were thinking clearly, I would have said 8:00 a.m. If Clovis was anything, though, he was dependable. If he were to live in a far-away place, he could run a little late. He happened to live nearby.

Clovis walked in promptly at 6:59 a.m., yawned, and said that were he to do this again, he would simply camp overnight in my living room.

When Clovis was younger, his father demanded that he grow his hair long and be another Mick Jagger. Clovis declared that if he were a rock star, he would be miserable. Clovis insisted that he study accounting instead. Clovis's mom said to his dad, "I suggest that you reconsider." He acquiesced but asked that Clovis play with a band once a month to keep his "guitar chops" in shape. Clovis agreed on the condition that his father take accounting classes at the local community college. His father concurred.

"Achoo!"

"God bless you, Clovis."

"Thank you," said Clovis. "Now, I recommend that Baxter insist that Aunt Ruth be with us on the big hunt today!"

Baxter said, "Today, Aunt Ruth, we are hunting … the elusive, evasive subjunctive!" He handed her this piece of paper.

HUNTING THE ELUSIVE, EVASIVE SUBJUNCTIVE

1 Would that I **were** to have another two hours of sleep.

2 Baxter, my butler for the weekend, recommended that Aunt Ruth
3 **cook** breakfast for us before the big hunt. I proposed that she also **eat**
4 breakfast with us. I knew that if I **were** she, I would want as much en-
5 ergy as possible for the day I was about to have.

6 I had requested that Clovis **be** here no later than 7:00 a.m. If I **were**
7 thinking clearly, I would have said 8:00 a.m. If Clovis was anything,
8 though, he was dependable. If he **were** to live in a far-away place, he
9 could run a little late. He happened to live nearby.

10 Clovis walked in promptly at 6:59 a.m., yawned, and said that **were**
11 he to do this again, he would simply camp overnight in my living room.

12 When Clovis was younger, his father demanded that he **grow** his
13 hair long and **be** another Mick Jagger. Clovis declared that if he **were** a
14 rock star, he would be miserable. Clovis insisted that he **study** account-
15 ing instead. Clovis's mom said to his dad, "I suggest that you **reconsid-**
16 **er**." He acquiesced but asked that Clovis **play** with a band once a month
17 to keep his "guitar chops" in shape. Clovis agreed on the condition that
18 his father **take** accounting classes at the local community college. His
19 father concurred.

20 "Achoo!"

21 "God **bless** you, Clovis."

22 "Thank you," said Clovis. "Now, I recommend that Baxter **insist** that
23 Aunt Ruth **be** with us on the big hunt today!"

24 Baxter said, "Today, Aunt Ruth, we are hunting … the elusive, eva-
25 sive subjunctive!" He handed her this piece of paper.

26 "Please, someone **tell** me how this works," said Aunt Ruth.

"Please, someone tell me how this works," said Aunt Ruth. "Wait a minute … how did you know I was going to say that?"

"Never mind," said Clovis. "Just imagine that verb hunters on safari were to capture (on camera, of course) the above subjunctives (marked in bold and underlined); and suppose the queen has decreed that the hunters be required to state why a marked verb is in the subjunctive mood. Our job is the latter. Why is each word that is marked in bold marked at all?"

"Well, great balls of fire, this will be fun!" exclaimed Aunt Ruth. "Bring it, baby!"

"Before we get started," said Clovis, "let's all go out on the front porch. It's such a beautiful day." With that, our party moved through the front door to the porch, where we all found chairs.

"Okay, Aunt Ruth. Since you are so pumped about this, why don't you take the first one? Why is **were** marked in bold on Line 1?"

"It's marked because it's a subjunctive."

"Well … yes, that's true, but why is it a subjunctive?"

"Ah, I get it. Well, my first clue was the word *that*. I know that subjunctives are sometimes found after the *that* conjunction. And I kind of guessed that '*Would that I*' meant something like '*I wish that I*.' Wishes, commands, and important things like that often use the subjunctive."

"Ding ding ding!" Baxter rang the bell.

"Yes?" asked a puzzled Aunt Ruth.

"Oh, the bell just indicates that you get a point," said Baxter.

"Oh, goodie! I love getting points."

"Okay, Aunt Ruth. Ready to tackle the next one?"

"Someone else can have a turn," she replied.

"Nope. It's like shooting basketballs with friends. Shoot until you make it, and then shoot until you miss. Keep going until you get one wrong."

"Wow, cool. Okay, the next bold word is **cook** on Line 3. That's bold because someone in Line 2 *recommended that*—there's *that* again—I **cook** breakfast. Recommendations are like wishes or commands and are sources of subjunctives. Actually, this applies for proposals as well. In Line 3 it was *proposed that* I **eat** with y'all, so **eat** would be subjunctive too."

Ding ding ding! Ding ding ding!

"That's two more points," said Baxter.

I noticed the mailman standing by the mailbox out near the street, watching and listening with curiosity.

"You're on a roll, Aunt Ruth," I exclaimed.

She stood up and looked over her shoulder at the chair where she had been sitting. "I don't see a—"

"Never mind, Aunt Ruth. How about the next one?" asked Clovis.

"Well, it's like this," said Aunt Ruth, gaining confidence by the minute. "*If I* **were** *she* in Line 4 is a hypothetical condition. My nauseating nephew is not she—or I—so the condition is false and it is in the subjunctive mood. So, we use **were** instead of **was**."

Ding ding ding!

"Baxter, stop ringing that confounded bell," Aunt Ruth muttered under her breath. "You're giving me a headache."

Several people were now standing outside, captivated with the event.

"What about Line 6, Aunt Ruth?" asked Clovis.

"Let's see," said Aunt Ruth. "Yes, the next one is on Line 6. Well, it is subjunctive because *requested* is another phrase that is in the importance category. Instead of using *is*, we use its present subjunctive form **be**."

"Excellent, Aunt Ruth," said Clovis.

There was a smattering of applause from our growing audience, and I heard someone say, "She's really good!"

"Let's examine this one for a moment," I said. "Using **be** like that may sound strange to our modern ears. Suppose this were not subjunctive. Suppose, instead, that the sentence said, '*I* **hope** *that Clovis* **comes** *here by 7:00 a.m.*' Hoping that something will happen does not make it subjunctive. So, in the non-subjunctive case, we use ***comes*** since that is the first person singular form that matches Clovis. However, using *requested* instead of *hoped* turns this into the subjunctive form. Just like we would say, 'I requested that Clovis come,'—note that *come* is the subjunctive form of *to come*—we need to use the subjunctive form of *to be*, which is *be*. The subjunctive mood form for all cases of present tense *to be* is simply **be**."

"Right," confirmed Clovis. "Keep going, Aunt Ruth."

By now there were probably over a hundred people clamoring to get a glimpse of the performance. One man sold his place in line for ten dollars to an old lady who claimed to be Aunt Ruth's hair dresser.

"At the end of Line 6—*if I* **were** *thinking clearly* is obviously hypothetical and so the subjunctive **were** is used."

"Fine," said Clovis. "What about Line 8?"

"Well, I believe that Clovis doesn't live far from here. I know that the conditional *if he* **were** *to live in a far-away place* is probably false.

The audience—now numbering four or five hundred—collectively gasped.

"Boy, she's amazing! So smooth!" said one on-looker, a heavyset man wearing a bandana and a sleeveless leather vest with "Grammar's Angels" written on the back. He was sporting an "I heart subjunctives" tattoo on his right bicep. His eyes were moist with emotion.

"Line 10, Clovis, is different. I'm guessing that **were** *he* means the same as *if he were* ... is that true?"

"Yep."

Two television sports news reporters, complete with camera crew, began broadcasting.

"Whaddya think, Vince. Can Aunt Ruth do it? She's got a hot streak going."

"I don't know, Al. This is so reminiscent of Dimaggio back in '41, when he hit safely in fifty-six consecutive games. Remember, you saw it here first, on the USA Grammar Sports Channel."

"And," continued Aunt Ruth, "I have no earthly idea whether you, Clovis, will do this again in the future. It's an unknown to me; hence, I can use the subjunctive."

"You got it."

A plane flew overhead, pulling a streaming banner with the words "Aunt Ruth 4EVER."

"Next, on Lines 12 and 13, the *demanded that* on Line 12 applies both to **grow** and to **be**. Then, Line 13 has the hypothetical situation *if he* **were** *a rock star*. I like Clovis a lot—I really do—but he ain't no rock star, as they colloquially say. So, we use the subjunctive **were** instead of *was*."

A roar erupted from a nearby stadium, where tens of thousands had gathered to watch on the big screen as Aunt Ruth attempted to conquer the subjunctive beasts at this great hunting event.

Then, as she readied herself for the next one, there was a deafening hush from all around. This was more stressful than watching golf on TV.

"Well, Line 14—*Clovis insisted that he* **study**—the *insisted* is like the other words of importance. So, we use the subjective form **study** instead of *studies*."

Clovis smiled.

"Can she do it?" I asked.

"I think she can."

"Do what?" Aunt Ruth asked.

"Can you figure out the next one?" I asked.

"Well, before the **reconsider** on Line 15, I see a *that*. Hmm ... *suggest that you* **reconsider** ... um ... that sounds normal. Oh! I know. The **reconsider** is indeed in the subjunctive form already. This is one of those cases—the second person, *you*—where the subjunctive and indicative forms are the same. To be honest, if it were not marked I probably would have missed it as being in the subjunctive mood. It's like hunting for something that is camouflaged."

"Nicely done," said Clovis.

The governor stopped by, followed by the full retinue of state dignitaries. The mayor gave Aunt Ruth a key to the city.

"Now, the next one is interesting," began Aunt Ruth, "because in Line 16 it says *asked that Clovis* **play**."

"Why is that interesting?" asked Clovis.

"Well, I wasn't sure if *asked* is a strong enough word to make the phrase important and therefore subjunctive. Evidently, at least in this context, it is."

"I do think you're right," agreed Clovis.

The president of Aardvark University momentarily interrupted to give Aunt Ruth an honorary doctoral degree. Millions world-wide on social media were chanting, "AUNT," followed by, "RUTH," over and over again.

"On Line 18, it's clear to me that the *that* is preceded by a phrase—*on the condition*— that somehow seems important, so the subjunctive **take** is used here."

A movie producer for MARVELOUS Comics signed Aunt Ruth to a contract which cast her in the starring role of the new superheroes movie, "Aunt Ruth and the Subjunctive Zombies." A new Aunt Ruth Grammar doll became the runaway best-selling gift item for the holidays. And "Aunt Ruth" became the Number One most popular name for baby girls (and Number Three for baby boys).

Somewhere in the distance, a drum rolled.

"Now," said Aunt Ruth, "I don't know why 'God bless you' is in the subjunctive, but maybe it is one of those phrases that is just that way. When someone sneezes, you don't say, 'God blesses you.' Maybe it's like saying, 'May God bless you.' Perhaps the *may* has something to do with it. You certainly aren't giving God a command, ordering that He bless you. Maybe sentences involving the majesty and glory of God are automatically subjunctive. I don't know. Is that acceptable?"

"That's fine," smiled Clovis. "Yes, there is a history behind it with some very good reasons explaining why it's a subjunctive, but that's beyond the scope both of this hunt and this book."

"Keep going, Aunt Ruth," I said. "You're almost done."

She wiped the perspiration from her brow. "Are you ready?" she exclaimed. "Watch this and weep, subjunctive beasts! In Lines 22 and 23, we see what I would call a double or nested subjunctive."

Cries of "ooo" and "aaaah" arose from the throng.

"The *I recommend that* opens up the first subjunctive, which is why we have *Baxter* **insist** rather than *Baxter insists*. Now, the *Baxter* **insist** also opens up a subjunctive, which is why we have *Aunt Ruth* **be** instead of *Aunt Ruth is*."

Over the airwaves, the voice of an astronaut standing on the surface of the moon called out, "One small step for Aunt Ruth, one giant step for grammar-kind."

"Then, finally," choked Aunt Ruth, quivering with excitement, her great jowls swinging back and forth like hams hanging in a smokehouse during an earthquake, "in Line 26, I demanded that someone **tell** me how this works. Surely, this was important. There's kind of an implied 'I am formally requesting that' before the *someone*. Good enough?"

"Good enough? It's perfect!" shouted Clovis.

The sports broadcasters cheered, "It's a no-misser, a perfect game, for Aunt Ruth!"

A great roar erupted over the whole earth. Confetti came down from the skies for forty days and forty nights. Well, okay, perhaps that is an exaggeration. However, even if it were merely one person tossing a shredded candy wrapper, it ensured the edict that Aunt Ruth go home happy.

28

Aunt Ruth Wants a Cheeseburger Bad

We had finished an exciting afternoon touring the cement company, including leaving our handprints in the fresh concrete poured for the new sidewalk in front of the visitor center.

"What was your favorite thing about the cement company tour, Aunt Ruth?" I asked as we sat down at a table in a greasy spoon diner across the street.

"Well, I liked the art museum a lot," she said. "Did you like it?"

"It was okay," I said, "I tend to prefer abstract art. The art at the cement company was a little ... too ... concrete."

She laughed. "What was your favorite part of the tour? What made the biggest impression?"

"Well, I enjoyed making handprints in the sidewalk. That was fun. The biggest impression, though, was when you fell backward and landed with your bottom in the fresh concrete. That was quite a big impression."

"I sure felt badly about that," she said. "Hey, look out the window. I see bright searchlights in the sky."

"Ahem," said the waiter, whom we found standing next to us, ready to take our order. "What can I get for you today?"

"I'll have a burger and fries," I said, "and just water to drink, thanks."

"And for you, Aunt Ruth?" asked the waiter.

Aunt Ruth thought a second. "You know what? I sure could use a cheeseburger, a big fat one with bacon and barbecued pork piled on top. I think I could just devour one of those in an instant. Okay, give me two of them, with some jalapeno peppers thrown in. Oh my, I want those cheeseburgers so bad!"

Suddenly, familiar superhero music started playing in the background. "Na na na na na na na na na na na na na na na na Bad man! Na na na na na na na na na na na na na na Bad man!" (Then the key changed and the song continued, with several more key changes along the way.)

A black car with "Bad Mobile" on its license plate swerved into the parking lot, squealing its tires and skidding to a stop just inches from the big picture window in the front of the restaurant. Two masked men in capes climbed out of the car and dashed into the establishment.

"We detected two flagrant violations of Grammar Code G407.23, incorrect use of bad or badly. I am Bad Man," said the taller of the two.

"And I am Bad Lee," said the other. "We're here to help."

"Yes," said Bad Man. "We're here to help. Now, nobody panic. Don't move—stay right where you are—and don't panic. I repeat. Don't move, don't panic."

"I think he's the one panicking," whispered Aunt Ruth.

"Shh!" said Bad Lee. "No talking, either."

"I think these guys take themselves a little too seriously," muttered Aunt Ruth.

"Madam," barked Bad Man, "grammar is something that needs to be taken seriously by us all. It is imperative to our educational upbringing that we understand how correct sentences are formulated and used. Otherwise, we end up knowing nothing more than a mere ... a mere ..."

"A mere mortal?" I offered.

"Yes, thank you. That's the word I was seeking. Anyway, who may I find is the infringer of G407.23?"

"May I ask," said Aunt Ruth, "if the infringer were to confess, what would happen to said individual?"

"Holy subjunctive!" cried Bad Lee.

Bad Man said, "Well, the confessing person would receive a lesson on how to use *bad* and *badly* correctly."

"No public scorn would be enacted? There would be no tarring or feathering to dread?"

"No, indeed. We only tar and feather for incorrect use of *hopefully*."

"And the *lie / lay / lain* thing," said Bad Lee.

"Oh, right. But we haven't done that for years," said Bad Man.

"Well, then I confess. That infringer would be I," offered Aunt Ruth.

There was a collective gasp in the restaurant crowd. Mothers put their hands over their children's ears.

Bad Man shook his head. Bad Lee wept, but only for a moment.

Bad Man cleared his throat and began. "Aunt Ruth, it's like this. There are two words: *bad* and *badly*. Now, *bad* is an adjective, which means it can be used to modify a noun.

"Examples of *bad* as an adjective include: bad dog, bad person, bad weather, bad news, bad fruit, or bad breath.

"When using a linking verb (is, am, are, and the other forms of be, and words like feel, seem, smell, appear, look, etc.), you would also use *bad* and not *badly*, because a linking verb can take an adjective.

"So, you could say: I am bad, I smell bad, I taste bad, I feel bad."

"Holy down in the dumps!" said Bad Lee. "Do you want to tell her about the other case for *feel* yet?"

"Let's wait on that a moment, Bad Lee. We mustn't overwhelm her."

"So, when I landed on my posterior in the squishy cement today, I should have said, 'I feel bad'?" asked Aunt Ruth.

"That's an affirmative, Aunt Ruth," replied Bad Man. "You may not have buns of steel, but the cement company now has buns of concrete."

"Holy bad-lib, Bad Man! That line wasn't even in the original script."

"Now, for the word *badly*," said Bad Man. "*Badly* is an adverb, which means it can modify verbs, adjectives, or other adverbs. Answer me this. You said you wanted a cheeseburger. What kind of word is *wanted*?"

"Well, in the case where I wanted a cheeseburger, *wanted* is the past tense of the verb *want*, so *wanted* in that example is a verb."

"Right. Now, do adjectives like *bad* modify verbs?"

"Um, no, I don't think they do," posited Aunt Ruth.

"That is correct," confirmed Bad Man. "One speaking correct English would not say: ate bad, slept bad, sang bad, showered bad, or ran bad. Therefore, if someone says that he wants his cheeseburger bad, *bad* cannot modify *wants*; *bad* must modify *cheeseburger*. So, what I'm saying is that you don't want your cheeseburger bad."

"No, in fact," offered Bad Lee, "you want your cheeseburger good."

"Well stated, Bad Lee," said Bad Man. "If your cheeseburger were bad, it might have mold, or it might be under-cooked or, more likely, overcooked; it might have sat out in the sun for seven days, thus turning into a glob that cannot be used for anything other than tricking some lake-bottom scavengers into taking your hook."

"Holy catfish bait," exclaimed Bad Lee.

"So, you don't want your cheeseburger bad. You want it badly."

"Oh, I get it!" shouted Aunt Ruth, the light finally turning on. She continued. "Saying I want my cheeseburger bad or good is like saying I want my water hot or cold. It's like saying I want my children happy or sad. It's like saying I want my sleep fitful or sound."

"Holy grammatical insight, Bad Man: she's got it!"

"Indeed, she does. Now, Aunt Ruth," said Bad Man, looking into Aunt Ruth's eyes, "let's talk about the case where you can feel badly."

"Like the time I glued my nephew's lips to the barbed wire fence?"

"Holy cow barrier!" exclaimed Bad Lee.

"No, Aunt Ruth," said Bad Man. "You should feel bad about that, not badly. The case I am talking about is the case where badly modifies a verb that is not a linking verb. For example:

>If your fingers were numb, you might feel badly.
>If your tongue were burned, you might taste badly.
>If your eyes were blurry, you might look badly.

"Of course, you can also badly do just about anything else. You can badly play piano, badly cook dinner, badly run a race, or badly tell a joke."

"Holy inferiority complex!" cried Bad Lee.

"Now, a word of warning," said Bad Man. "When you're using *badly* with *want* and the thing you want is a noun in the form of 'to verb,' you must be careful. Be sure to make it clear what *badly* is modifying."

"Holy infinitive!" shouted Bad Lee.

"Thank you, Bad Lee," said Bad Man. "For example, you badly want to play a Beethoven piece. However, you don't want to play it badly."

"Holy Moonlight Sonata!" interjected Bad Lee.

"Oh, you're right," said Aunt Ruth. "That could be confusing or misleading! Okay, you have convinced me. I resolve to be cautious in my handling of *bad* and *badly*."

"Once again, Grammar City is saved from *bad* (and *badly*) usage," stated Bad Man.

"Holy look at the time, Bad Man! Let's go!"

"Yes, we have done our duty, Bad Lee. To the people of this great city, I want to remind you that whenever you suspect you are encountering Bad grammar, you know where to find us—same Bad time, same Bad channel. Now, to the Bad Mobile, so we can drive to our favorite sporting event!"

"Holy badminton!" exclaimed Bad Lee.

Then, in a flash, they leaped into the Bad Mobile and drove off into the setting sun.

Aunt Ruth and the Comma Splice

The airline magazine article looked intriguing, and I plunged into it with gusto as the plane began its ascent into the friendly skies.

"What are you reading?" asked the ever inquisitive Aunt Ruth as she started working on a crossword puzzle.

"I'm reading an article entitled, 'How to Survive a Crash Landing in Piranha-Infested Waters,'" I replied.

"Sounds like a thriller," she mumbled.

"It is. Listen to this sentence: 'When traveling to piranha-infested waters, be sure to accompany someone who weighs far more than you do. The fish may find that person more attractive.'"

"Looks like you're safe there. So, that's why you invited me," Aunt Ruth laughed. "Hey, I'm looking for a six-letter word that completes the phrase 'Comma _____' and is a common grammatical error."

I thought about it a moment. "Splice," I responded.

"Splice?" she asked.

"Splice," I repeated. "A comma splice is a common grammatical error."

"What's a comma splice?" asked Aunt Ruth.

"Well, let's see ... look, here's an example from the article I'm reading.

> You think you're about ready to land in piranha-infested waters, it's time to update your will."

"What's wrong with that?" asked Aunt Ruth.

"The problem here is that the sentence contains two independent clauses that are joined by a comma."

"Wait, so you're telling me that each half of the sentence—before and after the comma—is an independent clause. Doesn't that mean that each half could be a sentence all by itself?"

"That's right, Aunt Ruth. If each independent clause were its own sentence, complete with periods and beginning with capital letters, the punctuation would be perfect. One way to fix a comma splice is like this:

> You think you're about ready to land in piranha-infested waters. It's time to update your will."

"So, when I recognize a comma splice, I should fix it by changing the comma to a period, right?" she asked. "In other words, I just have to turn it into two sentences."

"Putting a period in place of the comma and turning it into two sentences would fix it. That's correct," I agreed.

"That's all you have to do?" she asked.

"That's all you have to do, but it's not all you can do," I added. "If you wanted to, you could put a semicolon where the comma is, and that would work too."

"So, I could use a period or a semicolon there?"

"That's right."

"Cool. Do you have a recommendation on which one to use?"

"Well, if the independent clauses are related and flow together, a semicolon would be fine to use. If the clauses aren't closely related, perhaps a period would be better."

"Couldn't you just get rid of the comma and not replace it with anything?" asked Aunt Ruth.

"Nope, that's not good. That's called sentence fusion."

"Sentence fusion? That sounds like a new kind of music or something."

"Uh, no. Sentence fusion is just as bad as comma splicing. It looks messy.

> You think you're about ready to land in piranha-infested waters it's time to update your will."

"So, in this case you would want to insert a semicolon or a period?"

"Yes, that's correct," I said. "Either a semicolon or a period would work."

"Well, this all seems simple enough," said Aunt Ruth with a smile. "You either replace the comma with a semicolon or period, or you insert the semicolon or period if nothing is there but something is needed. Thanks for the explanation. Now, may I get back to my puzzle?"

"Not so hasty, my dear," I said. "There is another possibility in which you can keep the comma."

"There is? Good grief! Why do you have to make things so complicated? This story could have been finished after the first page."

"There is indeed another possibility," I said, ignoring her diatribe, "but you need to use a coordinating conjunction if you want to keep the comma."

"A what?"

"A coordinating conjunction. Your choices are: *and, but, or, nor, so, for,* and *yet.*"

"How do you use them with the comma?" she asked.

"I'm glad you asked," I said with a smile. "If you have a comma splice—two independent clauses and a comma in between—you can insert a coordinating conjunction as the first word following the comma. If you have sentence fusion, insert a comma followed by a coordinating conjunction between the two independent clauses. Watch what happens when we add the coordinating conjunction '*so*' to our sentence:

> You think you're about ready to land in piranha-infested waters, **so** it's time to update your will."

"Attention! Attention!" barked a voice over the plane's loudspeaker. "This is your pilot for our flight, Captain Clovis. I want to thank you all for flying on Grammar Airlines today. We will be distributing complimentary grammar crackers shortly. Now, I request that you turn your attention to Row One, where my friend, the nauseating nephew, will explain the following Important Grammar Rule to his beloved Aunt Ruth."

The other passengers on the plane cheered. I heard cries of "Aunt Ruth!" and "Grammar, yes!" and "Let's keep flying forever!"

"Hi, Clovis!" I shouted.

"Hi, buddy," he replied over the loudspeaker.

"Now, everybody"—I turned around to face all the passengers behind me—"we have a grammar lesson that is crucial to our understanding of commas, but it is a rule that many, many people get wrong."

Gasps arose from the crowd. I heard a little voice squeak, "Mama, is it true?"

"This rule has to do with independent clauses," I continued, "and it comes in two parts."

"You da man!" boomed a deep voice from the back of the plane.

"The first part is this," I said. "Use a comma and a coordinate conjunction to combine two independent clauses into one sentence. Most people get that right."

"Yeah, I knew that," I heard someone yell.

"Whoa, did you hear that, Maude?" someone whispered.

"I did, Henry," said the woman who apparently was Maude. "He said most people get it right. I wish he would give us some examples!"

"Your wish is my command," I said with a nod. "So, here are two sentences (i.e., each is an independent clause):

> Aria ate the avocado.
> Her chicken Amber danced and went to sleep.

"Combine those two independent clauses with a coordinating conjunction and a comma. For this example, let's use *and*.

> Aria ate the avocado, *and* her chicken Amber danced and went to sleep.

"If you don't have the comma, you might wonder if Aria ate the avocado and her chicken, or she ate just the avocado. You might interpret it as:

> Aria ate the avocado and her chicken; Amber danced and went to sleep."

"Oh, I see," said a teen-aged girl with purple hair. "Now, what if the part after the conjunction is not independent?"

"You mean that it's a dependent clause, not a standalone sentence?"

"Right," said the girl. "What if we had this:

> Aria ate the avocado.
> Went to the concert."

"In that case," I said, "you would not put a comma before the coordinating conjunction when attaching a dependent clause to the end of an independent clause unless the comma is needed for clarity. This is the rule that many people get wrong."

> Aria ate the avocado and went to the concert."

"Why wouldn't you put a comma there?" she asked.

"Well, with the comma, you would have:

> Aria ate the avocado, and went to the concert.

"This is incorrect. Think of it like this. The coordinate conjunction *and*, preceded by a comma, gives us a clue that the first independent clause has ended and a second independent clause is about to begin. We have established that *Aria ate the avocado*, but look at what happens next. We have the phrase *went to the concert*, which does not have a subject and thus is not an independent clause; however, if we leave out the comma, it's clear that the subject is still Aria."

The other passengers on the plane roared their approval with cheers; high-fives were given all around; and after the tears of joy were wiped away, we all returned to our normal flight routine, crammed into our seats like sardines and enjoying the measly in-flight snack of three peanut-sized grammar crackers and a drop of water per person. I made a mental note to complain to Clovis.

"Okay, I think I understand all my options," sighed Aunt Ruth, appearing anxious to get back to her crossword puzzle.

"Well, those aren't quite all your options," I said with a mysterious smile. Aunt Ruth looked at me, rolled her eyes, and looked back at her puzzle.

I remained silent, thinking it probably best. After all, I didn't want to annoy her with my tendency to talk about grammar all the time. I resumed reading the magazine article. After five minutes, however, I couldn't shake the nagging feeling that she was staring at me. I glanced up from the article. Indeed, she was staring at me.

"Well, what is it?" asked Aunt Ruth, impatiently.

"What is what?" I asked.

"What are the other options? You can't leave me hanging," she exclaimed.

"Do you really want to know?" I asked, delighted at the grammatical suspense I had created.

"No, you're right. I'm just asking to annoy you," she said quietly. "After all, why would I ever want to know the complete story? I mean, this is English grammar we're talking about. I guess I can be content with getting old and eventually dying without ever knowing what it was that you were going to tell me." She looked left and then right, and then she looked at me and took a deep breath. "Of course I want to know!" she shouted.

"Now, calm down," I said in a soft, soothing voice. "This is a fun grammar lesson, remember?"

"Yes," she said, clenching her teeth. "Right. This is terribly fun. Now, please tell me the other options for dealing with comma splices and sentence fusion before I bite off your head," she grimaced.

"Okay, I'll tell you," I whispered. I leaned toward her. She leaned toward me. "Subordinate conjunctions!" I exclaimed, startling her. If she hadn't been seat-belted, she might have gone through the ceiling of the plane.

"Subordinate conjunctions?" she said with a quizzical look in her eyes. "What on earth is a subordinate conjunction?"

I smiled. "There's not enough time to tell you about it right now. I'm afraid this will have to wait for another adventure."

Aunt Ruth rolled her eyes, but she didn't argue. Moments later, her eyes closed, and she was soon snoring in a deep sleep.

I leaned over and whispered in her ear, "Aunt Ruth, we're going down in piranha-infested waters."

Without flinching, she instantly whispered in reply, "I've already updated my will, and you'll be glad to know that you are mentioned."

Yes! At last, I was finally included in her will.

"I don't want to come across as materialistic or anything, but what do I get?"

"I'm giving you my toilet paper roll collection, along with a postcard of Fort Knox and a huge vault of gold." She closed her eyes and began drifting back to sleep.

"Wait! Wait! Wait! You can't leave me hanging like this," I exclaimed. "Is there a comma between Fort Knox and a huge vault of gold?"

"What difference does it make?" she asked with a wry smile.

"What difference? Well, with no comma, I can't tell if the postcard is of both Fort Knox and a huge vault of gold, or if the postcard is of Fort Knox and that another item you're giving me is a huge vault of gold."

"Well," she chuckled, "that's the beauty of it. Our language can be so ambiguous at times. Maybe I'll clarify it for you on another adventure."

"But Aunt Ruth, I ..."

Her snoring drowned out the possibility of saying anything further. I didn't know what she was dreaming, but she had a big smile across her face as we flew into the sunset.

Iowa Ruth and the Lost Commas

I was leaning back in my office chair, feet up on the desk, reflecting on the mystery of that cryptic phrase found in the bedrooms of nearly every home in America—"Do Not Remove Under Penalty of Law"—when the door burst open.

"Whatcha got there, Nebraska Nephew?" asked Aunt "Iowa" Ruth, towering over ... well, standing at four foot nothin' on a warm day, she didn't tower over much.

"Iowa Ruth, look at this treasure." I motioned to the small pile on my desk—a candy wrapper, an empty soda can, and a mattress tag. "What do you make of it?"

"Where did that come from?"

"I explored the garbage can in the office across the hall."

"You need to get out more, buddy, and this may be your opportunity. Take a look at the news," she said, flinging the morning paper at me.

Ancient Egyptian Hieroglyphics Decoded!

(Press Release from Egyptian Department of Grammar)—Inscribed on the inner walls of the famous Unknown Pyramid of an anonymous king and queen are hieroglyphics that have long been a mystery. In a breakthrough of ancient language, using modern grammar techniques, the code has finally been broken! After all these years, we are now able to read the hieroglyphics of what appears to be the final resting place of King and Queen Tuten.

    Famed archaeological scientist, Dr. Bones Jones, is being credited with the breakthrough. "It's absolutely astounding," said Dr. Jones. "I had stared at the first line of this hieroglyphic text for seven months without so much as batting an eye. I finally gave up, and then not thirty seconds after I quit thinking about it, what should happen to pop into my head but the solution! The first line, I finally realized, said the following:

When Queen Tuten was eating her cat a fluffy pet screeched loudly however while eating King Tuten the king of our great land noticed his royal commas had disappeared.

    "The commas appear to be missing, but commas really aren't important," Dr. Bones Jones is quoted as saying. He adds, "This hieroglyphic text only reveals what the Grammar Mafia has claimed all along—that the ancient peoples of Egypt were grammatical imbeciles!"

"What do you make of it, Nebraska?" asked Iowa excitedly.

"Something is amiss. He is devoid of commas and doesn't understand the gravity of the situation. It is as if he has been brainwashed into forgetting the power of the almighty comma. This is so unlike the Dr. Jones whom I know. I wonder if—say, I've got it! Dr. Jones is sending us a message!"

"How do you know?"

"Remember when I went to the Grammar Awards a few years ago?"

"Honey, at my age I can't remember what I ate for breakfast."

"Anyway, Dr. Jones was there. I remember sitting next to him while we watched our favorite grammarian singer."

"Perry Comma?"

"Perry Comma. Now, during this award ceremony, Dr. Jones and I came up with a special code in case one of us ever faced trouble from the Grammar Mafia, aka the Gob."

"The Gob? Really?"

"Really. Those guys have no qualms with stealing a shipment of commas or anything else. Periods, question marks, exclamation marks, single and double quotes, parentheses, you name it—if it's punctuation, they think they own it."

"Sounds brutal, Nebraska Nephew. How does the code work?"

"Well, it's complicated—it uses a combination of algebraic ring theory, molecular biology, and fresh eye of newt—so we should save that for another book. Anyway, let's see … if I take his first phrase—*It's absolutely astounding*—and convert it to Pig Latin and then factor it into prime numbers, we get …

> Nebraska Nephew, I need your help! The Gob is following me and watching my every move. They have possession of all the commas from the Unknown Pyramid. Be alert. Danger lurks around every corner. Have a nice day."

"What does that mean?" she asked.

"It means an adventurous trek to Cairo is in the offing," I replied.

"What did you say?" asked Iowa.

"Pack your bags; we're going to Egypt."

Twenty-four hours later, we landed in Cairo on a warm, sultry afternoon. "Where to first, hot shot?" asked Iowa Ruth as we disembarked.

"Let's go to the Egyptian Museum of International Language Punctuation," I suggested. "That's where Dr. Jones supposedly hangs out."

We hailed a taxi—it had been years, said the cab driver, since they had seen hail in Cairo—and he took us to the Egyptian Museum of International Language Punctuation, pronto.

Walking into the foyer, we saw furniture in the shape of various punctuation: an exclamation mark couch, a recliner and footrest that looked remarkably like a semi-colon, and several comma chairs.

"Look at that round dot thing over in the corner," said Iowa.

"Yes—that's a beautiful example of period furniture," I explained.

"Nebraska Nephew and, I presume, Iowa Ruth," boomed a voice from the balcony above. "I've been expecting you. Welcome to Cairo. I am Dr. Jones," said the clean-shaven man, who had a strange device hanging from his neck. "Pleased to meet you, Iowa Ruth."

"Dr. Jones, good to meet you," Iowa Ruth remarked. "What is that thing around your neck, if you don't mind my asking?"

"Oh, this? It's a colonoscope, and it helps, in my colonoscopy work—you know, finding colons, and even, semi-colons. I've been sifting through some relics, from our last dig, looking for punctuation."

Something didn't feel right about this situation. His commas were out of place. I had a hunch, and I decided to run with it.

"Dr. Jones, let me cut to the chase. You are an imposter," I declared.

His smile turned to an evil sneer. He ripped off a mask, revealing a visage that looked like a cross between "Jaws" (the heinous character in the James Bond movie *Goldfinger*) and the Metro-Goldwyn Lion (ask your parents (or maybe your grandparents)).

"Vhat do you vhant from me?" snarled the villain, dropping his pleasant British lilt and revealing his true, heard-only-in-the-movies, eastern European accent.

"First, what did you do with the real Dr. Jones? Second, we need to go over your punctuation knowledge, specifically for commas. It's hideous."

"I vill tell you about Doctor Jones, but first, tell me about zee comma. I thought zee rule vas, 'when in doubt, go all out.' I all-vays have doubts, so I all-vays go all out, and insert as many commas, as I can."

"It's a little more complicated than that," I gasped, looking at Iowa Ruth. "Another over-simplistic comma user, I'm afraid," I whispered to her.

"Be careful, Nebraska. I don't think he has a full appreciation for the power of the commas he may be wielding," she warned.

"Look, whoever you are," I said, shouting up to the balcony, "there are some rules governing comma usage. We'll cover three of the most frequently misunderstood and abused rules, namely these:

> 1. Use a comma after an introductory subordinate clause
>
> 2. Use commas to separate appositives.
>
> 3. Use a semi-colon to separate independent clauses that are joined with a conjunctive adverb."

Both the so-called Dr. Jones and Iowa Ruth appeared to be in stupors. I waved my hands and snapped my fingers, bringing them to their senses.

"First," I declared, "I will tell you about *subordinate* (or *subordinating*) *conjunctions*, which are words that begin *subordinate clauses*. A subordinate clause is a dependent clause (i.e., it cannot stand alone as a complete sentence) that tells you the *when, why, where, which, how,* or *what* of the sentence to which this subordinate clause is attached."

"Just out of curiosity," said the villain, "how many of zeez subordinating conjunctions are zere?"

"There are a bunch. They include: *because, although, after, before, once, since, until, when, while, so, in order that, if, unless, though, where, rather than, whether,* and a few others."

"May we stop now? My head's spinning," said Aunt Ruth.

"Not yet!" I insisted. "I need to show you some examples. Now, suppose we have these two sentences. Each, of course, is an independent clause, because all complete sentences are also independent clauses.

> The morning sun rose over the pyramids.
> I awoke and rode my camel to the sarcophagus.

"Suppose we want to indicate that the first independent clause marks the time of day at which the second independent clause occurred. One way to do this is to use a subordinate conjunction, like *when*, to change the first sentence into a subordinate clause.

> When the morning sun rose over the pyramids

"Note that this is now a dependent clause. It cannot be a sentence by itself. If we attach this subordinate clause to the beginning of the other independent clause, we use a comma to separate the two clauses.

> When the morning sun rose over the pyramids, I awoke and rode my camel to the sarcophagus.

"When using a subordinate clause, remember this: Order is important!"

"Vhat do you mean?" asked the villain.

"If the subordinate clause is before the independent clause, you should use a comma to separate the two, as we do above. However, if the subordinate clause follows the independent clause, you generally don't need a comma to separate them. Our example above, then, would look like:

> I awoke and rode my camel to the sarcophagus when the morning sun rose over the pyramids."

"Can we be done now?" Aunt Ruth asked again.

"See, it's like this," I continued, ignoring her question. "The comma after the subordinate clause tells us when the subordinate clause ends and when the main part of the sentence begins. In our adventure here, what we start with is this:

> When Queen Tuten was eating her cat a fluffy pet

"*When* is a subordinate conjunction, so we're looking for the subordinate clause. Now, we know that Egyptian queens did not dine on their feline pets. She was not eating her cat; therefore, what we want is this:

> When Queen Tuten was eating, her cat …

"That one comma makes everyone happier, especially both Queen Tuten and her cat. Let's look at the next few words, where we will be able to use the second rule that I stated above:

> her cat a fluffy pet screeched loudly however …

"We have two noun phrases in a row … *her cat* and *a fluffy pet*. The phrase *a fluffy pet* clearly describes the phrase *her cat* and is called an *ap-*

positive. Appositives are descriptive noun phrases and are often separated by commas, like this:

>her cat, a fluffy pet, screeched loudly however …

The appositive can also be thought of as a parenthetical clause, e.g., *(a fluffy pet)*. If we ignore that clause for a moment, we have *her cat screeched loudly*. It's pretty obvious that *screeched loudly* describes what the cat did.

Now, if we look at the next several words, we have:

>however while eating King Tuten the ruler of our great

"We will deal with *however* later. We see *while*, which is a subordinate conjunction. Now, we know that the ancient Egyptians were not a cannibalistic society, nor did they let their pet cats eat people; therefore, the subordinate clause *while eating* does not go with Queen Tuten, nor does it go with the fluffy pet cat. The subordinate clause, then, must go with King Tuten."

>while eating, King Tuten the ruler of our great land

"Just like we did before, we see two adjacent noun phrases—*King Tuten* is one, and *the ruler of our great land* is the other—and we need to separate them with commas:

>however while eating, King Tuten, the ruler of our great land, noticed his royal commas had disappeared."

"I had no idea zee comma could do all zis," remarked the villain. "Please tell me more," he begged. "Tell me about zee *however*."

"All right," I began, "it's simple. *However* is what is known as a *conjunctive adverb*, and they are not the same as coordinating conjunctions."

"You call zat simple? Vhat is a conjunctive adverb?"

"A conjunctive adverb is used to connect two independent clauses so that comparisons and differences between the clauses can be explained. Some of the familiar conjunctive adverbs include: *however, therefore, rather, although, hence, still, then, nonetheless,* and *meanwhile*.

"The standard way to arrange this is like this:

<Ind Clause 1> ; <Conj Adverb> , <Ind Clause 2> .

"Suppose your first independent clause was *Abbott ran east*, and your second independent clause was *Costello ran west*. If you used a coordinating conjunction to join them, it could look like this:

Abbott ran east, *but* Costello ran west.

"If, instead, you connected them with a conjunctive adverb, it could look like this:

Abbott ran east; *however*, Costello ran west.

"You can sometimes put conjunctive adverbs at the end or in the middle of an independent clause sentence, separated by commas. Your mileage may vary:

Abbott ran east; Costello ran west, *however*."

"Vait a minute," said the villain. "Couldn't vee have a period between zee two independent clauses; must it be zee semi-colon?"

"Good question!" I remarked. "Just about everybody uses *however* or *therefore* to begin or end sentences. The problem is that the conjunctive adverb depends on having two independent clauses. You wouldn't just say:

Costello ran west, however.

"You wouldn't begin a story that way, for instance. It just wouldn't make sense. Even though it is a sentence, it's a sketchy sentence at best. It can't stand by itself. You need the other independent clause—*Abbott ran east*—in order for the clause with the conjunctive adverb to make sense, n'est-ce pas?"

"Right."

"Incidentally," I added, "that's the same fundamental reason that we aren't supposed to begin a sentence with a coordinating conjunction like *and* or *but*. The conjunction is there to *conjoin* one clause with another, and if we add the conjunction but don't connect to another clause, we're sort of off-balance."

"But everyone does zat!" exclaimed the villain.

"I know, I know … I do it too sometimes. That doesn't make it right, though."

"Great balls of fire. Zis sounds serious!"

"Well, using a period instead of a semi-colon for a conjunctive adverb really is not a big deal. It's common in today's writing. If you use a period, just make sure that both independent clauses are apparent so that you know what the conjunctive adverb is doing there.

"What is serious, though, is how some people replace the semi-colon with a comma. That is an unacceptable violation of grammar sensibilities because it creates a type of comma splice.

> Abbott ran east, however, Costello ran west.

"That just doesn't work and it isn't good. You end up with two independent clauses incorrectly joined with a conjunctive adverb, and you don't really know to which independent clause the conjunctive adverb belongs."

"Okay, I zink I've got it. Now vhat about zee original example? Vee know zat vee have:

> When Queen Tuten was eating, her cat, a fluffy pet, screeched loudly *however* while eating, King Tuten, the king of our great land, noticed his royal commas had disappeared."

"Right. Notice that everything before *however* is one independent clause; everything after *however* is another independent clause. Let's try our standard usage model for dealing with conjunctive adverbs, putting a semi-colon after the first independent clause and a comma after the conjunctive adverb. Voila!

> When Queen Tuten was eating, her cat, a fluffy pet, screeched loudly; however, while eating, King Tuten, the king of our great land, noticed his royal commas had disappeared."

"I am most grateful to you, Nebraska Nephew, for zee grammatical explanation. Now, I have zis surprise for you."

Quickly and adroitly, the comma-confused villain ripped off another rubber mask he had been wearing. He was Dr. Jones again!

"I apologize for the ruse, my friend, but when I discovered the secret to the hieroglyphics, I knew I could only trust my Nebraska neighbor and his adventurous aunt to help me on the path to comma enlightenment. I had to ensure that you had not been compromised by the Gob. I had to protect the remaining commas."

"Glad to be of service," I smiled. Iowa Ruth curtsied politely. "Dr. Jones, where are the commas now?" I asked.

"They are in the lab, hidden between a pair of parentheses. Now that we know where they belong, all is well. The grammatical integrity of Egypt has been preserved. Furthermore," said Dr. Jones, "in honor of the two of you, we are renaming the king and queen who, at this location, will continue to rest in peace. Allow me to recognize you as the first honorary patrons of the Pyramid of King Nebraska Nephew Tuten-Comma and Queen Aunt Iowa Ruth Tuten-Comma, hereafter referred to as King and Queen Tut."

Later that afternoon, as Iowa Ruth and I were waiting on the sidewalk out front for our taxi to the airport, Dr. Jones rushed out of the building with a flustered look on his face.

"May I join you in a ride to the airport?" he asked. "I must dash to the capital of my home state, Indiana. I was just informed that someone has stolen all the native apples."

"You mean—" I began, sensing a punch-line coming.

"Yes, the capital of Indiana is Indiana-apple-less."

Aunt Ruth and the Independent Santa Clause

"Excuse me, sir, may I hail a cab for you?" I asked the jolly, white-bearded man in red who was standing on the corner.

"No, thanks. I can do this thing all by myself, and I don't really need help," he replied in a tone that exuded self-reliance.

Somewhere in the distance, a reindeer's red nose started glowing like a light bulb.

"Can I point you to a good restaurant for dinner?" I offered, determined to help the man in some way.

"Oh, I can do that too. I just ate, actually. I'm fine. Besides, I'm trying to cut back a little. You know, those elves make a lot of cookies."

I noticed that the guy had a large bag slung over his shoulder.

"Need help carrying that bag? It looks mighty full."

"No, thanks for your kindness, but I can manage it. I do this every year."

"Isn't there anything I can do for you? Oh, by the way, what's in the bag?"

"The bag is filled with red-and-white-striped peppermint candy commas, nice big fat ones, oh, and I've got two or three chocolate marshmallow semi-colons, topped with peanut butter, and strawberry jelly, and grape jam-filled colons, but they are kind of stale and dusty because people don't want them any more, and you don't need to help me, you see, because I like doing things myself, and I guess that's because I'm an independent Claus."

From somewhere in the distance, a drum roll followed by a cymbal crash was heard.

"You, Mr. Claus, do need some help."

"What kind of help, on a day like today, could I possibly need, where the sky is filled, with fluffy clouds, the air smells like snow, where I'm finding all kinds of bargains, from street vendors, selling really nice shiny, gold, name-brand watches, bright, colorful ties, and large, elegant purses, made of leather, fresh-grilled sausages, and teriyaki chicken, which may cause me to rethink whether to do the elf thing again next year, or just come down here, and shop for, like, everybody?"

Mr. Claus was careening into a comma disaster, I thought to myself.

"I was what?" he asked, furrowing his brow and glancing at me suspiciously.

"Uh, careening. To careen means to be swerving out of control; but … how did you read my thoughts?"

"You know what that Santa song says, something about 'He knows what you are thinking,' right?"

"This is almost sounding Orwellian."

"Well, my little friend, so far, you have asked to help, me, find, a taxi, even though, I'm not going, to take, a cab, and you've, asked me, if I need, or want, a good place, for dinner, and you've pestered me, about what's in, the bag, though, first of all, it's none of your business, and, second of all, well—ho, ho, ho—there, isn't,, really,,, a,,,, second,,,,,,,,.."

"Look, I know you are independent, Mr. Claus, but you're messing up this whole comma thing terribly."

"What do you mean?"

"Santa—"

"Please, call me Kris. Only my mom calls me Santa during off-hours."

"Kris, the literacy of children around the world depends on you. The example you set and the presents you give all add up to help shape and mold these youngsters around the globe."

"Mmm, okay, I'll buy that, and it sounds like you want to become my personal marketing agent."

"Not really. I do want to teach you about semicolons and colons though. You're giving away way too many commas. You need colons and semicolons in your life."

"You got it. Please, though, no digestive or anatomical jokes. You promise—cross your heart and hope to die?"

"Promise."

He smiled; I nodded; and we began our exploration into the world of semicolons.

"Kris, do you ever make lists?"

"Lists? I make lists all the time. I always check them twice. Thanks to modern technology and those little drone cameras, I can tell, too, whether you've been bad or good, naughty or nice."

"Creepy."

"Yes it is, isn't it?"

"Now," I began, "how do you put items together in a list?"

"I use commas," he replied. "If I have A and B and C and D, I'll put them in a comma list like A, B, C, and D."

"Very good. I notice that you used the Oxford comma."

"The Oxford comma? What's that?"

"That's the comma that comes after the next-to-last item in the list. Ironically, it's more common in America to use it; in England, they tend not to use it. It's okay to use or not use, but the main thing is to be consistent; otherwise, it can be terribly confusing for the reader."

"Got it," said Kris.

"Now, suppose four people—Person A, Person B, Person C, and Person D—go to a restaurant for lunch. Person A orders a cheeseburger, fries, tossed salad, and two cookies. Person B orders a tossed salad, fries, and iced tea. Person C orders two cheeseburgers. Person D orders three cookies and tossed salad. If you were to make a list of the orders and put that into a sentence that begins with *The people ordered*, how would you do it?"

"Well," he said, "I think I'd do this:

> The people ordered a cheeseburger, fries, tossed salad, and two cookies, tossed salad, fries, and iced tea, two cheeseburgers, three cookies, and tossed salad."

"If you were the waiter bringing the food to the table, would you know how to distribute the orders based on the sentence you just wrote?"

"Uh, no, probably not."

"Right. The problem is that each person's order has its own set of commas, and in the big list, you can't easily tell which commas are within a person's order and which commas separate the orders in the list."

"I guess so."

"It would be easier to understand if you used semicolons to separate each order, like this:

> The people ordered a cheeseburger, fries, tossed salad, and two cookies; tossed salad, fries, and iced tea; two cheeseburgers; and three cookies and tossed salad.

A good rule to remember, Kris, is that if one or more of the items in your list contain commas, you want to use semicolons to separate the list items."

"Okay, I think I've got that."

"Good. Now, Kris, do you know what a compound sentence is?"

"It's a sentence about multiple molecules or chemicals that get together."

"What?"

"You know, like a chemical compound.

> Uncle Wade mixed the hydrogen bi-carbonara with the

> nitro glycerin or something.

That's a compound sentence, right?"

"Wrong. That's not a compound sentence."

"What is it then?"

"A compound sentence is a sentence that contains multiple independent clauses, each of which could be a valid sentence all by itself."

"Oh, right!" said Kris. "I remember those."

"You do?"

"Sure, I do. If I have one independent clause that says:

> I went to bed early,

and I have another independent clause that says

> I woke up late,

I could combine them with *and* or *but* or something, with a comma, and—Hark the Herald!—we end up with:

> I went to bed early, but I woke up late."

"Very good!"

Kris was beaming.

"Now, in your example," I continued, "your independent clauses had no commas, so adding a comma with your *and* or *but* (remember, we call those coordinating conjunctions) is the right way to do it."

"I sense a *but* coming," said Kris.

"You are correct. If the independent clauses do have commas, or if the additional comma would make it more confusing, then use a semi-colon instead. Remember, too, that if you are using a conjunctive adverb, you want to use a semicolon instead of a comma."

"Uh, oh. My brain just froze."

"It's really not that bad. It sounds a lot more complicated than it is."

"You can't teach an old Santa new tricks."

"Yes, we can! You can do it, Kris. You just need to see some examples. Suppose we have the following clauses, and we want to put them together in a sentence:

> A honeybee went out one morning to collect some nectar.
> It visited the poplar tree, young and tall, down near the creek.
> It visited the picnic at the park, where Mrs. Smith was stuffing John, Lydia, and Silas with grapes.
> It visited the windmill up on the ridge, near the Thompson house.
> Finally, it visited the field of clover in front of the church, near where Alison and Albert were playing a game of catch with Albert's new baseball."

"You want me to combine all those sentences into one great big sentence? Is that legal?"

"Yes, it's legal. Now, how would you separate the sentences?"

"Well, let's see. Most of the sentences have commas, so that means I would use semicolons to separate the sentences from each other, right?"

"Bingo!" I confirmed.

"Okay, I'll give it a try," Kris said.

> "A honeybee went out one morning to collect some nectar, and it visited the poplar tree, young and tall, down near the creek; it visited the picnic at the park, where Mrs. Smith was stuffing John, Lydia, and Silas with grapes; it visited the windmill up on the ridge, near the Thompson house; and finally, it visited the field of clover in front of the church, near where Alison and Albert were playing a game of catch with Albert's new baseball."

"Nicely done, Kris. I like how you connected your first two sentences—or clauses—with the comma and then the rest with semicolons."

"Thanks. I did that because after the first sentence, each of the independent clauses was an item in a list of places."

"I see that you also put an *and* before the *finally* in the last independent clause."

"Yes. I thought it sounded better putting an *and* before the last item in the list."

"Right—a list where one or more of the things in the list have their own commas is one of the main places where semicolons are used. The other place where you'll frequently see a semicolon is in a compound sentence where the independent clauses are generally somewhat related."

"'Generally somewhat related'? That's a bold statement if I've ever heard one. What exactly do you mean?"

"Watch this.

> The rhinoceros puts his trust in his horn; the elephant, however, is afraid of a tiny mouse."

"That sounds like a mystical and wise saying."

"No, I read it in a bathroom stall somewhere. Anyway, see how the elephant's fear is juxtaposed next to the rhino's trust? If we use a period instead of a semi-colon, I don't think the comparison would be as strong."

"Okay, I'll buy that. Don't you want a semicolon there, anyway, since you have the conjunctive adverb *however* in the second independent clause?"

"You are absolutely right. Good catch. That whole saying could be rewritten as:

> The rhinoceros puts his trust in his horn; however, the elephant is afraid of a tiny mouse.

"Either way," I continued, "I think you want the semicolon instead of a period to separate them."

"Can you string more than two independent clauses together with conjunctive adverbs?" asked Kris.

"Sure, I think you can keep attaching them, as long as what you're saying makes sense. In the following example, *then* is a conjunctive adverb:

> It was dark; then, it was darker; and then, it was darkest."

"Brilliant writing," said Kris under his breath.

"Do I perceive a hint of sarcasm?"

"I don't know. How perceptive are you? Hey, what do you know about colons?"

"Let me tell you about them," I said. "A colon can introduce a list.

> In Edmund Spenser's *Faerie Queene,* he describes the Seven Deadly Sins: Gluttony, Sloth, Greed, Lust, Wrath, Envy, and Pride.

"You can also use a colon to separate two independent clauses where the first one is a statement and the second one expands upon the first.

> Be bold and daring in life, making a statement: playing the tuba is the easiest way to achieve that.

"Of course, you could use a semi-colon there instead."

"Wow, Nauseating Nephew, I think I understand this."

"What did you call me?" I asked, alarmed.

"I called you, uh ... Nauseating Nephew."

"Mr. Claus—uh, Kris—are you really Aunt Ruth? Or are you an Aunt Ruth impersonator?"

"What do you think?" said the bearded figure before hopping onto a large, red, gift-filled sleigh; revving up his nine spirited, enthusiastic reindeer; and cheerfully riding off into the twilight, singing a rousing rendition of "Jingle Bells."

Aunt Ruth Is a Short Short-Order Cook, etc.

RUTH'S
IF IT AIN'T
GREASY
IT AIN'T FROM HERE

The aroma of fresh-brewed coffee permeated the air as I opened the door and stepped into the diner. With just a brief, two-block walk from my house, I had enjoyed the cool, crisp air on that early Saturday morning.

"Welcome to Ruth's," cried a recognizable voice from the kitchen. "What'll you have today, kiddo?"

"Uh ... Aunt Ruth, what are you doing back there?"

"I'm building a new inter-planetary space station."

"You're ... what?" I asked.

"I'm frying eggs and am up to my elbows in bacon grease. Whaddya think I'm doing?" she snorted.

"When did you start working here?"

"Five o'clock."

"No, I mean what day."

"Today."

"Today is your first day of work?"

"You catch on fast. I needed some cash. The sign said they needed a short order cook. I was the shortest to apply. I got the job. Now look, I'm really busy. Place your order or go to the back of the line."

"Um … there's no one else in line."

"Well, all right then. Whatcha want?"

"Four eggs, sunny side up; two slices of bacon and two sausage links; a slice of toast with butter; a bowl of grits; a fruit salad; and a hot cup of coffee, no cream or sugar."

"What, you haven't eaten for a week?"

"I ate at your place last night, remember?"

"You did? What did I serve you?"

"Possum stew."

"Really?"

"Really."

"Was it good?"

"Why do you think I'm ordering such a gigantic breakfast?"

"So, what's your grammar point today? You'd better get to it soon, because this story is dragging on and on, *ad museum* or *ad infinite item* or something."

"You meant *ad nauseam* or *ad infinitum*, perhaps."

"It's Greek to me. What's it mean?"

"No, it's Latin. *Ad nauseam* is an adverb referring to doing something so often that it becomes annoying. *Ad infinitum* is an adverb referring to doing something over and over again, forever."

A long-stemmed red rose, thrown from somewhere off-stage, landed at my feet. Then a full bouquet of roses, again thrown from "out there," was tossed near me. Finally, a net containing thousands of flower petals was released from up above, creating a blizzard of color that was absolutely dazzling.

"Thank you, thank you," I said, waving and smiling.

"Whoa, whoa there," snorted Aunt Ruth. "You can't call this a grammar lesson. You say two little Latin phrases, and flowers are being thrown at you? Come on, Grammar Boy, you can do better than this."

"Aunt Ruth, a lot of serious English literature has lines intended for comic effect. Poe, for example, in his story *A Predicament*, had—"

THUD!

Startled by a loud noise behind me, I turned and saw a short, bearded fellow on the floor.

"Bill the Grammar Fairy, what are you doing here?" I asked.

"First things first. You call this serious English literature? This is a grammar book, remember? That's hardly *Paradise Lost*. Second, though the book is written in the English language, the book focuses on American usage and grammar minutiae, not English usage. Third, Poe was American, not English. Now, where were we? Oh, yeah. You got any pastrami? Maybe a little provolone, mayo, and mustard to go with it? Oh, and a big slice of tomato would be great. Rye bread this time. How about it?"

"I, uh … Aunt Ruth, this is your restaurant."

"Hi, Bill."

"Hi, Aunt Ruth. How's things?"

"How's things? You're supposed to be a Grammar Fairy, and you're asking me, 'How's things?'"

Bill shrugged. "Don't panic, Aunt Ruth. I'm officially off duty."

"Oh, okay. Well, you know how it is. Trying to make ends meet, dealing with difficult customers, and eclectic."

"Eclectic?"

"Yes, eclectic, you know. It means "so on and so forth," or something like that."

"Okay, looks like I'm back on duty. I think you're talking about *etcetera*. That is commonly used and is written as '*etc.*' for short," said Bill.

"How would you use it?" asked Aunt Ruth.

"*Etc.* can be used in multiple ways, but generally it is used to complete a thought or sentence with an implied 'and you know the rest' type of meaning."

"For example?"

"Yes, for example. Suppose someone came to you and said, 'I will paint your house for free, but I will only use one of the colors of the rainbow. You know the colors: red, orange, yellow, etc.'"

"Ah, I see. They used *etc.* instead of saying 'green, blue, indigo, and violet.' That's very clever. May I try?"

"Yes, please do," said Bill.

"Okay," began Aunt Ruth, "let's see. The positive even integers are 2, 4, 6, 8, 10, and etc. How's that?"

"Mmm, not quite right," sighed Bill.

"Is it 1, 3, 5, 7, and etc.?"

"Nope. Don't say the *and*. If you had said, '2, 4, 6, 8, 10, etc.,' then you'd be correct."

"Question, Bill."

"Yes, Aunt Ruth?"

"Do you always have a period at the end of *etc.*?"

"Yes ma'am, you do."

"What if it's at the end of a sentence?"

"Then the period with *etc.* is used as the sentence's closing period too."

"What if *etc.* is the last word in a question?"

"Can you list the Brady Bunch kids' names, like Greg, Marsha, etc.?"

"Oh, I see. You still kept the period on *etc.*, and then you put the question mark on the end."

"Right."

"Is that true for abbreviations in general?"

"Yep. I can say that I live in Washington, D.C. Have you ever lived in Washington, D.C.? I love Washington, D.C.!"

"Oh, cool. So ... if a sentence ends with an abbreviation, the final period in the abbreviation is also the final period in the sentence. If the sentence ends with an abbreviation and happens to be a question or exclamation, you use a question mark or exclamation mark, respectively, after the abbreviation."

"Now, what kind of food do you have here?"

"I cooked something up just for you: Four eggs, sunny side up; two slices of bacon and two sausage links; a slice of toast with butter; a bowl of grits; a fruit salad; and a hot cup of coffee, no cream or sugar."

"Perfect!" Bill cackled.

"But, Aunt Ruth!" I exclaimed.

"Go to the back of the line, Nauseating Nephew," Aunt Ruth retorted.

I made my way to the back of the line, moping, griping, complaining, whining, pouting, etc.

33

Aunt Ruth Is Spaced Out

"Houston, we've got a problem," said a recognizable voice that somehow seemed out of context. Standing in the Mission Control Room—I was on a sight-seeing tour at NASA—I thought at first that perhaps this false crisis was part of the entertainment.

"Houston, I repeat, we've got a problem," I heard the same voice repeat. It couldn't really be the voice I thought it was, could it? I thought Aunt Ruth was somewhere in the Caribbean on a luxury cruise.

The Mission Control staff quickly scrambled into their places, leaving me standing in the corner.

"Space Commander Aunt Ruth, what is it?" asked the head honcho.

"One of our engines isn't firing."

"Uh oh, that's not good. You need that engine to make it home."

"Do you mean that I might not make it home?"

"We'll do our best to get you home. It's considered bad form to leave an astronaut in Space."

"I need to make it home. I'm hosting the garden club on Saturday."

"We'll get you home, Space Commander Aunt Ruth. Just follow the instructions that we'll give you. Now, which engine is not firing?"

"I'm not sure yet. Either engine A or engine B are not firing."

Before I knew what I was doing, I leaped from the corner and grabbed the microphone from the man in charge.

"It's not 'either are firing' Aunt Ruth, it's 'either is firing.'"

There was a long pause on the other end. I heard what sounded like a gasp, followed by choking.

"Aunt Ruth! Aunt Ruth! Are you okay? Are you running out of oxygen?"

"Uh, no. I'm ramming my finger down my throat. That's a whole lot more fun than getting a grammar lesson at the moment. Besides, there are two engines—plural engines—so I should use *are*, not *is*, right?"

"Wrong, my space-borne aunt. When you have compound subjects connected by *or, nor, either ... or*, or *neither ... nor*, the verb has to agree with the subject that is nearer to that verb. So, in this case, engine B is closer to the verb. Since you would say, 'engine B is not working,' you would also say, 'engine A or engine B is not working.'"

"What about my pet yaks, Yally and Yolly?"

"Are your pet yaks not working either?"

"No, I mean if I said something such as, 'I like it when either my pet elephant Binky or my pet yaks, Yally and Yolly, licks my face.'"

"That would be wrong," I replied. "Your pet yaks are closer to the verb than Binky is, so you should use the third-person plural form of the verb *lick*, which is *lick*. Since you would say, 'I like it when my pet yaks, Yally and Yolly, lick my face,' you should have said, 'I like it when either my pet elephant Binky or my pet yaks, Yally and Yolly, lick my face.'"

"Let me ask you another question."

"Fire when ready," I said.

"If I say, 'I'm not sure if my yaks or Uncle Norman smell worse,' is that correct?"

"No, dear aunt. Uncle Norman is closer."

"But I'm closer to my yaks than I am to Uncle Norman. I'm not close to Uncle Norman at all, ever since the incident with my pet goose Mildred."

"What happened with Mildred?"

"Uncle Norman ate her for Thanksgiving dinner."

"Uncle Norman ate your pet goose?"

"Yep, feathers and all. He was a little … down in the mouth," chortled Aunt Ruth.

The staff in the Mission Control Room began laughing, breaking the tension of an otherwise serious situation.

"Anyway, it's not a matter of your relationship to the subject," I continued, "but how close the last part of the compound subject is to the verb. Since you would say, 'Uncle Norman smells worse,' you should say, 'I'm not sure if my yaks or Uncle Norman smells worse.'"

"That sounds awkward," sighed Aunt Ruth.

"I'll have to agree with you on that. It does sound awkward. In fact, some literary stylists say that when you have a compound subject with at least one plural subject, put a plural subject closest to the verb. The sentence just sounds better that way.

I'm not sure if Uncle Norman or my yaks smell worse."

"Oh, right. Anyway, thank you, NASA Nephew. Now, may I speak with a real person? I have more urgent fish to fry."

"One more point on this, first," I insisted. "Not only do you need to make sure of verb agreement, but pronoun agreement is important too."

Deafening silence was the reply.

"Aunt Ruth, are you there?"

"No, I jumped out of my spaceship," she replied.

"Do I detect a little sarcasm?" I asked.

"Not sure. How perceptive are you?"

"Anyway, it's like this. Neither Aunt Ruth nor her yaks could fathom what *their* next garden club meeting would be like if Aunt Ruth didn't make it back."

"I see," said Aunt Ruth. "Since the plural yaks are closer to the pronoun than the singular Aunt Ruth, it's *their* garden club meeting rather than *her* garden club meeting."

"Yes, indeed." I handed the microphone back to the man in white.

"Space Commander Aunt Ruth," he began, "have you tried repairing engine A or engine B?"

"Oh, I've been so busy up here, I haven't tried repairing either engine A nor engine B."

Before you could say Neil Armstrong, I had the microphone back in hand. "Aunt Ruth, we've got a problem."

"Tell me about it," she sighed. "What did I do now?"

"You used the dreaded *either … nor* combination. That's a no no."

"Ugh. What should I have said?"

"You should have said, 'I haven't tried repairing *either* engine A *or* engine B.'"

"Is there someone else down there with whom I may converse?" asked Aunt Ruth.

The man in white assumed control of the microphone again. "Space Commander Aunt Ruth, did you run through the required safety checks before your launch yesterday?"

"Yes sir, I did," replied Aunt Ruth. "I checked the oil, the windshield wiper blades, the coolant, and the tires."

"I appreciated having the NASA Parking Lot Shuttle Bus serviced. I think you forgot about the rocket though."

"The—oh my," she gasped. "I should have checked either engine A or engine B."

"Well, that would be a problem too," the man in white said.

"Why is that?" asked Aunt Ruth.

"Engine A or engine B implies one or the other but not necessarily both."

"That's not what I meant."

"It's what you said."

"What's wrong with what I said?"

The man in white handed me the microphone. "She's your aunt. You deal with it," he sighed.

"Aunt Ruth, it is I, here once again in all my glory to save the day."

I heard more gasping and coughing in the background.

"Finished?" I asked impatiently.

"Uh, no," came the reply.

"Let's continue anyway," I persisted. "Now, when you have *either ... or*, you have to remember that it does not mean the same as *both ... and*. If you mean *both ... and*, then say it that way."

> The Engine Safety List was checked for *both* engine A *and* engine B.

"Question for you," said Aunt Ruth, almost giggling.

"Sure, what's up?" asked the man in white.

"Did you send someone to pick me up?"

"Uh, no we didn't. Why?"

"Oh, just, uh, wondering. There's a spaceship circling me at the moment with 'USS Enterprise' written on it. Oh!"

"Aunt Ruth? I mean, Space Commander Aunt Ruth? Are you okay?"

"Oh, quite all right," she said a moment or two later. "A man just appeared in my spaceship. He's talking about captains' logs and star dates and stuff like that. He said he'll beam me home, whatever that means, if I go to dinner and a movie with him first."

"Dinner and a movie?" I asked.

"Dinner and a movie," she repeated. "Where? I don't know. He said something about meeting some friends from another movie at a cantina in a galaxy far, far away. And tell Binky, Yally, and Yolly that I'm bringing home a new friend for them."

"A new friend?"

"Yeah, something called a Tribble. He looks sort of like the Pillsbury Doughboy decked out in a shag carpet suit. Oh, and NASA Nephew, could you tell Binky, Yally, and Yolly that I miss either of them?"

"Each of them, Aunt Ruth."

"Whatever. Now, I go boldly … where no grammarian has ever gone."

34
Aunt Ruthii

WHAM!

The thud rattled my apartment, causing two pots—each containing a cactus—to fall from the window seat and shatter on the floor.

I dashed to the window and looked, expecting to see a meteorite in place of where Mrs. Thigglethorpe's home had once been. Mrs. Thigglethorpe's home was still there, and, in fact, Mrs. Thigglethorpe was on the front lawn with her pet hippopotamus. There were no signs of a natural disaster outside.

"Excuse me," said a voice behind me.

"Ay!" I screamed, startled. I whipped around only to find Bill the Grammar Fairy lying in a heap on the floor.

"Calm down, calm down, it was I who crashed," said Bill.

I calmed down. "Bill, what are you doing here?"

"You got any pastrami?"

"Uh, no."

"Liverwurst?"

"Nope."

"A thick, tangy pimento cheese spread, and a nice loaf of pumpernickel?"

"Yep. The pumpernickel came out of the oven just an hour ago, and a container of pimento cheese spread is on the bottom shelf in the fridge, next to an unidentified container that I'm afraid to open."

"Now you're talking," said Bill. "Thanks. I'll be right back. Oh, and sorry about the cacti."

"Cacti?"

"Cacti—the plural of cactus."

"It's not cactuses?"

"Well, actually, both are used. In Arizona, they just use the word *cactus* to be both singular and plural. Using -i for plurals is common with words pulled into English (or Anglicized) from the Latin."

"Okay, then. Let me go clean up the cacti mess."

"Cool. See ya," remarked Bill as he darted into the kitchen.

I began whistling that old favorite tune about whistling while you work. "I love having Bill around," I thought to myself. "He adds such clarity to my grammar life." I quickly put the pieces of cactus onto a tray and set it on the dining chair that was near the window, just to get it out of the way so that I could sweep the dirt and broken chards of pottery. In a moment, I had the floor as clean as a whistle.

As I turned to remove the cacti from the chair, I heard Bill's voice call out, "You got any mustard?"

"Uh, no. Sorry," I apologized.

The doorbell rang. I stood there for a second, debating whether to remove the cacti from the chair or open the door.

Bill stepped out of the kitchen. "Nauseating Nephew?" he asked.

"Yes?"

"The doorbell rang. Shouldn't you answer it?"

"Uh, yes. Good idea," I said, moving toward the door.

"I'll just, uh, you know, go finish the pimento cheese spread. You weren't going to use that tonight for anything, were you?"

"Uh, no," I answered. Bill darted back into the kitchen.

"Come in, come in, dear birthday aunt," I said, opening the door and motioning for Aunt Ruth to enter.

She smiled. "Why, thank you."

"Now, let's get down to business. Food is ready," I said, gleaming with pride. With a flourish, I lit the candles on the table. After all, I wanted this to be a nice birthday dinner for Aunt Ruth. "I'll bring in the food."

"Food is ready? Oh my, you're so efficient. May I sit down?"

"Yes, please do," I said, "just be sure to watch out for the—"

She plopped into the chair next to the window before I could stop her. For a moment, her eyes were as big as saucers and her cheeks turned beet red, and then she let out a scream and exploded off the chair and over the table, where her apparently highly-flammable garment made unfortunate contact with the flaming candles. The dress instantly caught fire.

"Water! Water!" I yelled, not quite sure to whom but hoping somebody would hear.

In full football gear, Bill ran into the room carrying a big orange bucket of water, and he dumped it on Aunt Ruth, drenching her. Wisps of smoke curled from her dress and dissipated into the ceiling.

"Hi Bill," sighed Aunt Ruth, "and thanks. I'm glad you were here!"

"Oh, you know me. I was just minding my own business quietly in the kitchen, but then I heard the call for water and I smelled the acrid odor of burnt underwear. I figured something was awry. Anyway, back to your regularly scheduled programming. I'll be in the kitchen if you need me for anything."

I brought in the food, and we sat down and commenced eating.

"Mmmm, this is delicious, Darling Nephew," remarked Aunt Ruth as she swallowed the first bite of my new culinary creation. "What did you say this was called?"

"I'm glad you like it, Aunt Ruth. This is my Jules Verne Special."

"What's in it, if I may ask?"

"The key ingredient is octopus," I said rather nonchalantly.

Aunt Ruth turned all the colors of the rainbow in less than a second, going from red to orange to yellow to green to blue to indigo to violet faster than you can say, "Roy G. Biv."

She began coughing violently. "Quick!" she gasped. "Get me (cough) some (cough, cough) water!"

"Water!" I yelled, feeling a sudden sense of deja vous.

In fireman garb, Bill ran back into the room carrying one end of a fire hose, and before I could stop him, he blasted Aunt Ruth, drenching her for the second time in less than five minutes. I'm not sure how it worked, but it did stop Aunt Ruth from coughing.

Dripping, Aunt Ruth sat there and stared at the large tray that I had used to serve the Jules Verne Special. She swallowed and asked, "How many octopi did you use for this recipe?"

"Hold it right there," said Bill.

"Don't tell me that *octopi* isn't the right word," muttered Aunt Ruth.

"Okay, I won't tell you that," said Bill. There was a large pause.

"Well, is it or isn't it?" sighed a flustered Aunt Ruth.

"It's accepted; but formally, the correct plural is *octopuses*."

"How come I hear everyone saying *octopi*?"

"Well, in Latin the plural is *octopi*, but the word *octopus* has Greek roots, and the more proper English plural form for a Greek word is *octopuses*. Octopi* is a cool word, but it's not grammatically correct. We have a lot of unusual plural nouns in English and it behooves us to learn them."

At that moment, I heard the roar of animals outside my window. A quick investigation revealed that Mr. Ledbottom had brought his pet hippopotamus over to play with Mrs. Thigglethorpe's hippopotamus.

"What's the noise?" asked Aunt Ruth.

"Just a pair of hippopotami out on the lawn," I said.

"That's *hippopotamuses*," said Bill, "just as it's *rhinoceroses*. Well, actually, the plural of *rhinoceros* could also just be *rhinoceros*."

"How about *rhinoceri*?" I asked.

"Listen," said Bill, "people do use -i endings when writing scientific journals or because it's fun. If you're going to use a noun, you've got to know the plural for that noun. That's called Plurality Responsibility, or *Pluronsibility*."

"Is it really?" I asked.

"No, not really," responded Bill. "I do like that word though."

"Well," sniffed Aunt Ruth with an air of superiority, "I think we should continue to keep our relative focuses on real words, not pretend (cough) words. You guys think you're such geniuses. Or is it genii?"

"Actually, either *geniuses* or *genii* will suffice, Aunt Ruth. Geniuses is probably more conventional, but in my opinion *genii* is pretty cool. And it's *foci*, not *focuses*."

"Wow," she said. "Anyway, (cough) I think some of the octopi—octopuses, excuse me—accidentally went down my sarcophagus."

"That's esophagus," said Bill with a smile.

"Oh yeah, that's right. I had forgotten that word. I should remember esophagus. It'll come in handy some day. My mommy said you never know when we might need to talk about esophaguses."

"*Esophagi* is preferred," said Bill.

"No way," said Aunt Ruth.

"Yes way," he responded. "And just in case you're wondering, it's *sarcophagi*."

"My mommy never told me about sarcophagi."

"No," said Bill, "but I'll bet your mummy did."

35

The Aunt Who Baked the Fruitcake

Ring! Ring! Ring!

"Hello?" I sleepily answered. I looked at the clock. It was three in the morning.

"Good morning, darling Nephew. Do you remember the fruitcake which I gave you last Christmas?" The voice was unmistakably Aunt Ruth's.

"That you gave me," I said, correcting her.

"Right. The one which I gave you," echoed Aunt Ruth.

"No, Aunt Ruth. Not *which*, but *that*," I sighed. Hadn't we gone over this before?

"Wait. Why is it *that* and not *which*?" she asked.

"Boy, am I glad you asked," I said with a smile. "I think it's time for a short grammar lesson."

"You want to give me a grammar lesson? Are you crazy? It's three o'clock in the morning."

"Well, you called me at this early hour to ask me about a fruitcake."

"Oh, right," she muttered. "I guess I deserve to be punished. Couldn't we try bamboo shoots under my nails or something else that might be a notch or two more tolerable than your grammar lessons?"

Undaunted, I continued. "It's like this. If the information in the clause is essential to the meaning or intent of the sentence, use *that*. If it's not, use *which*. I guess the other way to remember it is this: the *which* clause goes inside commas, and the *that* clause does not go inside commas."

"I think I need some examples," she sighed.

"Coming right up," I said cheerily. "Take a look at this. I have two stuffed pterodactyls. One was given to me by my aunt and the other by my uncle.

> The stuffed pterodactyl *that* my uncle gave me shrieked last night."

There was silence on the other end of the phone. Then I heard her clearing her throat. "So ... the '*that my uncle gave me*' is essential to the meaning of the sentence, and therefore you used *that* instead of *which*."

"You got that right, Babe," I replied.

"Why ... um ... why is it essential?"

"It tells the listener which pterodactyl shrieked. It wasn't the one that I won at the fair, and it wasn't the one that grew up in my basement. It was the one that my uncle gave me. And now listen to this one.

> The pterodactyl, *which* is my favorite dinosaur, could fly."

Again, silence, followed by a throat clearing. Then she spoke. "This time, the expression '*which is my favorite dinosaur*' is not essential to the meaning of the sentence, so you used *which*."

"You got it. It is not essential because it doesn't matter that it's my favorite dinosaur. The pterodactyl would be able to fly regardless of my affinity for it."

"Good," she sighed. "Anything else?"

"Just a general note that *which* gets used way too often. If it's essential to the sentence, use *that*. Now, about the fruitcake ... "

"Oh yeah, the fruitcake. I was calling to see if you still had it."

"Why?"

"Edna she is having a birthday tomorrow, and I don't have time to bake her a fruitcake this year."

"You have less time than you think."

"What? Why?"

"You'll be in Grammar Jail, Aunt Ruth, for using a double subject!"

"What's a double subject?"

"You said, 'Edna she is having a birthday ….' You used 'Edna' as a subject and 'she' as a subject, and you can't have both."

"You're just upset because you didn't get invited to her party."

"No, that's not it. You just can't use two subjects like that unless you're a poet trying to do something … uh … poetical, or if you are trying to come across as illiterate. Other examples of double subjects are things like:

> All of us we are going to the movies tonight.
> My uncle he's not a good golfer.
> Aunt Ruth she makes a fruitcake that'll kill you if it hits you in the head.

"Oh, and speaking of which, the fruitcake I have is the one that you gave Edna last year."

There was a long pause. "How, uh, how did you know that Edna was the person that received it?" she asked.

"Who received it," I said.

"Edna."

"No, I mean you said *that received it* when you should have said *who received it*."

"Am I sensing another grammar violation?" she asked.

"Actually … well … yes. Generally, you want to use *who* when referring to people and *that* when referring to things.

> He's the guy *who* found my sandwich.
> He's the dog *that* ate my sandwich.
> We are the folks *who* called for reservations.
> They are the goats *that* ate my rhubarb patch last night.

"You won't generally be thrown into grammar jail on this one—many writers use *that* for people—but note that it's pretty much universally agreed upon that one never uses *who* for non-human things."

"Okay," she sighed. "Thanks for the warning. Now, then, how did you know that Edna was the person WHO received it?"

"You crossed her name off the label and wrote mine over the top, and you also included her birthday card. Apparently she re-gifted the fruitcake back to you, and you proceeded to give it to me at Christmas."

"Oh dear, how careless of me."

"Well, and actually, this fruitcake happened to be the very same one that you gave me for Christmas four years ago. I suspect that this cake has been in existence since, oh, 1966, and that it's gone around the world a few times by now."

"Impossible. I didn't start baking fruitcakes until 1967."

"How many times have you given your fruitcakes as gifts?"

"Oh, I think perhaps some fifty odd times."

"Why were they odd times?"

"What?"

"You said fifty odd times. Why were the fifty times odd? Did you deliver the fruitcakes down the chimney, or were you wearing your Hawaiian luau outfit in the middle of winter and doing a hula dance on the front porch? I wouldn't call that fifty odd times. I'd call it fifty nauseating times."

"I said fifty odd times because I'm not sure if it's fifty or fifty-one or fifty-two or fifty-how-many."

"So, you should have said *fifty-odd*, not *fifty odd*. It's ambiguous otherwise."

"They sound the same. That hyphen thing between *fifty* and *odd* doesn't make any noise, does it?"

"A hyphen making noise? Now, that would be odd. The reader can see it, though. As long as this isn't being listened to as an audiobook, the difference between *fifty-odd* and *fifty odd* will be apparent."

"Audiobook? You're dreaming."

"Anyway, we've established that you've given fruitcakes as gifts fifty-something times."

"Right."

"How many fruitcakes have you actually made?"

"Three, I think. I don't remember, really. I haven't made one since 1981."

"Why not?"

"I lost my pan. I suspect, actually, that I accidentally left it on one of the fruitcakes, and over time the pan dissolved and was absorbed into the cake."

"Scary," I said.

"Tell me about it. Say, I know what you can get me for my birthday this year—a new pan for making fruitcakes!"

"There will be much rejoicing."

"Yes," she said, "the people that get freshly-made fruitcakes will be happy indeed."

"The people *who* get the fruitcakes, you mean."

"Whatever. All I know is that I have a list of twenty odd people who will want fruitcakes this year."

"You mean twenty-odd people."

"No, I mean twenty people who are odd—nineteen of my friends and you!"

36

Aunt Ruth and the Queen's Baseball Card

"I think I will donate your fruitcake to the Smithsonian. After all, it's a natural treasure. Well, at least, someone ought to take it out to the backyard and bury it," I said half-jokingly.

Aunt Ruth and I were on the Mall in Washington, D.C., enjoying a stroll from Washington Monument to Lincoln Memorial in the midst of prime cherry blossom season.

"Oh," said Aunt Ruth, "did I tell you that I'm now a patron of the Smithsonian's?"

(Grammar sirens blared in the background. The theme song to "Grammar Impossible" played briefly.)

"Oh no, what did I do now?" moaned Aunt Ruth.

"Incorrect double possessive usage," I kindly but firmly stated.

"Double possessive? What's that? Sounds like the name of a really scary movie or something."

"Well, you said, 'patron of the Smithsonian's.' The word *of* shows possession (the Smithsonian possesses you, in a sense; that is, you are of the Smithsonian; you are one of the Smithsonian's patrons). The apostrophe-s that you tacked onto the end also shows possession and likewise indicates that you are in the group of people labeled Smithsonian's patrons. You are not allowed to come within thirty miles of a double possessive UNLESS the object of the 'of' phrase is human!"

"What? Who came up with that rather arbitrary, silly rule? So, I would be allowed to say, 'patron of my nephew's'?"

"Well, yes, you can say that, but do you want to?"

"No way, Jose´."

"Okay then. What you could say is something like:

> I had lunch with a sister of my boss's.
> Aunt Ruth was a fan of hers. (Note that 'hers' is a possessive pronoun, so, coupled with 'of,' it becomes a double possessive.)

"So, suppose we have:

> Aunt Ruth is a fan of the fruitcake's.

"Can you say that? No, this is not correct. The noun in the 'of' phrase must be a human. That is the cardinal rule in this form of double possessives."

By this point, Aunt Ruth had collapsed into a conveniently-placed, overstuffed comfy chair. She was snoring to beat the band.

Noticing two ducks, a squirrel, and a hairy-chested leather-jacket-shorn biker sitting on a bench, all rapt in attention to my words, I continued. They were all the audience I needed.

"So, is it always wrong to use double possessives?" I asked.

The biker looked at the squirrel, who looked at the ducks. The ducks shrugged. The squirrel shrugged. The biker shrugged.

"The answer is: No, it's not always wrong, and it is used in America to a high degree of frequency. However, many people do consider it informal—if they consider it at all—so in formal settings you may want to think about sentence structure before you speak."

The biker looked at the squirrel, who looked at the ducks. The ducks nodded. The squirrel nodded. The biker nodded.

"Imagine that," I chortled, "the possibility that someone is actually thinking before speaking."

The biker looked at the squirrel, who looked at the ducks. The ducks did nothing. The squirrel did nothing. The biker did nothing.

My laughter ceased. "Tough crowd tonight, boss," I said under my breath, forcing a smile.

"Now," I continued, "a common problem with double possessives is that they can lead to ambiguity. We need to be careful to protect ourselves from ambiguity as much as possible."

The biker jumped up. "I'll protect you, mister, from ambi … ambi—"

The ducks whispered to the squirrel; the squirrel leapt onto the biker's shoulder and whispered in his ear.

"Ambi-chew-ity," said the biker.

I liked that. Ambi-chew-ity. *Ambichewity* could be a new word, meaning to eat something but not be quite sure of what exactly it is.

"We can see ambiguity—or ambichewity—in the following example.

> I found the Queen of England's baseball card at a trade show."

I could see that the biker's eyes were tearing up with emotion. The crowd began growing rapidly and in the space of a paragraph was teeming with excitement.

"Now, the question I submit to you is the following: Did I find a baseball card belonging to the Queen, or did I find a baseball card that had the Queen's likeness on it (i.e., it was a card of the Queen, perhaps an 'action shot' of when she stole home in the bottom of the ninth in the last game of a recent World Series)?"

"You tell 'em, No-nonsense Nephew!" shouted the biker.

"If I want to say that the card belongs to the Queen—she owns it, she got the bubble gum that came along with it, and she likes it because it's a card with a picture of baseball player Prince Fielder on it—then I could say:

> This is a baseball card of the Queen's.

"That double possessive seals the deal."

"Woo hoo!" cried the biker. "Did you hear that? That double possessive seals the deal!"

"Now, if I want to say that the card is of the Queen—she's represented on the card; the card is about her—then I could say:

> This is a baseball card of the Queen."

"Brilliant, simply brilliant," exclaimed the biker.

The crowd was cheering; it had been a while since my last standing ovation. I picked up a microphone and asked, "What example is it you wanna hear?"

Somewhere from the back of the crowd came a voice that cried, "Chihuahuas."

"Okay folks, you're in for a real treat tonight. I came prepared, believe it or not, with a chihuahua example. Here goes:

> I picked up a toy of my chihuahua off the floor.

What does that mean?"

My question was met with silence. Then the biker stood up and said, "Tell us, big guy. What does it mean?"

"Was the thing I picked up a plastic replica of my chihuahua? It's unclear," I explained.

"It's ambi-chew-ous!" said the biker with a grin.

"Indeed, it is ambiguous," I echoed. "I'm not even sure what I would do with a plastic replica of my chihuahua. If I said it like this, however:

> I picked up a toy of my chihuahua's off the floor.

then does that solve the problem for me?"

"Yes!" shouted the biker.

"Yes!" shouted the crowd.

"No!" shouted I.

The crowd instantly became so quiet that you could have heard a participle dangle.

The biker meekly said, "It doesn't?"

I shook my head.

"I tricked you," I confessed. "Don't forget the cardinal rule that this double possessive thing only works with humans. As much as we love dogs, they aren't human and are not allowed to participate in this double possessive usage. In this case, I would simply say:

I picked up my chihuahua's toy off the floor."

"Aw, you kid," guffawed the biker, giving me a soft punch in the shoulder.

The crowd roared. Aunt Ruth was still asleep in the comfy chair.

"Just remember, folks, the double possessive has been around at least since the 1500s. Chaucer used it; Shakespeare used it; and you can use it too. Good night. You've been a great audience. Thank you and good night."

37

Aunt Ruth Is Non-Nonplussed

"Clovis, look!" I shouted.

"Her voice recorder!" responded Clovis, clearly as excited as I was. "Maybe this will provide clues."

Though the discovery alleviated some of my anxiety, I still felt responsible for the afternoon's misadventures. I had worked so hard at convincing Aunt Ruth to go hiking with Clovis and me, and finally she relented. She was right behind me when we left the car to walk the five hundred yards to the trail head, but when I reached the trail head and turned around, she was gone. Now Clovis and I were trying to find her.

Clovis turned on the device, and sure enough, we heard Aunt Ruth's voice:

> "Aunt Ruth's Log, Star Date ... uh ... Thursday, sometime in the twenty-first millennium. I have discovered that which I believe to be a rare arthropod. Precisely stated, this is of the phylum Arthropoda, Subphylum Hexapoda, Class Insecta, Order Aburgertogo, Suborder Largefries, Family Awifeandfourkids, Genus Abracadabra, and Species Americana."

Clovis pushed pause.

"What does that mean?" I asked.

"Aunt Ruth either found a mayfly, or—"

"A mayfly?"

"A mayfly—or she found a plastic-wrapped slice of American cheese."

"Interesting," I remarked. "I know that she collects both bugs and slices of American cheese from around the world. Wonder which it is?"

"Don't know. Let's listen." Clovis pushed the play button.

> "And now I will take a photograph of this little gem of a bug, this precious specimen of creation, this delicate, fragile example of the wondrous beauty of life, before dousing it with a blast of ether. Then I will—"
> "Hands up!" cried a voice in the background. "Give me that bug. It's mine."
> "Mister," replied a startled Aunt Ruth, "you can't take my bug from me. It's not nice, nor is it ethical. I found it. I claim it. Now put your gun down. I can show you how to find another bug like this, or a slice of plastic-wrapped American cheese, for that matter. It's not difficult."

Clovis pushed the pause button. "Who do you think this guy is?"

"I don't know. I do know that he's a thirty-five-year-old white male from the United States."

"How do you know that?" asked Clovis, clearly impressed.

"That's the only answer that would be politically correct here."

Clovis pushed the play button.

> "Madam," said the man, "why are you so calm? I am pointing this gun at you, threatening to wipe you off the face of the planet, and yet you remain entirely nonplussed."

Then we heard siren noises on the recorder, and I quickly realized that Aunt Ruth was imitating a squad of police car sirens.

> "What is that noise?" said the man.
> "The grammar and language usage police are here. Now drop it!"
> "I will not drop it! I have done nothing wrong," declared the man. "That noise was from you. You made those siren

sounds."

"Of course I did," stated Aunt Ruth. "In the absence of my knucklehead nephew, I am the defacto Grammar Police and SWAT Team. Indeed, you certainly have done something wrong. You have violated the sanctity of definitions of words in the English language. You told me I was nonplussed. I am not nonplussed."

"You surely look nonplussed to me!"

"Do you know what nonplussed means?" asked Aunt Ruth.

"It means calm, collective, serene, a prairie of peace portraying pastoral pictures of perfect ... uh ... pineapples?"

"Nonplussed means disturbed, upset, or maybe discombobulated," said Aunt Ruth.

"How can I possibly remember that?" he asked.

"I'm glad you asked," said Aunt Ruth. "The way I remember it is like this. I think of 'plus' as things coming together (e.g., two plus two is four); then I think of 'nonplus' as things coming apart. So I remember that nonplussed is like things falling apart at the seams, things becoming unglued, or things going kind of crazy and chaotic. Make sense?"

"Sigh," said the man. "Yes, it makes sense. I'll put the gun away. Hold on a sec."

"Why did you pull out your cell phone?" asked Aunt Ruth.

"Need to call Mama. She's got the definition of nonplussed all wrong. Just a moment ... ringing ... Hello, Mama? It's me, Jimmy ... no, your son Jimmy ... right, yes ... well, Mama, I wanted to tell you that you raised me wrong. I'm wallowing in a cesspool of crime because you sent me down the wrong road in life. You know how there's a proverbial road less traveled? Yes, well, throwing me into the abyss of incorrect vocabulary is apparently not how one gets to that road. ... What am I talking about? Oh, nothing more than the definition of *nonplussed*. Where did you get that definition? ... Oh, I see ... oh, okay ... yeah, I guess that makes sense. Well, thanks for playing. Have a nice day."

"What did she say? Where did she get her definition?"

"It's the new math they're teaching in schools these

days. They can't call subtraction 'subtraction' or 'minus' anymore because it is taking something of value away. They can't change it to adding negative numbers, because it's not politically correct to call any number negative. So they talk about 'nonplussing' numbers. That is, it's like taking numbers and de-adding them. This keeps the numbers calm and collected, hence the new (and wrong) definition."

"Wow, that's sad," remarked Aunt Ruth.

"Yes, certainly. So I have a question for you. How were you able to remain non-nonplussed—or plussed, I guess—while I was pointing this gun at you?"

"I don't think that plussed is a word," said Aunt Ruth.

"Non-minused? I don't know. Anyway, how did you remain so calm?"

"Well, first of all, I recognized your gun as a 1966 J-Mart Six-Shooter Cap Gun."

"Wow, you're good. Are you a weapons expert of some sort?"

"No, I had one of those guns when I was a kid."

"Oh. You said 'first of all.' Is there more?"

"Yes. Second, I'm not afraid of guns, or more precisely, bullets. I do not have ballistophobia, which is the fear of bullets, nor do I have hoplophobia, the fear of guns."

"Those are real phobias?"

"Indeed, there are phobias for everything."

"Everything?"

"Everything. Try me."

"All right," said the man, "What's the fear of chins?"

"Geniophobia," Aunt Ruth responded.

"Knees!"

"Genuphobia."

"Hair!"

"Chaetophobia."

"Hmm ... how about ... fear of the figure eight?"

"Octophobia."

"Fear of opinions, fear of youths, and fear of chopsticks!"

"Allodoxaphobia, ephebiphobia, and consecotaleophobia, respectively."

"Fear of cheese and fear of the moon!"

"Turophobia and selenophobia."

"Wow, you're good," said the man admiringly. "How do you know all these?"

"Social media, hashbrowns weirdphobias."

"Hashbrowns? I think you mean hashtag."

"Whatever. You know, the thing that TwitFace uses."

"Okay, I've got more for you … fear of flutes!"

"Um … aulophobia," said Aunt Ruth.

"How about the fear of long words?"

"Sesquipedalophobia."

"Finally, the fear of developing a phobia is?"

"Phobophobia, of course," replied Aunt Ruth.

"I'm amazed," said the man. "There certainly are a lot of phobia words that one could learn and use."

"I'm afraid so."

"Hey, what's the word for fear of grammar?"

"I … I don't know!" gasped Aunt Ruth.

"I'm keeping this bug!" shouted the man.

At that moment, the recording abruptly ended.

I looked at Clovis. "Clovis, my great aunt is in trouble! Let's go rescue her!"

"But we don't know where she is!"

"She's in the field behind Farmer Brown's barn."

"How do you know that?"

"I read the script."

"Ah. Okay, let's go."

One paragraph later, we arrived and found Aunt Ruth facing the ruthless phobia interrogator.

"Villain!" I stated, raising my head and sneering in disgust. "Hand over my aunt's mayfly, pronto!"

"You talkin' to me, grammar boy?" he retorted. "What makes you think you have the right to just barge in here and boss around whoever you want?"

I gasped; Clovis gasped; and even Aunt Ruth gasped.

"Should I tell him, or do you want to take this one?" asked Clovis.

"I've got it," I said softly, taking a deep breath. "Mister, whoever you are, you have mistakenly used the pronoun *whoever*."

"No way," he said.

"Yes way," I wittingly replied. "You used *whoever* when you should have used *whomever*. In your sentence, you said *boss around whoever you want*. The noun phrase *whoever you want* is the object for *boss around*. Within the phrase *whoever you want*, the word *whoever* is the object of *you want*. You need to use the object form. You want *whom*? You want *whomever*. You should have said *you want whomever*, not *you want whoever*."

He responded, "But you said, 'Mister, whoever you are.' How come you could use *whoever* instead of *whomever*?"

"In my noun phrase *whoever you are*, the verb *are* is a linking verb; therefore, this is the same as saying *you are whoever*, and with linking verbs the personal pronouns take on the subject form (*whoever*) and not the object form (*whomever*)."

"Okay, consider me enlightened. I'll revise my question: What makes you think you have the right to just barge in here and boss around whomever you think deserves it?"

"Wrong again," I sighed.

"Argh!" he groaned. "What is it this time?"

"This one is trickier, but look at your phrase carefully. The noun phrase that is the object of *you think* is *whomever deserves it*. By using the noun phrase *whomever deserves it*, you are saying that the subject is *whomever*. That is not a subject pronoun. You should be using *whoever* instead."

"Good grief," mumbled the grammatically challenged villain. "Would you please give me a couple of examples?"

"Certainly," I said. "My pleasure.

    1. The birthday cake is for *whomever*.
    2. The birthday cake is for *whoever wants it*.
    3. The birthday cake is for *whomever I want*.
    4. The birthday cake is for *whoever I say can have it*.

"In the first example, *whomever* is the object of the preposition *for*. It's pretty straight-forward that the object form *whomever* should be used.

"In the second example, the noun phrase *whoever wants it* is the object of the preposition *for*. Within the noun phrase itself, *whoever* is the subject of the phrase and thus is correctly in the subject form.

"In the third example, the noun phrase *whomever I want* is the object of the preposition *for*. In that phrase, *whomever* is the object (i.e., the phrase can be stated *I want whomever*) and is correctly in the object form.

"Finally, in the fourth example, *whoever I say can have it* is the object of the preposition *for*. Within that noun phrase, which can be reordered as *I say whoever can have it*, the noun phrase *whoever can have it* is the object of *I say*. Within that phrase, however, *whoever* is the subject (*whoever can have it*). That means that we want the subject form *whoever*."

"Wow, that actually seems reasonable!" remarked the villain.

"See? It's not that hard once you know how to look at it."

"Right. I feel better. Thanks. I guess we can all go home now."

"Sir!" I exclaimed. "I still have another bone to pick with you. Just a little while ago, you queried yonder aunt about the word meaning *fear of grammar*. Boy, do I have a surprise for you!"

He gave me a "you've got to be kidding" look, but then his attention was turned to the sound of trumpets arising in harmony from just over the horizon, accompanied by a choir of angels singing, "Ahhhhh," heralding the proclamation of a revelation with no insignificant import.

"There is no such word," I explained. "No one needs to fear grammar. After all, grammar is your friend. It enables you to communicate your ideas."

"Okay," said the man, "I can agree that there is no such word, but there should be such a word. After all, is it not true that many phobias are irrational?"

Clovis whispered, "The guy makes a good case."

"He does," I admitted. "Yes, you may be right. Okay, this is your chance for fifteen seconds of fame. If you give the bug back to Aunt Ruth, I will let you determine the word that means fear of grammar."

"It's easy," said the man, handing Aunt Ruth her mayfly. "The word is ruthaphobia!"

38

Bored of Aunt Ruth

As the perspiration rolled off my nose and my skin baked under the shining spotlights, I took a deep breath and finished the closing song with a flourish:

> ... mind your commas and your verbs ...
> ... even if you're just writing blurbs ...
> ... and with your grammar be cautious ...
> ... you may be nauseated, but we don't think you're nauseous.

The curtains closed. The final dress rehearsal for our new Broadway smash hit—*Aunt Ruth Grammar: The Musical*—was done!

"Did anyone throw roses to you?" asked Aunt Ruth, standing off to the side. She had finished her dancing just moments earlier.

"Not just roses, but a whole salad!" I exclaimed. "I saw tomatoes, apples, eggs, and even some avocado pits. I guess they loved it. Anyway, I'm so excited about our opening show this weekend."

"Nephew, I have something to tell you," said Aunt Ruth, quietly.

"What is it, my dear aunt?"

"I'm bored of this show."

I coughed. I felt dizzy. My world started spinning and everything turned black. Before I knew it, Aunt Ruth was standing over me, waving smelling salts in my face.

"What ... what happened?" I asked.

"I said I was bored of this show, and you fainted. I guess you are more excited about the show than I am."

"Oh, no, it's not that, really," I said, standing up. "I was shocked at your word usage, not at the fact that you are bored."

"What do you mean?"

"You can be bored *with* something or bored *by* something, but you are not bored *of* something."

"Really?" she asked.

"Really," I said. "Now, we Americans use *bored of* pretty regularly, but that doesn't make it right."

"Well, no, but do you think that you are going to get people to stop using it?"

"Probably not," I reflected, "but we can still point out the rule, the standard, so that people understand whether they're speaking correctly versus bending the language a little. After all, you never know when you might be presenting a paper or writing something on the Internet that might be read or heard by people world-wide."

"True. So tell me how this bored rule works?"

"Hit it, Hal," I shouted. Somewhere in the distance, a piano began playing. Someone from off-stage tossed me a cane and top hat.

"You may be bored with the new neighbors who don't ever take a bath;

you may be bored with too much homework if you're only doing math.

You may be bored with heavy traffic if you're always in a jam.

You may be bored with TV dinners if you only eat a yam."

"Yeah?" asked Aunt Ruth.

"Yeah!" I said. "Further ...

You may be bored by big white elephants whose snouts are really long;

you may be bored by big brass church bells that go ding-a-ling-a-dong.

You may be bored by cheetahs, cougars, and a hippopotamus;

you may be bored with getting coffee when the waiter's name is Gus.

You may be bored by pointy antlers if you find them on your head;

you may be bored by great big pillows if you see them on your bed.

You may be bored by a big tuba if its notes are way too deep;

you may be bored by fluffy penguin dolls that never say a peep."

"Really?"

"Really."

Aunt Ruth then began singing.

"I get bored with doing grammar when I'm stuck on lie or lay;

I get bored with conjugation—yuck—whose rules I must obey.

I get bored with me—the novice—using well and using good,

I get bored with trying to figure out I shall or if I should.

I get bored with trying to know if it is bad or badly done;

I get bored with sentence adverbs when they really aren't so fun.

I get bored with lots of commas and those semi-colons too;

I get bored with participles and I only know a few.

I get bored when I'm confused with using they're or there or their;

I get bored by trying to know if data is or data are.

I get bored by trying to see where my apostrophes should go;

I get bored by the subjunctive case—I wish it were not so."

"But never!" I sang.

"Never!" Aunt Ruth sang.

"Never!" I repeated.

"Never!" she echoed.

"Never," we sang together, "are we bored **of** anything!"

The piano played a final chord, and we were done.

"Gosh," said Aunt Ruth. "I won't be bored **of** anything ever again!"

39

Aunt Ruth and the Solar ... Ellipsis

Knock! Knock! Knock!

It was true that I was expecting company, but the invitation stated 10 a.m., not 9:30 a.m., the current time.

I opened the door and found Aunt Ruth standing there in dark sunglasses and with a rather large telescope strapped to her back.

"I'm here to see the ellipsis," she said with a smile. "I brought my shades to protect my eyes—"

"Uh, Aunt Ruth, I think—" I interrupted.

"I wasn't sure," said Aunt Ruth, interrupting my interruption, "if we're going to see a solar ellipsis or a lunar—"

"Well, Aunt Ruth, I need to explain to you that the—" I began, interrupting her interruption of my interruption.

"I brought my telescope," she continued, interrupting my interruption of her interruption of my interruption, "hoping it would help with our astronomical adventures today, and—"

"Aunt Ruth," I interjected, interrupting her interruption of my interruption of her interruption of my interruption, "there are no astronomical adventures today."

"No?"

"No."

"What about the ellipsis?"

"I think you're thinking eclipse, not ellipsis. They aren't the same thing."

"They aren't?"

"No. The solar / lunar thing you're thinking about is an eclipse."

"Then ... what's an ellipsis?"

"An ellipsis is the three-dot thing like the one that you just used in your last sentence."

"You mean ... like this?"

"Yes ... precisely."

"Hey, you did it too."

"Yes, I ... I like using them," I blushed.

"So, today isn't an astronomy day? It's a grammar day?"

"You've got that right, Aunt Ruth. That makes it a glorious day!"

She turned pale. "I ... I suddenly don't feel so well. I think I need to sit down in the comfy chair. I also need an ice pack for my head. I feel extremely nauseous right now."

"Nauseated."

"Whatever."

"Now, Aunt Ruth, let me introduce to you a very special guest for today's grammar adventure. Introducing ... a former president, general, and grammar aficionado, Ellipsis S. Grant!"

On that cue, a man wearing a blue circa 1865 army uniform fell out of the sky and onto the floor of my living room with a crash. He stood up, brushed the dust off his jacket, and began.

"Ladies and gentlemen, I am hear to teach you the fundamentals of the mighty *ellipsis*, the plural of which is *ellipses*. Now, before I dive into this juicy topic, I must give credit where credit is due—my parents. Mama and

Papa had the foresight to name their three daughters Dorothy, and when I was born, being the fourth child, the family had three Dots and an Ellipsis. Ha ha … ha ha … ha ha."

Aunt Ruth simply stared at him, glassy eyed.

"Just kidding, folks," said Ellipsis. "We'll all try to loosen up a bit, won't we? But seriously, ellipses are powerful friends, especially (well only, really) in the written language.

"Ellipses can be used to indicate silence during deep thought:

> As the general watched the army in gray advance, he pondered out loud, *I wonder what would happen if … yes, I have a plan!*

"Ellipses can be used to indicate pauses or the passing of time:

> 'It was the best of times, it was the ….' As Gerald read Dickens, he began day-dreaming of publishing a newspaper devoted to sausages. He would call it 'The Wurst Times.'

"Ellipses can be used to indicate stuttering or stammering:

> 'Hon … honest … Gen … General … I … I was aim … aiming for … for your hat.'

"Ellipses can be used to show a change in thought:

> 'I'm so hungry, I could eat a … uh … oh never mind.'

"Ellipses are perhaps more commonly used for providing a partial quote from some other source. For the next few examples, let's take our quotes from the following passage by esteemed author Joel Schnoor's book, *A Spoonful of Dirt*.

> With chubby cheeks and curly blond hair that made him look a whole lot nicer on the outside than he was on the inside, Eugene Dinwidden III had the rare ability to get under my skin, and he knew it. I'm not sure if it was because his name sounded too city-like, or if maybe I was just jealous that he had a III behind his name and I didn't.

"Suppose you wanted just the beginning and end of the first sentence.

You can do something like this:

> With chubby cheeks and curly blond hair ... Eugene Dinwidden III had the rare ability to get under my skin, and he knew it.

"Note that the form or syntax is:

> <phrase1><space><ellipsis><space><phrase2>

"If you have a complete sentence on the immediate left side of the ellipsis, use a period (or whatever ending punctuation mark that sentence has) and then a space, then the three dots, then another space, followed by the remaining material.

> With chubby cheeks and curly blond hair ... Eugene Dinwidden III had the rare ability to get under my skin, and he knew it. ... [M]aybe I was just jealous that he had a III behind his name and I didn't.

"Notice that phrase1 is replaced by a complete sentence, including ending punctuation. So here, between *it* and *[M]aybe,* we have a period, a space, three dots, and a space.

"In this example, the M in *Maybe* is capitalized even though in the original quote it wasn't. The reason is that because the text before the ellipsis ends in a complete sentence, a new sentence starts after the ellipsis. The M is then marked with a bracket so that the reader will see that it was not originally capitalized."

Aunt Ruth's hand shot up in the air. "Question from the audience, President Grant."

"Yes, darling," he replied.

Aunt Ruth blushed. "Ahem ... what if you don't end the excerpt at the end of a sentence?"

"Well, if you don't end your quote at the end of a sentence, then you would take your phrase, add a space, add the ellipsis, and add the ending period (or whatever ending mark the original quote uses). So, for example:

> With chubby cheeks and curly blond hair ... Eugene Dinwidden III had the rare ability to get under my skin ....

"Now, I need to give you two warnings about ellipses. First, you must only use ellipses in a trustworthy manner. A cardinal rule is that the text with the ellipses should mean the same thing, or have the same tenor, as the text without ellipses. Don't use ellipses to bend the truth. That's just not a good thing to do.

> With chubby cheeks and curly blond hair … maybe I was just jealous …."

"Gosh," said Aunt Ruth, "that means something totally different!"

"You're right."

"What's the second warning?"

"The second thing this shows is that when you are reading a quote that has ellipses, approach it cautiously. Unless you trust your source, it's possible some treachery has occurred."

"This all sounds kind of complicated," sighed Aunt Ruth.

"Well, first of all, don't get too frazzled by it. When you're quoting something, the basic idea is that the ellipsis—the three dots—is replacing the text that you are leaving out. As to whether a space goes here or there … well, the general consensus seems to be to use spaces as we talked about, but there certainly are magazines and books that have their own ways of doing this. If you're a writer, it all depends on what your boss says. So … does anyone have any questions?"

"Oh, oh, I do, I do," said Aunt Ruth, raising her hand.

"Yes, Aunt Ruth, what is your question?"

"Well … I was wondering … I've heard that you don't have a middle name. Is that true?"

"Well, yes and no … my middle name is the letter S."

"Really?"

"Really.

"How did that happen?"

"It's a long story. You got time?"

"Looks like we have about a page left, maybe less."

"Okay, I'll be quick. Are you familiar with Morse Code?"

"Only a little. I know SOS—Save Our Ship—which is three dots, three dashes, and three dots."

"Right. Very good. So what is the S?"

"Three dots."

"And what's my first name?"

"Ellipsis … oh, I get it! Your middle name is the Morse Code representation of your first name! Now, is that cool or what!"

"I think we're done with this story."

"Must you leave so abruptly? Are you heading back to Grant's Tomb?"

"Well, you know what they say: Old soldiers never die; they just …. Actually, I'm going to Mississippi to have a new suit tailored for me."

"Why Mississippi?" Aunt Ruth braced herself for the punch-line.

"I've heard good things about the famous 'serge of Vicksburg.'"

40

Aunt Ruth Letters from Aunt Iquity

My dearest Ruth,

With great remoras, I am swimming without you at the beach. Really, those suckerfish are huge. I am still looking for my porpoise in life, at least hoping to find a ray of meaning. "Live each day to the fullest"—that's always been my manta. Sometimes I flounder, but other days I have a whale of a time.

Oh, I'm such a kidder. Enough with the puns already. Anyway, just dropping you a line to say howdy. I'm doing laundry today and I hanged my clothes outside on the line. It's humid though. I was hoping my clothes would be dryer than they are by now.

Later Gator,

Iquity

Dear Aunt Iquity,

You're "punny," but you're also erroneous. Things are hung; people are hanged. Why would your clothes become an appliance?

Yours,

Ruth

Dear Ruth,

What are you talking about?

Later Crocodile,

Iquity

Dear Aunt Iquity,

You said you wished your clothes were a dryer. A dryer is something that makes things more dry than they were. You want your clothes to be drier. A dryer makes clothes drier.

Yours,

Ruth

Dear Ruth,

I'm glad you set my mind at ease on that point. I've been worrying about it all week. I can breath more easily now.

Later Babe,

Iquity

Dear Aunt Iquity,

If the word *can* is a helper verb, why did you put a noun after it? You said, "I can breath." The word *breath* is a noun, so that's like saying, "I can porcupine" or "I can chihuahua."

I believe you wanted to say, "I can breathe," not, "I can breath."

Sincerely,

Ruth

Dear Ruth,

Picky, aren't we? I think your girdle is too tight. Relax, girl. Losen up.

Your distant relative,

Iquity

Dear Aunt Iquity,

Sticks and stones may break my bones, and names do hurt me sometimes. You meant loosen up, not losen up.

Affectionately yours,

Ruth

Ruth,

Can we talk about something else now? You're driving me bonkers.

A distant relative whom you will never see again,

Iquity

Dear Aunt Iquity,

Yes, we *may*.

Yours,

Ruth

Dear Ruth,

Arrrrrrrg! Say, I just saw lightening in the sky. Perhaps we'll get some rain.

Iquity

Dear Aunt Iquity,

Lightening? Really? Lightening is when something is being made lighter. The opposite of lightening would be darkening. The lamp is lightening the room. Lightening could also refer to weight. The opposite of lightening here would be some word that means to make heavier. The hiker poured all the water out of his canteen, lightening his load.

The weather phenomenon to which you are referring is lightning.

Cordially,

Ruth

Ruth,

When did you start raining on my grammatical and word usage parade?

Iquity

Iquity,

My "reign" began when I was crowned the Queen of English. :-)

Ruth

41

Aunt Ruth and the Synonym Bun

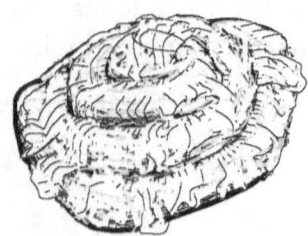

I can't really explain how I ended up in this position, but I found myself playing the unlikely role of patient in a psychiatric office, lying on a psychiatric couch, and being interrogated by my psychiatrist, Aunt Ruth.

I was hoping it was a bad dream, but I wasn't sure. I had the hardest time, though, accepting what she was trying to tell me.

"Could you go over it one more time, Aunt Ruth? I just can't believe my ears."

"Sure, Nincompoop Nephew. It's like this."

Before Aunt Ruth launched into her explanation, my entire life played before my eyes. In one scene that I had nearly forgotten, I climbed a mountain in Tibet to seek the answers to the questions of life from a wise seer. I remember approaching him as I reached the summit.

The wise man on the mountain asked me, "Tell me, my son, what is the difference between a homonym and a homophone?"

With the gentle wisdom that I've learned in my relatively few years of life here on this great planet, I answered with the confidence of a man who has heard it all. "It depends," I responded. There was a pause, and I realized that the wise man was waiting for the complete answer. So I decided to continue.

"It depends on what a homophone is," I triumphantly stated, "and what a homonym is. I came here seeking the answer from you to this very same question."

"Man," said the wise man, "I was hoping you knew. I'm writing a letter to my brother Larry in Brooklyn. He and I are having this argument. Sigh. I can't find good help anywhere these days. Next customer please."

"Wait—is that all the time from you that I get?"

"What, you want me to tango with you or something? Scram, kid."

Wisely, I evacuated the premises. Such was my experience with the wise man on the mountain and my attempt to learn homonyms and homophones.

Somewhere between third and fifth grade I was given a definition of *homonym*, and it stuck. Homonyms are words that sound the same. Period. Yes, they do sound alike. That is true. But that's not the end of the story.

Apparently, deep in the bowels of my elementary education, I was either:

    A) misinformed,

    B) not paying attention, or

    C) the victim of a government plot by Communists somewhere to lead American children astray in an attempt to hinder national productivity and intelligence.

I suspect it was C, but I cannot prove it. (C, incidentally, is also responsible for video games and cell phone text messaging.)

"Ahem!" grunted Aunt Ruth, breaking the silence and snapping me out of my reverie. "Allow me to expound upon the nature of the homonym."

Sigh. At this point in the story, it was too late to switch roles. I would just have to lie here and listen to her.

She continued. "**Homophones** are words that sound alike. *Two*, *to*, and *too* are homophones.

"**Homographs** are words that are written alike. *Lead* (as in 'to be in front') and *lead* (the metal used to make fishing weights) are homographs.

"**Homonyms** are words that are both homophones and homographs.

"In other words, all homonyms are homophones, i.e., all homonyms sound the same. The converse is not true—not all homophones are homonyms. Why? Remember that a homonym must also be a homograph. That is, not all words that sound the same are spelled the same, and vice versa."

"That's all fine and dandy, Aunt Ruth, and you've taught me some words that aren't homonyms. Could you show me some words that *are* homonyms?"

"Of course. Stalks."

"Stalks?"

"Stalks. Let us go to the great plains of America and examine corn stalks.

"Stalk and stalk—the former being the base of a corn plant and the latter being the action of clandestinely following somebody (or is it the other way around, and how do you know?)—are examples of homonyms. They are spelled the same and they sound the same."

"Wow, so it's true," I said, aghast. Talk about having your world turned upside down. This is akin to thinking for years that it was Neil Armstrong who first set foot on the moon, only to find (decades later) that it was really Neil Young.

Why didn't anyone tell me? Not that I'm paranoid, but what other facts out there have I gotten wrong all my life? It makes one wonder.

"Fortunately, antonyms and cinnamons are a lot easier," I said.

"Are they?"

"Yes indeed. Try me," I challenged.

"Let's try antonyms first. We'll start with wet."

"Dry."

"Cold."

"Hot."

"Full."

"Empty."

"Smart."

"Dumb."

"Liberal."

"Conservative."

"Black."

"White."

"Dog."

"What?"

"Dog: D-O-G."

"It doesn't have an opposite."

"Certainly it does. Think feline, something that goes 'meow.'"

"Aunt Ruth, a cat is not the opposite of a dog."

"Why not?"

"A dog has four legs. A cat has four legs. Dogs have fur. Cats have fur. Dogs are pets. Cats are pets. Dogs are cuddly. Cats are cuddly."

"Are you saying a dog and a cat are identical?"

"No, of course not. But they have many similar characteristics. Since a dog is an animal, should I choose a non-animal? How about a cactus? Maybe the opposite of a dog is a cactus. Oh, but wait. A cactus is a living thing, as is a dog. So the answer isn't cactus. Hey, I know! It's a rock. A rock isn't living. No, that's not it. A rock is opaque, and so is a dog. I should choose something transparent, like plastic wrap. That's it! The opposite of a dog is plastic wrap. Hmm, hold on. That can't be right."

"Any why not?" demanded an exasperated psychiatric aunt.

"Because dogs and plastic wrap are both solid materials. One of them should be liquid, air, or plasma. Or something. Maybe the opposite of a dog is pink lemonade. Or ... or maybe it's carbon monoxide."

"Carbon monoxide?"

"That's it! That's it! Aunt Ruth, we're geniuses! Or geniuii perhaps."

"No, I don't think it's geniuii. Why are we geniuses?"

"We've solved the 'changing climate phenomenon.'"

"We have?"

"Yes! Since the climate supposedly is changing because of too much carbon monoxide in the atmosphere, and since dogs are the opposite of carbon monoxide, all we have to do is launch dogs into orbit. Woohoo! We'll be famous!"

"Look," said Aunt Ruth, "the opposite of dog is cat, and I can prove it."

"How?" I asked in disbelief.

"Look at the audience. Gentle readers, raise your hand if the first thought that crossed your mind regarding a dog's opposite was 'cat.' See? That's nearly everybody. The only person who didn't raise a hand was your mother."

"Okay, I stand corrected," I sighed. "Can we do cinnamons now?"

"Cinnamons?" asked Aunt Ruth. "That's my line. Sure, let's do cinnamons. After all, we're on a roll! Okay, but seriously, let's do synonyms. We'll start with the word *shut*."

"A synonym for shut is close."

"Perspires."

"A synonym for perspires is sweats."

"Shouts."

"A synonym for shouts is yells."

"Angry."

"A synonym for angry is mad."

"Funny."

"A synonym for funny is comical."

"Speaks."

"A synonym for speaks is talks."

"I think that's enough to get the point across."

"Thanks, Aunt Ruth. Note that synonyms should mean exactly or near enough to the same thing that there's no doubt as to the meaning and usage. For example, *warm* and *hot* are not synonyms. *Good* and *great* are not synonyms either."

DING! DING! DING!

"Oh, time's up," said Aunt Ruth. "You're psychotherapy session is over, Nutty Nephew. That would normally be $7489.15, but for you it's free."

"Free? Really?"

"Yes, didn't you see the sign on the door? It said nuts are complimentary."

42

Aunt Ruth Has Got to Be Kidding

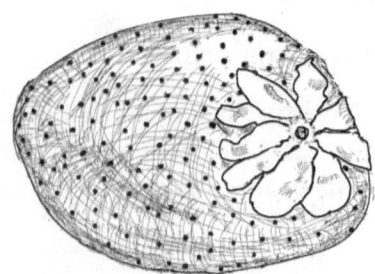

"Clovis, these are great seats! Wow, front row behind the centerfield wall here at Grammar Stadium—this is the place to be! Boy, oh boy, I hope someone hits a ball our way."

Clovis, chewing on a mouthful of peanuts, merely nodded in agreement.

No sooner had the game begun than my wish was granted. The leadoff batter blasted the first pitch, sending a towering fly ball toward centerfield.

"I got it, I got it," yelled the centerfielder in an unmistakably familiar voice.

"Aunt Ruth! You're playing centerfield!" I blurted in astonishment. Clovis was so surprised that he choked and coughed. Peanuts riddled out of his mouth like bullets from a Gatling gun.

Positioning herself beneath the still-sky-high fly ball, Aunt Ruth retorted, "Thanks for reminding me, Rookie Relative. I almost forgot. Now, what can I do for you while I'm waiting for the ball to return to earth?"

"First of all," I said, never one to miss an opportunity, "you can correct your claim to the ball."

"Pardon?" she asked, before muttering under her breath, "I think I'm going to regret this."

"The phrase 'I got it,' is simply incorrect when used in the present tense. Yes, it's common to hear it that way, but that doesn't make it correct English."

"Can we talk about something more pleasant, like the time you stapled your tongue to a giant windmill?"

"Uh, no. Look, Aunt Ruth, this isn't too hard. Just bear with me." I looked up. The ball was still hundreds of feet from the ground.

Her silence encouraged me, so I continued.

"Let me start by saying that one usage of *get* that we do share with other English-speaking nations is to indicate possession or ownership.

"Examples of using *get* to mean ownership or possession:

(Present Tense *get*)
- I am going to get a new crocodile today.
- I will get the pizza on my way home from work.

(Past Tense *got*)
- I got an autographed picture of that guy Aristotle for my birthday.
- He got the flu from Aunt Ruth.

(Past Participle *got*)
- She's got the comb that once belonged to actor Yul Brynner (ask your parents), even though he said he would never part with it.
- I have got a baseball at home that was autographed by Homer, the famous Greek slugger.

"Are you with me so far?"

"Uh huh," she yawned. "Homer, the famous Greek slugger."

"Before I go on, let me also point out that American English tends to use *get* in ways that are totally, uh, foreign to some of the other English-speaking places on Earth."

"For example?"

"For example, we use *got* to mean *must*. I got to be going. We use *got* to mean permission or capability. I got to go salmon-fishing on the Kenai Peninsula. We even use *got* to mean *have got*. Yes sir, I got one big, old, mean, tough aunt."

"You got one big, old, mean, tough aunt? Have I ever met her?"

I ignored her question and continued. "In American English, the present tense is get, the past tense is got, and the past participle form is *gotten* or *got*, depending on meaning. Generally, Americans use *gotten* for the past participle when talking about ability or permission, and they use *got* for the past participle when talking about possession or ownership, as we saw above.

"Examples of using *get* to refer to ability or permission:

(Present Tense *get*)
- Today, I get to go to a ballgame.
- I won my semi-final match, so I get to go to the Finals!

(Past Tense *got*)
- Yesterday, I got to go to the Grammar Zoo.
- I was so popular in school that I got to be the Third Grade Class President two years in a row!

(Past Participle *gotten*)
- I recently have gotten to go back stage to see Aunt Ruth after one of her rock concerts.
- I have gotten through the first chapter of Tolstoy's *War and Peace* five times.

"Now, in British English—"

"You mean English English?" she asked.

"Uh, I guess so. In English English, the meaning of *get* is much more restrictive than you will find in America. *Get* is pretty much confined to mean *to receive* or *to obtain*. The present, past, and past participle words are *get*, *got*, and *got*, respectively.

> I get strawberries and cream for lunch today.
> I got strawberries and cream for lunch yesterday.
> I believe I have got strawberries and cream in the larder; would you care to join me for an afternoon snack?"

"Really? The Brits don't use *gotten*?" she asked with an incredulous look on her face.

"That's right."

"At all?"

"Well, they have words like *forgotten* and *begotten*, but they don't use *gotten* by itself, unless of course they've picked up an Americanism."

"You got to be kidding."

"The British would say that *you got* is not correct."

"You have got to be kidding?" tried Aunt Ruth.

"Technically, that's not correct either, because the British don't generally use forms of *get* to mean *must*. Now, well-respected writers have been using that phrase for the past four hundred years or so, but even current grammarians will admit that one shouldn't overuse *have got* or *has got*, because it gets tiresome. One suggestion often heard is to elide (i.e., put in contraction form) the phrase *have got* so that it comes out as *I've got* or *you've got*. That just sounds less awkward. But really, what's wrong with just saying, 'You have to be kidding'?"

"Why is the distinction important? Why do we care if Americans do it one way and the British another?"

"I am merely putting a stake in the ground and saying there is a right way of using *get* and there is the American way that deviates from the norm. I am not saying that we shouldn't use the American way, but I want to make it clear what is proper or not proper in formal writing."

"Oh, brother," sighed Aunt Ruth.

Unperturbed, I continued. "There may come a time when you need to make a presentation at a formal conference or have high tea with the queen of England, and you want to be sure to speak or write correctly and accurately."

"High tea with the queen of England? Yeah right, and maybe monkeys will fly before the game is over."

I glanced up. The ball was now just dozens of feet from Aunt Ruth's head.

I yelled, "Get it!"

Aunt Ruth raised her mitt high in the air and exclaimed, "I do believe that, of the nine of us in the defensive field, I am located in the most suitable position for being able to stake my claim as the player who should try to catch this ball. In other words ... I'LL GET IT!"

The ball ended its meteoric descent with a crisp POP! as it landed in Aunt Ruth's glove. She raised the ball triumphantly and shouted, "Got it!"

At that moment, an elegant, regal figure stepped out from the shadows. Recognizing her, the crowd instantly became silent. The woman said, "Well done, Ruth. You have got the ball, indeed!"

"Thank you, Your Majesty," said Aunt Ruth.

"Ruth, I believe I have got strawberries and cream in the larder; would you care to join me for high tea?"

"High tea with the queen? You better believe it—yes, I would love to join you. Forget this game. I'm outta here!"

She threw her mitt onto the field and leaped over the centerfield wall. Moments later, the two of them—the queen of England and the queen of English grammar—linked arms and walked out of the stadium, whistling, "God Save the Queen."

Clovis smiled. "Aunt Ruth has **got** to be the luckiest person alive."

"It can't **get** any better than that!" I agreed.

43

Aunt Ruth and the Peach Cobbler's Kitten

"It's mine," grumbled Aunt Ruth. "Give it back to me at once, my nemesis nephew. Or else!"

"You're being too possessive, my dear Aunt Ruth," I said as I set down the now-empty plate of what had been a delicious serving of Aunt Ruth's peach cobbler. "Besides, you are distracting me from being able to concentrate on this fascinating topic of possessives with appositives."

Aunt Ruth yawned. It was time for her morning nap.

I tried hard to ignore Aunt Ruth's occasional tantrums—not an easy task, certainly, but every now and then it worked—and this morning I had been in deep thought about some of the odd (and correct) possessive statements I have witnessed through the years.

Unfortunately (or perhaps fortunately), Aunt Ruth's new pet kitten had taken a liking to me, and it was now sound asleep on the floor at my feet. Aunt Ruth followed suit (in her favorite comfy chair, not on the floor at my feet) and in moments was sawing wood like a lumberjack on steroids.

Anyway, back to odd possessives. The most bizarre possessive statements that I've seen involve appositives.

Appositives, you may recall, are noun phrases that are used to clarify or further describe the noun immediately preceding it in the sentence. For example, look at the sentence:

> Marjorie, the lady who sat next to us in church this morning, has a dog and two cats.

In that sentence, Marjorie is the subject, and *the lady who sat next to us in church this morning* is the appositive. The appositive is a description or identification of Marjorie.

Now, suppose I accidentally sat on Marjorie's hat. Suppose, also, that I am not sure if you remember who Marjorie is. For clarification, then, I want to include the appositive when I tell you about sitting on Marjorie's hat.

The rule for creating a possessive with a statement that has an appositive is NOT to put the apostrophe on the subject, but put the apostrophe at the end of the appositive (i.e., add apostrophe -s to the last word of the appositive, and then remove the comma that normally immediately follows the appositive). So, that would look like this:

> I sat on Marjorie, the lady sitting next to us in church this morning's hat.

Note a couple of things. In the phrase before the appositive, it indeed says *I sat on Marjorie*. However, I did not sit on Marjorie. I sat on her hat. The second thing to notice is that the apostrophe -s is attached to *morning*, as in ... *this morning's hat*. And the comma after morning has been removed.

Weird? Certainly. And I must confess that the grammar books that discuss this also say that in such cases, the writer should seriously consider restructuring the sentence for clarity, e.g.,

> I sat on Marjorie's hat; she was the lady sitting next to us in church this morning.
> Or ... I sat on the hat of Marjorie, the lady sitting next to us in church this morning.

That works, certainly, though *the hat of Marjorie* sounds a little stuffy, kind of like the title of a murder mystery, perhaps.

"Tonight, on 'Hitchcock Presents,' we will watch *The Hat of Marjorie*." That sounds sinister, indeed.

One can contrive scenarios that produce word combinations that are visually funny.

> I was bitten by Marjorie, the lady sitting next to us at the concert's dog.

Of course, I was not bitten by Marjorie but by her dog. The dog was probably upset with me for sitting on (and undoubtedly ruining) Marjorie's hat.

> I vacuumed up Marjorie, the lady who always went to the park with her husband's ashes.

I did not actually vacuum up Marjorie; and Marjorie did not go to the park every day with her husband's ashes. She simply went to the park every day with her husband. I did vacuum up Marjorie's ashes, but we don't know from whence those ashes came. Maybe Marjorie is a chronic chain-smoker. As far as we know, her husband is still alive and has not (yet) been reduced to ashes. The possessive statement leaves a lot of wiggle-room for ambiguity.

> I sat on Marjorie, the lady sitting next to me's hat.

This is similar to the first example, but I like the *me's hat* combination. It just sounds so wrong.

> I ate a bowl of Marjorie, the next-door neighbor who liked to go to Africa to hunt elephants' soup.

I ate a a bowl of Marjorie? I'm not even sure what that means. She does go to Africa to hunt elephants (I am not condoning that, by the way). She does not go to hunt elephants' soup, though that could be an interesting hobby. Tusk, tusk. Note, also, that in this case we merely added the apostrophe to elephants; we did not add the "s" because the word already ended in "s" (and elephants's just doesn't sound right).

> We must get Steve Berry, the attorney handling the case of the missing elephant's signature.

This seems to indicate that the elephant's signature is missing. I can see why we might be concerned.

Now, suppose Steve Berry has a piano, and suppose that I went over to his house to play his piano. I could say this:

> I played Steve Berry, the attorney handling the case of the missing elephants' piano.

I did not play Steve Berry. He is a fine actor and can play his own part quite well. He's still handling the case of the missing elephants, not the *elephants' piano*. It's interesting to consider, though, that multiple elephants would have only one piano. I can't imagine two elephants playing a one-piano duet. That could be awkward.

"What are you saying, Notorious Nephew?" asked Aunt Ruth, yawning as she slowly awoke. "Are you violating our grammatical agreement to not stretch out there into the strange world of intentional weirdness and ambiguous writing?"

> I acknowledged but tried not to focus on Ruth, the aunt who likes to take me out to eat's warts.

"What did you say? Eats warts?"

"Uh, never mind."

> I am wearing Marjorie, the neighbor who has the llamas' argyle socks.

"Marjorie's llamas wear argyle socks?" gasped Aunt Ruth. "Really?"

> In my rush to pack up and get out of here at the end of the story, I accidentally stepped on Aunt Ruth, my relative who makes the best peach cobbler's kitten.

44

Aunt Ruth in the Oval Office

"Ahem." I cleared my throat, hoping that would be sufficient to garner the attention of the person sitting in the chair, facing away from me, on the other side of the desk.

Standing in the Oval Office of the White House after being summoned to the nation's capitol to provide grammatical expertise to America's commander in chief, I was looking forward to this encounter. Of course, I was nervous, but golly, I saw this as the opportunity of a lifetime. I had rehearsed my speech over and over so that I would be firm but gentle, knowledgeable but not arrogant, humble but not exhibiting false modesty—in short, I resolved not to tell the president everything I knew and to tell nothing that I didn't know.

"Ahem!" I tried again in a larger font and with more emphatic punctuation. That, indeed, seemed to do the trick.

"Here, try one of these," said a voice as the chair swiveled slightly toward me and a hand flung a jellybean my direction. "This may soothe your throat." I caught the jellybean in the air, popped it into my mouth—raspberry, yummy!—and then turned to say thank you.

I screamed.

"Aunt Ruth! What are you doing in the president's chair?"

"I'm doing the macarena. What do you THINK I'm doing? I'm presiding. That's what a president does, *n'est-ce pas?*"

"Wait a minute. You used that phrase in an earlier story. What does it mean?"

"All I know is that it's French and it means something like *isn't that so,* or *isn't that right?*"

"Huh. Anyway, I know that television can do remarkable things with digital special effects, but I had no idea that I was voting for you in the last election. I thought I was voting for a really old, kind of heavyset candidate from Topeka."

"No, no, no, I'm not presiding over the United States. I'm presiding over the president's garden club. I'm the head gardener for the White House. I think I sent that info to you on last year's Christmas card."

"Christmas card?"

"You know, the one taped to the fruitcake. You did get the fruitcake, didn't you?"

I thought quickly back to last Christmas. I think I used the fruitcake to replace a broken brick on the front steps of my house. The bricks, I knew, would eventually crumble and break to pieces; Aunt Ruth's fruitcake, however, was guaranteed indestructible.

"Hey, could you send me maybe thirty more fruitcakes this Christmas?"

"Anyway," she continued, ignoring my comment, "I was outside gardening this morning and it got so warm that I came in for a break. The president has always said I could come into the Oreo Office if I needed a respite. I was hungry, and oreos sounded good. I couldn't find much food, though—just this jar of jelly beans on the desk. Here, have some." She handed me the jar.

"Aunt Ruth, this is the Oval Office, not the Oreo Office," I said, chewing the jelly beans and reaching into the jar for more.

"Oval Office? Maybe that's why the mirrors make me look short and dumpy. It's one of those elliptical illusions or something." She grabbed another handful of jelly beans. "These things sure are good."

"You're sitting in the president's chair, you realize," I warned, implying that she may want to get up and find another place to sit.

"So tell me, National Nephew, what brings you here?" she asked just as I stuffed more jelly beans in my mouth.

"Well ... (chew, chew) ... in the most recent State of the Union speech ... (chew, chew) ... the president used *hopefully*, *nauseous*, and *lie / lay / lain* all incorrectly ... (chew, chew, swallow) ... in the same sentence!"

"Horrors."

"Yeah, I know. I wrote a letter explaining my dismay, and the president invited me to come in for a chat. Here I am, in all my glory."

"Well, that's pretty cool," said Aunt Ruth. She helped herself to more jelly beans. "Hey, I have an idea."

"Yes?"

"After you finish meeting with the president, let's you and I go out to celebrate. I know a restaurant downtown that makes the best ... hey, what's wrong? Why are you shaking?"

"Aunt Ruth, you just committed a grammar offense so grievous that I'm ashamed I never taught this to you."

"That bad, huh?"

"Remember when Godzilla destroyed Tokyo?"

"Yep."

"Well, that's nothin' compared to this. You said, 'Let's you and I.'"

"Well, yeah? I know that 'Let's' means 'Let us,' so I was basically saying, 'Let us, you and I.'"

"I know. But think about it. The word *us* is the third person plural objective (also called nominative) pronoun. *You and I*, or *we*, is the third person plural subjective pronoun. You can't mix them."

"That sounds serious."

"It is."

"Zounds!"

"Exactly."

"Now, what can I do to remedy the situation? Should I say, instead, 'Let's you and me …'?"

"Well, you could do that, but since you are already saying, 'Let's,' which includes the 'us,' how about you simply say, 'Let's go celebrate.'"

I took the last jelly bean from the jar and set the jar on the desk. It was then that I noticed an empty gift box and a purple ribbon.

"Wonder what was in this box?" I mused.

"Oh, the jelly beans were in there," said a nonchalant Aunt Ruth.

"What? You opened the box—apparently a gift to the president—and we've eaten all his jelly beans! Oh my, this isn't good."

"I guess you're right," said Aunt Ruth meekly. "I wasn't paying attention. It's kind of obvious, isn't it, that there are less jelly beans in the jar now than when we started."

"That should be *fewer* jelly beans, not *less* jelly beans."

"Really? Why?"

"It's like this. Use *fewer* when the item you are talking about is countable. Use *less* when it's not countable."

"What do you mean by countable and not countable?"

"Well, um, if you can count them, then they are countable."

"But there were hundreds, maybe thousands of jelly beans in that jar."

"Right, but if I told you to take twenty jelly beans out of the jar, could you do it?"

"No."

"No? Why not? Surely, you can count to twenty."

"There aren't any jelly beans in the jar. That's why I can't take twenty from the jar. I can't even take one from the jar!"

"Okay. If the jar were full, could you remove twenty jelly beans?"

"Of course."

"Then you could say the jelly beans were countable; therefore, we could say that we now have fewer jelly beans than when we started."

"When would you use *less*?" she asked.

"Suppose we filled the jar with water," I said. "Could you remove twenty waters?"

"Twenty waters? What does that even mean?"

"That's precisely my point. We don't know if we mean molecules of water, ounces of water, inches of water, or what. It's not countable."

"Okay, I think I get that," said Aunt Ruth. "Now, we should—"

"Wait a minute. I'm not done," I exclaimed.

"Yes, but—"

"Let me finish!" I demanded.

"Oh all right," she sighed. "Please finish."

"When talking about the *number* of something, don't use *less* or *fewer*. Instead, use *smaller*.

> The *number* of tubas in our band is *smaller* than we had last year.

"Of course, if you don't use *number*, you could simply say:

> We have fewer tubas in our band than we had last year."

"That's very interesting," said Aunt Ruth in a rather unconvincing tone. "Now, I really think—"

"Just one more thing," I insisted.

"Sigh. Okay. Proceed, but make it quick."

"There are certain kinds of countable objects with which you are allowed to use *less*. This occurs for objects that we typically (or often, at least) think of in quantities. Specifically, quantities of money, time, and distance belong in this category."

"You're confusing me, Countable Nephew."

I ignored her and forged ahead. "Suppose you want to buy a car. You see a car at a car dealership, and the dealer tells you that the car costs ten thousand dollars. Now, even though that amount of money is countable, a person may not think of it that way. He or she may think of it in more fluid terms."

"Fluid terms, like gallons of money?"

"Not exactly," I said, "but instead of thinking of it like ten thousand one-dollar bills, the buyer may think of it in relative terms, e.g., "That car costs twice my salary," or, "I only have one-quarter of that amount in the bank."

"Oh! I think I get it," said Aunt Ruth, almost appearing to be actually excited. "It's like when I ask for water and I might want a full glass, or half of a glass, or a quarter of a glass."

"Right, sort of," I said. "Now, you could tell the dealer that you have *fewer* than ten thousand dollars available; but, you could also tell the dealer that you have *less* than ten thousand dollars available. Either one is fine."

"Wow, that's neat."

"Agreed! Now, with time and distance, you have the same kind of thing.

> We drove there in less than ten hours.
> He lives less than one hundred miles away.

"Again, you could use *fewer* in either case, but *less* is also permitted."

I heard voices in the hall.

Thinking quickly, I shoved the jar back into the box and wrapped the box with the ribbon.

Suddenly the door opened, and I heard a voice say, "To express my appreciation to you, my esteemed comrade, for your willingness to travel so far to converse with me at our summit meeting to help prevent conflict arising from the fragile tension of the currently sensitive international arena, I have a special gift that I ordered custom-made for you. These are the most exquisite jelly beans in the world, sweetened solely with honey produced by a rare Alaskan honeybee from the nectar of an even rarer (and almost unknown) fruit, the Puerto Rican Demomo Berry. The cost of one jar of these jelly beans is approximately equivalent to the cost of one of our high-end aircraft carriers."

I had the sinking feeling that I didn't want to be there.

It was too late. In walked the president and his entourage. He saw me standing at the desk—Aunt Ruth was still in the chair—and he said, "Hello," with the sort of rising tone that means "Hello, who are you, what are you doing here, and don't you think it's about time to leave" all at the same time.

"Hello, uh, hi," I began. "I ... I was just ... um ... waiting here in the offal orifice ... the oreo edifice ... I mean the oral officious ... the, uh, orthodontic oligarchy ... oh my, look at the time. By the way ... the grammar person you were going to meet ... well, he had to go ... and me? I'm just the nephew of your gardener, you know. Well, see ya," I said, grabbing Aunt Ruth's hand and dragging her out of the room as I closed the door behind me.

"Whew," gasped Aunt Ruth. "You got out of that one."

"Yeah, but it's too bad that I couldn't correct the president's grammar."

"I have a feeling you'll have more opportunities someday," she mused.

"Oh, perhaps," I said.

"Anyway, I'm feeling kind of stressed. I sure could use some ice cream."

"Good idea. I wish now that I had eaten *fewer* jelly beans," I lamented.

"Me too. I guess we'll just have to eat *less* ice cream. Anyway, let's go."

"You and me?"

"You and me."

45

Aunt Ruth and the Train to Gettysburg

> ✗ One Century minus
> ✗ 13 years ago...
>
> ✗ Three-fourths of a
> ✗ century plus 12...
>
> ✗ Six decades and
> ✗ an additional 27...

"While I'm in the time machine, I still can't get over the fact that we're doing this," declared an excited Aunt Ruth. "I know it's a long ways there, but you know I'm not adverse to travel, and I'm so anxious to speak with Abraham Lincoln that I can almost taste it. All I'm waiting on is for this machine to go as fast as it can go. All right, are we ready to precede? Let's get on with it. I want to meet Mr. Lincoln; plus, I'm hungry as a bear."

At that moment, though, I put my hands to my mouth and did perhaps my best grammar police call ever: "One Adam Twelve, One Adam Twelve, we have numerous and severe shreddings of the English language in a time machine located at the corner of Fourteenth and Vine. Be on the lookout for a handsome nephew, accompanied by the perpetrator, a vastly overweight and senile, old—"

WHAM! The umbrella came down on my head with a fury that hasn't been felt since early on in the grammar classic *I Laid an Egg on Aunt Ruth's Head*. I definitely deserved it, and I didn't even complain as a lump on my head began forming.

"I am not old," croaked Aunt Ruth. "Now, what were the grammatical difficulties that you encountered in my earlier utterance? Are you, indeed, concerned about the following?"

At this point, she began rattling off the following list of grammatical errors:

"1. Avoid using *while* instead of *although* if it can lead to ambiguities. *While* could mean *at the same time*, but it also could mean *although* or *whereas*. I said that *while* I am in the time machine, I still can't get over the fact that I am doing this. Do I mean that if I were not in the time machine, I would be able to get over that fact?

"2. When referring to distance, one place is a long way from another place, not a long ways.

"3. When using *adverse* or *averse*, remember that *adverse* means difficult or unfavorable; *averse* means being opposed or reluctant. I said I am not adverse to travel, but I should have said I am not averse to travel.

"4. *Anxious* carries with it the sense of worry or apprehension. Though I may be anxious in the time machine, I was attempting to express that I was eager to get there. *Eager* would have been better than *anxious*.

"5. I said I was waiting *on* the machine to go as fast as it can go. I should have said I am waiting *for* the machine. To wait on someone is what a waiter or waitress does. To wait for something is to be ready or in some state of preparedness for something.

"6. *Precede* means to come before something; *proceed* means to continue. I should have used *proceed*.

"7. Do not use *plus* as a conjunction to connect two independent clauses. When I said, 'plus, I'm hungry as a bear,' I should have used *and* or *but* or some other appropriate conjunction."

Aunt Ruth had finished her list. I was stunned. "Aunt Ruth, you mean you knew that you were saying those things incorrectly?"

"Well of course, my dear nephew. I've been hanging around you a long time … don't you think I'm going to do some preemptive research so that I can avoid these grammatical stumbling blocks?"

"I suppose so … but how long have you been doing this?"

"Longer than you think," she said with a wink. "Now, let's get going. I'm eager to meet perhaps the greatest president of all time. Beside, I want to give him a surprise."

"*Beside*? You mean *besides*, right?"

"Uh, what's the difference? I figured since it's forward and not forwards, and it's backward and not backwards, that it would be *beside* and not *besides*."

"Well, *beside* means next to; *besides* means also or in addition to. Anyway, what's your surprise for Mr. Lincoln?"

"Oh, I just wanted to give him a copy of the biography that Carl Sandburg wrote about him."

"You can't do that, Aunt Ruth."

"I cannot? Watch me."

"Okay, I mean you shouldn't. Of course you can—you are able—but it's not a good idea. We shouldn't mess with history."

"Why not?"

"Well, what if Mr. Lincoln read ahead in the book and found out what was going to happen in the future?"

"That could certainly change things, couldn't it. Okay, you're right. I won't mess with history. So I suppose that means that I shouldn't give him a copy of the picture of me standing at Mount Ruthmore."

"Right," I sighed.

We arrived almost instantly. After all, the year 1863 really wasn't all that long ago. We found ourselves on a train bound from Washington, D.C., to Gettysburg, Pennsylvania. The president's security staff were surprised at our arrival initially, but they quickly got over it and allowed us to mingle with the other passengers on board, including the president himself.

As usually happens when I have an opportunity to speak with someone famous, I stumbled with my conversation with Mr. Lincoln. I had thought of all these great questions, subjects of tremendous historical import, but when it came right down to it, all I could really talk about was the weather.

Aunt Ruth, on the other hand, somehow turned on her charm, and she spent over an hour conversing with the president in a corner of the car.

I watched them closely, mostly to make sure Aunt Ruth wasn't overstepping her bounds by trying to change history. The president had a solemn, somber look on his face at first, but eventually he was smiling, and I thought I even heard him chuckle a time or two.

The train conductor announced our imminent arrival to Gettysburg, and Aunt Ruth approached me. "We best be going back home now, Nephew. I've done my part."

As we were getting into the time machine, Mr. Lincoln walked up to say good-bye. "Ruth, thank you for your thoughts on the introduction. *Four score and seven …* that's brilliant. I think I'll use it. Perhaps I will be able to give you a copy of the speech someday. And Nephew, I enjoyed talking with you. I share your fascination with the weather. Good-bye, my friends."

Aunt Ruth and I stepped into the time machine and closed the hatch. "Ready?" I asked.

"Ready!" she said.

"Okie doke. Let's go!"

With the push of a button, we were gone, headed back to real life so that we could fight the good fight for the preservation of English grammar and usage in the free world. What adventures lay before us? I had no idea, but I knew that any adventure with Aunt Ruth, the indomitable one, was worth it.

Common Rough Spots in English

Active Voice Verbs

21 *The Ripcord Was Pulled by Aunt Ruth*

> **Rule:** A verb in the *active* voice is a verb whose action is performed by the subject. Active verbs can be either transitive or intransitive. If the verb is not in active voice, it is in *passive* voice.

- Aunt Ruth kicked the football through the goalposts. What is the subject? *Aunt Ruth.* What is the verb? *Kicked.* Who did the verb? *Aunt Ruth.* So, Aunt Ruth kicked the ball. *Kicked* is an active verb.

- The football was kicked by Aunt Ruth. What is the subject? *The football.* What is the verb? *Was kicked.* Who did the verb? *Aunt Ruth.* In this example, the subject was not the person "doing the verb," so *was kicked* is a passive verb phrase. This is a valid sentence, but it is an example of passive voice and not active voice.

- Aunt Ruth gargled. What is the subject? Aunt Ruth. What is the verb? Gargled. Who did the verb? Aunt Ruth. The subject did the verb, so gargled is an active verb. Note that gargled is also intransitive (the sentence has no direct object).

- Aunt Ruth gargled the mouthwash. What is the subject? Aunt Ruth. What is the verb? Gargled. Who did the verb? Aunt Ruth. The subject did the verb, so gargled is an active verb. In this sentence, gargled is transitive—the direct object is mouthwash.

- The mouthwash was gargled by Aunt Ruth. What is the subject? Mouthwash. Who did the verb? Aunt Ruth. This is a valid sentence, but it is an example of passive voice and not active voice.

Adverse and Averse

45 *Aunt Ruth and the Train to Gettysburg*

Rule: *Adverse* means difficult or unfavorable; *averse* means being opposed or reluctant.

- Aunt Ruth, *averse* to going outside because of the *adverse* weather conditions, changed her mind when she learned that it was raining chocolate.
- Aunt Ruth was *adverse* to raising her own chickens until she discovered the joy of having eggs laid on her head.
- I know that *adversity* is supposed to make us stronger, but I am often *averse* to having to go through it.

Antonyms

41 *Aunt Ruth and the Synonym Bun*

Rule: Antonyms are words whose meanings are opposites.

- **hot / cold**   **light / dark**   **fast / slow**

Anxious and Eager

45 *Aunt Ruth and the Train to Gettysburg*

Rule: *Anxious* carries with it a sense of apprehension, a feeling of worry or even dread. *Eager* has the connotation of simply looking forward to something.

- At first I was *anxious* about the grammar portion of the exam, but after reading *I Laid an Egg on Aunt Ruth's Head*, I was *eager* for the exam day to arrive.

Bad / Badly

 Aunt Ruth Wants a Cheeseburger Bad

Rule: *Bad* is the adjective; *badly* is the adverb.

- You feel bad.
- The sour cream is bad.
- Aunt Edna's casserole went bad in the fridge.

Advice: Be careful when wanting to badly do some verb (e.g., want to run badly). Does this mean you want to run in a poor manner, or does it mean you really want to run? It's ambiguous. Putting *badly* closer to the word it modifies can help, but it doesn't always make it clearer.

- You *badly* want a banana with peanut butter.
- You *badly* want to eat a banana with peanut butter. This means the same as the previous example.
- You want to eat a banana with peanut butter *badly*. (Grammatically this is okay, but it is ambiguous because eating something badly may mean that you stick it on your forehead instead of in your mouth).

Beside / Besides

 Aunt Ruth and the Train to Gettysburg

Rule: *Beside* means next to; *besides* means also or in addition to.

- *Besides* spilling his orange juice on my copy of *I Laid an Egg on Aunt Ruth's Head,* the man sitting *beside* me on the plane was using dangling participles as though they were going out of style.
- Little Miss Muffett, *besides* eating her curds and whey, startled the poor spider that had sat down *beside* her.

Bored of

38 *Bored of Aunt Ruth*

> **Rule:** One cannot be *bored of* anything. One may be *bored by* something (e.g., bored by the television that is showing nothing but commercials all day long); one may be *bored from* something (e.g., bored from having to wash dishes every night); and one may be *bored with* something (e.g., bored with having to read from a grammar book that tries really hard to be fun, but it's a grammar book nonetheless).

- Even though the Grammar Channel expanded its lineup to include a weekly primer on Linking Verbs, Al became *bored with* the shows.

- *Bored by* the flying monkeys, Dorothy decided to return to her home in the Midwest.

- Larry, *bored of* staring at his aquarium day after day and week after week, decided to buy some fish to put in it.

Borrow / Loan / Lend

13 *Queen Ruth Borrows Your Ear*

> **Rule:** You may borrow some item from somebody, but that person does not borrow it to you. Rather, that person lends it to you.
>
> In American English, loan can be a noun or a verb. The past tense of loan is loaned; the past tense of lend is lent.

- May I borrow a pencil please?

- Could you borrow a pencil to me?

- Will you lend me a pencil?

Breath / Breathe

40 *Aunt Ruth Letters from Aunt Iquity*

> **Rule:** *Breathe* (long "e" sound) is the action that involves inhaling and exhaling.
>
> **Rule:** *Breath* (short "e" sound) is a volume of air that has either been inhaled or exhaled.

- When a doctor says take a deep *breath*, you should *breathe* in a lot of air.
- When a friend says that you have bad breath, it's time to start regularly brushing and flossing, buddy.

Bring / Take

8 *Aunt Ruth Brings It*

> **Rule:** A person arriving may *bring* something; a person going may *take* something. The person himself may see it as either bringing or taking.

- Don't forget to *bring* Aunt Ruth's fruitcake when you come.
- Don't forget to *take* Aunt Ruth's fruitcake when you go.

Colons and Semi-colons

31 *Aunt Ruth and the Independent Santa Claus*

> **Rule:** In a compound sentence (a sentence with multiple independent clauses), semi-colons can be used to help clarify meaning. If one or more of the independent clauses contains commas, you may want to use semi-colons to separate the clauses.

- Yesterday, I washed the car; I took my old, worn tuba to the mall, and I played it for an hour; I caught a favorite, old mystery show at the discount movie theater; and I made it home in time for lunch.

Rule: Semi-colons can be used to separate items in a list, especially if individual list elements already contain commas.

- I ate two ham biscuits; sausage, wrapped in tortillas; freshly squeezed mango juice, poured into a coffee mug; and three eggs, sunny-side up.

Rule: Colons can be used to introduce complex lists (lists of items separated by semi-colons).

- Here is what I ate for breakfast: two ham biscuits; sausage, wrapped in tortillas; freshly squeezed mango juice, poured into a coffee mug; and three eggs, sunny-side up.

Rule: A colon can also be used to separate two independent clauses with the second clause an example of the first clause.

- Make someone's day: Be a Grammar Buddy.

Commas

Aunt Ruth and the Comma Splice

Rule: A comma splice occurs when two independent clauses that should be separated by a period or semi-colon are separated by a comma with no coordinating conjunction.

- Jane sat down to eat a small slice of cake, she ended up eating the whole thing.

The preceding sentence should have had a semi-colon or period in place of the comma, or a conjunction could have been added, e.g.,

- Jane sat down to eat a small slice of cake, *but* she ended up eating the whole thing.

30 Iowa Ruth and the Lost Commas

> **Rule:** If an independent clause is connected to a second clause with a coordinating conjunction (*and, but, yet, etc.*) and the second clause is not independent, there should be NO COMMA between clauses.

- Jim ate bagels for breakfast this morning, and shrimp for lunch.

This should be either of the following:

- Jim ate bagels for breakfast this morning and shrimp for lunch.
- Jim ate bagels for breakfast this morning, and he ate shrimp for lunch.

> **Rule:** When a subordinate conjunction (e.g., *when, since, if, until,* etc.) begins a sentence, a comma should separate the subordinate clause from the rest of the sentence. If the subordinate clause is at the end of the sentence (or following the verb), a comma should not be used unless it is needed for clarity.

- If Aunt Ruth is approaching by land, put one candle in the window.

Because the subordinate conjunction *If* starts the sentence, the subordinate clause should be separated from the sentence with a comma.

- Put two candles in the window if she is approaching by air.

> **Rule:** When a sentence contains an appositive (a noun phrase that modifies the noun phrase immediately adjacent to it), the appositive is separated by commas if it is a non-essential phrase and is not separated if it is essential.

- The guy who mowed my lawn this morning scared my chickens.
- Aunt Ruth, who visits frequently and is my source of eternal exasperation, scared my chickens.
- The green car sitting in the driveway is the one that needs to be washed and polished this afternoon.

Comparatives / Superlatives

6 *Aunt Ruth Is the Superlative Super Relative*

Comparatives are used to compare attributes of two entities (people, things, circumstances, etc.), and superlatives are used to compare three or more. Most comparatives end in -er and superlatives in -est. Ready for more fun than you were expecting (in fact, this could be the most fun you'll have all day)? Let's talk about how to form comparative and superlative words!

> **Rule:** You can only make comparatives and superlatives from adjectives.
>
> For one-syllable words ending in a single consonant, often it's the case that the consonant can be doubled and then -er is added for the comparative and -est is added for the superlative. Notable exceptions are *bad* and *good* (see below).

- mad, madder, maddest
- big, bigger, biggest
- sad, sadder, saddest
- bad, worse, worst
- good, better, best

> **Rule:** If the one syllable word ends in two or more consonants, the comparative can be made by adding -er, and the superlative can be formed by adding -est.

- old, older, oldest
- sick, sicker, sickest
- bald, balder, baldest

> **Rule:** For one syllable words ending in -e, the comparative is made by adding -r, and the superlative is made by adding -st.

- nice, nicer, nicest

- brave, braver, bravest
- cute, cuter, cutest

Rule: For two syllable words ending in -y, the comparative is often made by changing 'y' to 'i' and adding -er; the superlative is made by changing the 'y' to 'i' and adding -est.

- runny, runnier, runniest
- nosy, nosier, nosiest
- holy, holier, holiest

Rule: For two-syllable words ending in something other than -y, and for words that have three or more syllables, use *less / more* or *least / most* for the comparative or superlative, respectively.

- solemn, more solemn, most solemn
- ginger, less ginger, least ginger
- ambiguous, ambiguouser, ambiguousest

Rule: As the story illustrates, the word *fun* is not an adjective. It is a noun. Do not use *funner* or *funnest*. They are not real words!

Could / Couldn't Care Less

Queen Ruth Borrows Your Ear

If I *could care less*, that means I am capable of caring less than I do care, which of course means that I do care.

I couldn't care less. (That literally means that I am not capable of caring less than I care, which of course means that I do not care at all. I couldn't care less about the score of the game, i.e., I had no interest.)

- I couldn't care less that she doesn't like my new book.

Deep / Deeply and other Adjectives Used as Adverbs

Aunt Ruth: Fishes Tight, Fishes Deep

> **Rule:** Some adjectives can be used as adverbs even though they may also have -ly forms of the words that function as adverbs. Generally the non -ly form comes after the verb, and the -ly form may come before or after. For formal English, the -ly form of the adverb is preferred.
>
> Adjectives that are used as adverbs and that also have -ly adverb forms include: *easy, silent, slow, quick, deep, tight, fast, hard, late,* and *long.*

Easy / Easily

Easy as an adverb can mean gentle, careful, or relaxed:

- Go *easy* on him. He's new here.
- Take it *easy*; you've worked hard enough already.
- You've got a big fish on your line. Reel him in nice and *easy*.

Easily as an adverb means something that is done without difficulty.

- I was *easily* able to pry the tuba loose from Aunt Ruth's grip.

Quick / Quickly

Quick can be an adverb for verbs of movement or action; also, often in the imperative (e.g., a command) quick will be used as an adverb.

- Get there *quick*! The queen is waiting.
- Get there *quickly*! The queen is waiting.
- *Quickly* get there! The queen is waiting.

Silent / Silently

Silent as an adverb is rarely used.

- Run *silent*, run deep. (This is also a movie title.)
- The sleigh silently crossed through the woods.

Slow / Slowly

- Go *slow*. It's raining hard outside and the roads may be slippery.
- *Slowly* he turned to the jury and asked, "Do you really believe Aunt Ruth has a time machine?"

Tight / Tightly

When *tight* is used, it tends to mean "close and make tight," but the action of closing may not necessarily itself be done in a tight manner.

- Please shut the windows *tight*.

When *tightly* is used, it means something is done in a tight manner but it may not reflect the end state of something.

- She hugged him *tightly*.

Deep / Deeply

Doing something *deep* generally means to do it in deep areas, whereas doing something *deeply* tends to mean to do it in a profound or intense way.

- He hit the ball *deep* into centerfield.
- She cares *deeply* for her country.

Fast, *hard*, *late*, and *long* are other adjectives that can be used as adverbs.

- Run *fast*! The crowd is getting restless.
- He arrived *late*, but that was okay because Aunt Ruth's time machine was somehow hung up in traffic.
- With his new fishing pole, he could cast *long* and accurately.
- If we push *hard*, I think we can get Aunt Ruth through the door. (This one is especially interesting because if we use the -ly form instead (i.e., *hardly*), do we say it as *push hardly* or *hardly push*?)

Different of / different from / different than

9 *Aunt Ruth and the Okay Chorale*

Rule: Something may be *different from* something else, or it may be *different than* something else. We never say that it is *different of* something else.

☹ • How is today's lunch *different of* yesterday's?

Double Negatives

16 *Aunt Ruth Doesn't Not Know About Double Negatives*

Rule: Double negatives don't always mean the same thing as the positive version of the same sentence. Be careful to avoid ambiguity.

- Aunt Ruth wants to have spaghetti for dinner.
- Aunt Ruth wants to not have spaghetti for dinner.
- Aunt Ruth doesn't want to not have spaghetti for dinner.

The first sentence is clear. The second sentence is also clear. The third sentence (the double negative) literally means that Aunt Ruth has no intent regarding not wanting spaghetti. She may be ambivalent regarding spaghetti, which is different than what the first sentence says.

Warning: To avoid ambiguity when asking a yes/no question, exercise caution when using negatives. The implied double negatives can be confusing.

- Wouldn't you like to see what is on the menu? (Technically this is not incorrect, but it can lead to ambiguity depending on the understanding of the listener / reader.)
- Would you like to see what is on the menu?

Double Possessives

36 *Aunt Ruth and the Queen's Baseball Card*

> **Tip:** Double Possessives can be useful for removing ambiguity.

- *I have the president's photograph.*

This is ambiguous. Do I have a photograph that is the likeness of the president, or do I have a photograph that belongs to the president (e.g., maybe it's a selfie he took while riding a roller-coaster at Grammar Theme Park)? To remove the ambiguity, I can rewrite the sentence as one of the following:

- *I have a photograph of the president.* (The president's image is on the photograph.)
- *I have a photograph of the president's.* (The photograph belongs to the president. How I ended up with it, I'll never know.)

> **Rule:** The one thing you cannot do is put the apostrophe-s on a noun that is not a human. For example, this is bad:

- I have a photograph of my dog's. (As much as you love your dog, it is not human and does not actually have ownership.)

Double Subjects

35 *The Aunt Who Baked the Fruitcake*

> **Rule:** Double subjects are not always easy to identify. The common theme linking the obvious offenders is when a subject noun phrase is immediately followed by a pronoun with no comma in-between.

This example has a double subject:

- My uncle he said I should have my head examined.

It is a double subject because *he* does not add any information to the sentence. *My uncle said I should have my head examined* will work perfectly well. What about this next example?

- My uncle Bob said I should have my head examined.

This is a valid sentence because Bob adds information to the sentence (in fact, here it is essential information because we are differentiating between Bob and some other uncle, e.g., Larry). Note that here we can use "uncle Bob" as written, or we can use the titular "Uncle Bob."

- My uncle, Bob, said I should have my head examined.

This is also a valid sentence. Here, Bob is not essential information to the meaning of the sentence, but it is additional information nonetheless.

This brings us back around to *he*. What if we tried the following:

☹ • My uncle, he, said I should have my head examined.

This example is still a double subject. The issue is that *he* is a pronoun that modifies *my uncle*. Having both the pronoun and the noun phrase that the pronoun represents—together in the same sentence—just doesn't make sense.

Drier / Dryer

40 *Aunt Ruth Letters from Aunt Iquity*

> **Rule:** *Drier* is what you want your clothes to be. You put them in the *dryer* (the appliance that usually is next to or above the washing machine) to make them *drier*.

The appliance is the dryer. The way I remember this is to reference other appliances. When I want to mix, I use a mixer. Then I want to blend, I use a blender. When I want to wash, I use a washer. For all of these, I add -er to the end of the task I want to do, and—eureka!—I have named the appliance. Similarly, if I want to dry, I use a dryer.

Either (see Neither)

Ellipses

 Aunt Ruth and the Solar ... Ellipsis

Rule: When using ellipses to leave out part of a quote, the general rule is: insert a space; follow the space with the ellipsis (three dots or periods); and follow that with another space. Suppose, for example, we have the sentences:

- *Ralph, Dusty, and Henry are the first three batters due up next inning. Then, we see that Orlando and Felix are after Henry.*

Rule: When removing words from the middle of a sentence, replace them with a space, the ellipsis, and another space. Also, if the quote ends at the end of a sentence (i.e., in the original text it is the end of a sentence), just use a period at the end. Don't use an ellipsis for the next sentence.

- *Ralph, Dusty, and Henry are ... due up next inning.*

Rule: When leaving out words at the end of a sentence, indicate this by inserting a space, then the ellipsis, and then a period to end the quote.

- *Ralph, Dusty, and Henry are the first three batters due up ....*

Rule: When including the end of one sentence but leaving out the beginning of the next sentence, use a period to end the first sentence, then insert a space, ellipsis, and space, and proceed with the remainder of the quote.

- *Ralph, Dusty, and Henry are the first three batters due up next inning. ... Orlando and Felix are after Henry.*

Rule: The ellipsis can also be used to indicate the fading of a thought or uncertainty in what to say:

- *I think ... well, I ... I will have to take a pass on your lasagna.*

Eminent (see Imminent)

Etc. Usage

32 *Aunt Ruth Is a Short Short-Order Cook, etc.*

> **Rule:** The common abbreviation, "etc.," is pronounced "etcetera" and it means "and so on." Note that the "and" is part of the definition, so it is incorrect to say "and etc."

- The picnic was a normal family reunion banquet, complete with lizard tongue, eye of newt, toe of frog, *etc.*
- The Jones's picnic, on the other hand, was bizarre, featuring potato salad, hot dogs, brownies, *and etc.*

Fragment / Sentence Fragment

19 *Aunt Ruth Fragments*

> **Rule:** A sentence contains at least one independent clause, and that independent clause has at least a subject and verb. If there is a string of words that does not have an independent clause, then that string is a sentence fragment.

- A really great hot dog. (This is an example of a fragment.)
- This is a great hot dog.

In the 1970s, there was a popular song on country radio with the title "Mamas, Don't Let Your Babies Grow Up to Be Cowboys." Similarly, I've often felt that the modern child suffers from educational abuse when the parent or teacher allows the child to use sentence fragments. Mamas, don't let your babies grow up to use fragments!

Fragments do have their place, especially in dialogue (the response to the question, "How are you?" is often a fragment such as "Great!"), but be sure to get a solid handle on what constitutes a correct sentence before dabbling in the black art of sentence fragments. My high school English teacher required that we mark all of our written fragments with "I.F." (for Intentional Fragment). I think that's a fine idea.

Gerund

3 *Aunt Ruth and Lou Gerund's Practicing*

> **Rule:** A gerund is a word that is in a verb's present participle form but is used as a noun. Gerunds end in -ing. Be sure to determine whether the -ing word is a noun or part of a verb phrase. Gerunds are also sometimes called "verbal nouns."

Verb	Gerund
hit	hitting
dance	dancing
swim	swimming
talk	talking
walk	walking
play	playing

- *Hitting* was one of Lou Gehrig's most valuable strengths.
- *Dancing* is not my strong suit.
- *Swimming* with sharks is not my favorite thing to do.
- I was hoping to find some good music on the radio, but all I heard was a lot of *talking*.
- ☹ I have been walking for two hours. (This is not an example of a gerund; here, the present participle *walking* is being used as part of the verb phrase *have been walking*.)
- *Walking* in the rain is one of my favorite pastimes.
- ☹ He will be playing the tuba in the marching band at the football game. (This is not a gerund; *will be playing* is the verb phrase.)
- In his copious leisure time, he loves *playing* the tuba.

Get, Got, Have Got / Have Gotten

42 *Aunt Ruth Has Got to Be Kidding*

Rule: Americans and British agree that *get*, with past tense *got* and past participle *got*, is used for possession or ownership. This is generally the most accepted usage of *get*.

- I will get the granola if you get the kippers.
- I got a brand new pair of roller skates for my birthday.
- I have got a chocolate chess set in the freezer.

Rule: Americans use *get*, with past tense *got* and past participle *gotten*, for ability or permission. This is accepted in American English, though prudence should be exerted so that it is not overused.

- I get to use Aunt Ruth's old catcher mitt!
- I got to sit next to Coach Tom Osborne at the meeting!
- He had gotten used to Aunt Ruth's nonsensical rambling.
- I've gotten to sit in the dugout with the Grammarville Commas.

Rule: Americans also use *got* (usually with *have*) more informally to mean *must*. Do not use *gots* ever. (In the early 1970s, the movie "Dirty Harry" featured a scene in which one of the plot's antagonists (i.e., a bad guy) uttered the line, "I gots to know." That line, though perhaps famous in itself, did not bring fame or fortune to the person speaking it. Neither will it do so for you. Avoid *gots* at all costs!)

- I have got to go! (This is okay, but *I have to go* is much better.)
- ☹ I gots to know!
- You've got to be kidding.

282 | *Common Rough Spots in English*

Go / Went / Gone

4 *Aunt Ruth's Go-Cart Has Gone*

> **Rule:** The verb *go* is an irregular verb with past tense *went*, past participle *gone*, and present participle *going*.
>
> Do not use *went* as the past participle.

- Aunt Ruth has gone in her time machine, but she'll be back tomorrow.
- Aunt Ruth had gone to the doctor twice this month before she took ill.
- ☹ The nauseating nephew has went with her. [The verb *went* is the past tense of *go*. Saying "has went" is like saying "has ate."]
- The nauseating nephew went with her.
- ☹ She gone and did it. [The verb *gone* is the past participle of *go*. Saying "She gone" is like saying "She eaten."]
- She went and did it.
- ☹ If she had went earlier, they could have avoided the entire fiasco.

H-words with Articles A / An

7 *Aunt Ruth Is a Historic Anomaly*

> **Rule:** There is a scene in *My Fair Lady* where Eliza Doolittle, behind a lit candle, pronounces words that begin with the letter H. If the H is a "hard H" (also called *aspirated*), the flame should flicker. If the H is not aspirated, the flame will not flicker.
>
> For all words beginning with the hard (aspirated) H, use the article *a*. For all words beginning with the soft H, use the article *an*.

- a Herculean effort   an herb garden
- a historic event   a Hawaiian vacation

Homographs, Homonyms, Homophones

41 *Aunt Ruth and the Synonym Bun*

> **Rule:** A homophone is a word that sounds like another word. Blue and blew are homophones.
>
> **Rule:** A homograph is a word that is spelled the same as another word (though it may be pronounced differently). Lead (to be in charge, with a long 'e' sound) and lead (the metal, with a short 'e' sound) are homographs.
>
> **Rule:** A homonym is a word that is both a homophone and a homograph. Another way of looking at it, I suppose, is that a word has a homonym if there is more than one definition for that word with the same spelling and same pronunciation.

Examples of homonyms include:

- charge: 1) to rush forward in battle; 2) to purchase on credit
- bank: 1) the side or boundary of a lake; 2) a place where money is stored

Hopefully, Frankly, Seriously, Actually, and a host of other Sentence Adverbs

11 *Frankly, My Dear Aunt Ruth*

> **Rule:** *Hopefully* is the most popular example of an adverb that is frequently misused as a sentence adverb. *Hopefully* means *in a hopeful manner,* but some use it to mean *I hope that.*

- Hopefully, I went to the job interview. (That is, I went hoping the interview would go well.)

- Hopefully, the rain will go away. (The rain cannot experience hope, nor can rain do anything in a hopeful manner.)

- *Basically*, the rocket to Mars was launched this morning at 0700

hours. (There is nothing *basic* about a rocket launch to Mars. If you replaced *basically* with a phrase such as *The gist of it is that* or perhaps *The bottom line is that*, that would work.)

- *Basically*, she lives in a log cabin and tries to live as simple a life as she can. (Here, *basically* is fine because it describes the subject's lifestyle.)
- *Honestly*, the bank was held up and robbed less than an hour ago. (A bank cannot be held up and robbed honestly. If it were honest, it would not be a hold-up, nor would it be robbery.)
- *Honestly*, the old man who found the purple-haired teen's cell phone on the ground returned it to her. (The man was behaving in an honest manner when he returned the phone to the teen.)
- *Thankfully*, the lion did not eat my pet chihuahua for lunch. (Why would the lion be thankful that it didn't eat the little canine morsel for lunch?)
- *Thankfully*, the lion took the bologna sandwich that I left out for him and devoured it for supper. (I'm sure the lion was quite thankful for din din.)

Imminent / Eminent

Aunt Ruth Fragments

> **Rule:** *Imminent* refers to an event that is going to happen soon; impending. *Eminent* refers to a highly respected person or persons.

- Ray Bradbury is an *eminent* modern writer who is a favorite of many.
- According to reliable weather sources, the arrival of the hurricane is *eminent*.
- The outlaw, sweat dripping from his brow, stood at the crossroads. The townspeople were hidden behind doorways and drapes. The arrival of Sheriff Aunt Ruth was *imminent*.

Imperative Mode / Mood (see Modes / Moods of Verbs)

Indicative Mode / Mood (see Modes / Moods of Verbs)

Ingenious and Ingenuous

19 *Aunt Ruth Fragments*

> **Rule:** *Ingenious* means clever or brilliant.
> *Ingenuous* means naïve or lacking in cunning; also, deceitful.

- He held the *ingenuous* belief that running for public office would be mere child's play.
- ☹ The telephone was an *ingenuous* invention.
- Thomas Edison was a man of *ingenious* ideas.

Into / In to

2 *Aunt Ruth, QE-II*

> **Rule:** *Into* is a preposition that generally means to head toward or to the inside of something. There are nuances to this, including heading toward a circumstance / situation or accidentally meeting someone.
>
> **Rule:** *In to*, on the other hand, generally means either moving to some location in order to do something or giving something to somebody.

- I had trouble keeping my eyes open as I drove *into* the sunrise.
- I ran *into* Aunt Ruth at the First Annual Grammar and Barbecue Festival on Saturday.
- ☹ I ran *into* eat a snack before the next story began.
- After I went *in to* take the test, I found out that it has been rescheduled to next Friday instead.

Intransitive Verbs

22 *Intransitive Day Rocks*

> **Rule:** Intransitive verbs take no objects. The intransitive verbs need not be weak and wimpy. See Transitive Verbs for other examples.

- Marvin *shouted*!
- Marilyn *shrieked*!
- Franklin spontaneously *combusted*.
- Isaiah *sang* quite loudly.
- Hector and Svetlana *waltzed* into the kitchen on a bright Saturday morning. (*Waltzed*, of course, is the verb. There is no direct object.)
- Petunia and Beauregard *laughed* hysterically throughout the evening.
- Waiting in the shade of the bus stop, Aunt Ruth and Queen Elizabeth II *conversed* quietly.
- We *worked* all day.

Irregular Verbs (see Verb Tenses)

Let's

44 *Aunt Ruth in the Oval Office*

> **Rule:** *Let's* is the contraction for *Let us*.
>
> *Let's you and me* is okay because *you and me* is an appositive for *us*.
>
> *Let's you and I* doesn't work because *us* is an object pronoun and *I* is a subject pronoun.

- Let's go to the ice cream store.
- Let's you and I go to the opera tonight.

Lightening and Lightning

40 *Aunt Ruth Letters to Aunt Iquity*

> **Rule:** *Lightening* means to become less heavy or less dark.
> *Lightning* is the natural weather phenomenon that is rather striking.

- I was on the beach when dawn broke, and the darkness of night began lightening all at once.
- ☹ I had a great round of golf today until I was struck by lightening.

Linking Verbs

13 *Queen Aunt Ruth Borrows Your Ear*

> **Rule:** A key point to remember about Linking Verbs is that the "thing" on one side of the linking verb is the same, or is described by, the "thing" on the other side of the linking verb.

- Jay is my dad. (A man named Jay is the same man who is my dad.)
- My dad is Jay. (The man who is my dad is the same man who is named Jay.)
- He is Jay. (The man referred to by "he" (perhaps he's mentioned in an earlier paragraph, or perhaps I'm pointing him out in a crowd) is the same man who is also named Jay.)
- Jay is he. (Remember, Jay and "he" are the same person. Jay is the subject, so we use the subject pronoun form "he.")
- ☹ Jay is him. (This is wrong because "him" is the object pronoun form, and we want (and with linking verbs, we always want) the subject form "he.")
- My dad is tall. (Tall is an adjective that describes my dad.)
- Dad is the church organist.
- Mom is the church pianist.
- Omar Tariff was the middle-eastern import duty collector in the movie.

> **Note:** Linking verbs are not limited to *to be* verbs.

- I *feel* good about last night's game. (If you are commenting on your health or if you have particular sensitive fingers, you could say you feel well. It's okay to feel good, too. Note that "doing good" is not correct grammar unless you really are doing something that is good.)
- I *feel* bad about missing Grandma's recital. (If your fingers are numb or you're wearing thick gloves, you might feel badly. Otherwise, you probably feel bad.)
- The food *smells* burnt, but that's the way food usually smells after Aunt Ruth cooks it.
- The soup *tastes* great!
- You *appear* to be rather cheerful today.
- The plan to roast marshmallows at the park *looked* flawless in every detail but one—we forgot the marshmallows.
- That Aunt Ruth should have been nominated for a position on the U.S. Supreme Court *seems* obvious to all of those who know her.
- This plan to replace the English language with Pig Latin certainly *feels* all wrong to me.
- That's him! (Technically this is incorrect because the contraction *That's* expands to *That is*, and since we're using the linking verb *is*, we need to use the subject pronoun *he* and not *him*.)

Modern society dictates that casual usage such as *That's him* be allowed. Do with this information what you will. I am not going to hover over your escritoire like a grammatical vulture greedily seeking the remains of your particular English carnage for the day. If your conscience can handle it, then fine, be that way. (You at least know what is correct and why it is correct. And I do confess that occasionally (once or twice a year) I will whisper, "That's him!" just to experience a clandestine thrill.)

Masterful and Masterly

19 *Aunt Ruth Fragments*

> **Rule:** *Masterly* is something done in the manner of an expert or by someone who is a master. *Masterful* can mean that as well, but it can also mean haughty, arrogant, imperious, high-handed, or despotic.

- There's no doubt that the Ninth Symphony was masterly written.
- The little king sat on his little throne, ruling his little country in a most merciless and masterful manner.

Metaphor

 Aunt Ruth and Metaphors

> **Rule:** A metaphor uses words to describe something that isn't really the thing the words normally describe.

- The bear's eyes lit up when he saw Aunt Ruth; to him, I was only the appetizer or perhaps a small garden salad. Aunt Ruth was both the main course and the dessert.
- "O lente, lente, currite noctis equi." ("Run slowly, slowly, horses of the night.")—from *The Tragical History of Doctor Faustus* by Christopher Marlowe.
- In the grand royalty of musical instruments, the tuba is king and all others are subservient.
- Driving to Boston's "Little Italy" in the north end, I found the countless exits and entrances and side roads a big mass of spaghetti noodles all tangled in one hopeless knot.
- One bite of Aunt Ruth's fruitcake laid me flat on the mat of the boxing ring. I was knocked out, down for the count.
- It was when we were eating hors d'oeuvres that Aunt Ruth let the bomb drop—she was married to a chihuahua!

Modes / Moods of Verbs

 Aunt Ruth and Verbs Ala Mode

> **Rule:** Without going into nauseating detail (though I'll leave that to your judgment), there are three verb modes (also called moods) in English that are good to know: *indicative, imperative,* and *subjunctive.*

The mood can almost be thought of as, "What kind of mood was the writer/speaker in?" or perhaps, "What kind of mood does the sentence emote in me?" That, of course, is an exaggeration—three moods cannot possibly capture the fine-grained possibilities that the sentence creator experienced.

> ### Indicative Mood
> This is the standard, good-old meat and potatoes English sentence. The sentence can be a statement or a question.

- The water buffalo leaped over the fence on his way to the bowling alley.
- When was the last time you had a fire-roasted marshmallow?

> ### Imperative Mood
> This is the command or the urgent statement, the haven of the bossy and the paradise of the exclamation mark maven.

- Martha, get your sweet buns off the table, and I mean now!
- Kick it now! Kick it now!

> ### Subjunctive Mood
> This is the realm of the imaginative, the philosophical, the investigative, and the speculative. These are not statements on *what did* happen but on *what if it* happened. See **Subjunctives** for examples.

Myself, Yourself, Himself, Herself, Ourselves, Themselves

5 *Aunt Ruth Herself and Henry VIII*

> **Rule:** These object pronouns are best used in **reflexive** and **emphatic** contexts. The **reflexive** context is when the subject performs an action to, on, or for himself. The **emphatic** case stresses that the subject is doing the action, rather than someone else. Outside of those contexts, do not use the -self words in place of the object pronouns me, you, him, her, us, or them, if those object pronouns will work. Note that *hisself* is not a valid word.

- (Reflexive) For my birthday, I gave myself a chocolate blackberry carmel cheesecake. I was sad because I don't like cheesecake.
- (Reflexive) Don't do this for me, do it for yourself.
- (Reflexive) With her Type A personality and a busy schedule, she ended up giving herself the appendectomy.
- (Emphatic) With her Type A personality and a busy schedule, she herself did the appendectomy.
- (Emphatic) For my birthday, I myself made the key lime pie.
- (Emphatic) Tired of waiting for his breakfast, Henry walked into the restaurant kitchen and cooked the omelet himself.
- (Reflexive) Peter unwittingly tried to play the trick on Frank, but something went horribly wrong, and he ended up burying himself in a mountain of shaving cream.
- ☹ For my birthday, she gave a copy of *I Laid an Egg on Aunt Ruth's Head* to myself.
- For my birthday, she gave a copy of *I Laid an Egg on Aunt Ruth's Head* to me.
- We cooked breakfast for ourselves.
- ☹ They cooked breakfast for ourselves.
- ☹ He served hisself the biggest slab of chocolate cake.
- We must defeat the foes of correct grammar ourselves!

Neither

33 *Aunt Ruth Is Spaced Out*

Rule: For formal writing, use the singular verb agreement by default.

- Neither of us *is* ...
- Neither A nor B *is* ...

Rule: When one of the premises is plural, use the plural verb form.

- Neither Steve nor the others *feel* like playing at the polka festival.
- Neither the girls nor Jim *feel* comfortable serving Aunt Ruth's potato salad at the funeral reception.

Rule: There are certain conditions where *neither ... or* has been accepted in the past, but they are few and far between. It's safer (and more likely to be correct) if you stick to *neither ... nor* and *either ... or*.

- Either Susan or Janet is sufficient for the job.
- Either candidate is going to do a great job.

Rule: Just as you would say "Are you" instead of "Is you," use "Are either of you" instead of "Is either of you." It just sounds better.

- Is either of you dining with the president tonight?
- Are either of you dining with the president tonight?

Advice: Put *either* as close as possible to the first item in the list.

- I am tired of ballplayers <u>who either ask for too much money</u> or too many perks. (Not as good as the following:)
- I am tired of ballplayers <u>who ask for either too much money</u> or too many perks.

Common Rough Spots in English | **293**

Nonplussed

 Aunt Ruth Is Non-Nonplussed

Rule: Nonplussed simply means "to be coming apart at the seams." A person who has lost his or her calm demeanor, patience, or composure is nonplussed. The word is often used (incorrectly) as having the opposite meaning.

- Usually a calm and collected mathematician, Dr. Boudreau became nonplussed when he momentarily forgot how to add two numbers.
- Despite the fact that her chocolate souffle collapsed moments before the party began, Beverly remained nonplussed, both cool and calm.

Numbers

 Aunt Ruth by the Numbers

Rule: Rules for numbers vary based on different style guides, but the general rule is that if the number can be written in one or two words, write it out; otherwise, use the numeric figures.

- six, forty-four
- *Fahrenheit 451*

If the number is at the beginning of a sentence, write it out.

- One hundred thirty-two lumberjacks showed up for our first Grammar Street Festival.

Numbers in a series should be consistent in form.

- one billy goat, four chickens, eight iguanas, sixteen llamas
- one billy goat, 4 chickens, eight iguanas, 16 llamas

> For clarity, you may want to use both numeric figures and words:

- "This will cost you only eighty (80) dollars."

Examples of **Dates:** December 7, 1941 or 7 December 1941

Examples of **Years:** the forties; 1940s; the nineteenth century; 1994-1997

Examples of **Time:** 8:46 p.m. (or P.M.), 9 o'clock at night

Examples of **Addresses**: 1017 Fourteenth Street, 1862 East 169th Street

Examples of **Decimals:** 3.1415926535, 23.2%

Examples of **Formulas:** 57 / 11 instead of fifty-seven / eleven

Examples of **Large Whole Numbers: one million instead of 1,000,000**

Only

Aunt Ruth Is Only in a Quandary

> **Rule:** *Only,* for clarity, usually modifies the immediately following word.

- *I ate only the burrito.* This means that I didn't eat the taco, the french fries, or Aunt Connie's guacamole dip.
- *I only ate the burrito.* This means that I ate it but didn't do anything else with it. I didn't put it on my head; I didn't use it as an explosive; and I didn't put a stamp on it and try to mail it.
- I only smelled the roses (I didn't water them, fertilize them, or cut them).
- I smelled only the roses (I didn't smell the tulips, the daisies, etc.).

This is not a hard, fast, you're-gonna-be-arrested-by-the-grammar-police type of rule. Give the speaker / writer some leeway. If someone says, "I only smelled the roses" instead of "I smelled only the roses," it's fine. Stay calm and collected. Life will likely go on.

Passive Voice Verbs

21 *Aunt Ruth Learns Verbs*

> **Rule:** A *passive* verb is a verb that acts on the subject. All passive verbs are also transitive.

- The pomegranate *was eaten* by the old stork. (The verb phrase *was eaten* is passive and was done to the pomegranate by the stork.)
- The mosquito *was squashed* by the eager kindergartner. (*Was squashed* is a passive verb phrase and was done by a rambunctious youngster.)
- Aunt Ruth *was embarrassed* from all the publicity surrounding her nascent grammatical fame.
- ☹ The publicity surrounding her nascent grammatical fame embarrassed Aunt Ruth. (Here, *embarrassed* is active, not passive, because it is done to the direct object Aunt Ruth. The sentence, however, is a valid sentence.)

Past and Passed

17 *Aunt Ruth Passes the Pesto Test*

> **Rule:** *Past* describes a time that has already occurred.
> **Rule:** *Passed* is the past tense of pass.

- The bill for Aunt Ruth's new hat is *past* due.
- The age of chivalry is in the *past*.
- The age of chivalry has *passed*.
- ☹ Aunt Ruth *past* Mario with one lap to go in the race.
- ☹ Somehow, deep in Aunt Ruth's sordid *passed*, no one took the time to teach her how to use "hopefully" correctly.

Plurals ending in -i or -ii

34 *Aunt Ruthii*

> **Rule:** The plurals of words can have surprising endings. It's best just to learn them. The "just add an -s" rule is a good start, but there are many variations as seen in the example singular / plural pairings below:

- cactus / cactuses or cacti
- octopus / octopuses (octopi is considered ungrammatical)
- hippopotamus / hippopotamuses (preferred) or hippopotami
- rhinoceros / rhinoceroses (preferred) or rhinoceros or rhinoceri
- esophagus / esophagi
- sarcophagus / sarcophagi

Possessives with Appositives

43 *Aunt Ruth and the Peach Cobbler's Kitten*

> **Rule:** This is a language feature that can generate ambiguous prose and hours of fun at the dinner table (try it!). The grammar rule is that when you want to give a possessive attribute to a noun that has an appositive, you put the apostrophe-s at the end of the appositive (and remove the second comma of the appositive).

- Phil, the brother of my wife, is going to let me drive his new car. So I could say ... I put the keys in Phil, the brother of my wife's car.
- I saw my wife, the lady sitting on the fat white horse, smiling at me ... so I kissed my wife, the lady sitting on the fat white horse's cheek.
- Last weekend I played Tom, the uncle who runs a pizza restaurant's harp.
- This morning I mowed Mrs. Bergstrom, the neighbor who owns a yellow canary's lawn.

Plus

45 *Aunt Ruth and the Train to Gettysburg*

Rule: Do not use *plus* as a conjunction.

☹ • I didn't go to the party because I wasn't feeling well; plus, I heard that Aunt Ruth's fruitcake would be there.
- I didn't go to the party because I wasn't feeling well; and, I heard that Aunt Ruth's fruitcake would be there.

Precede and Proceed

45 *Aunt Ruth and the Train to Gettysburg*

Rule: *Precede* means to come before something; *proceed* means to continue.

- The letter A precedes the letter B in the alphabet.
- At the stoplight, I will turn left and proceed to the store.

Sentence Adverbs (see Hopefully)

Simile

 Aunt Ruth and Metaphors

Rule: A simile uses *like*, *as*, or *than* to compare two things that are typically unrelated. Similes are often used to highlight aspects of one thing in terms of the other. A simile is a type of metaphor.

- I was feeling about as speedy *as* a Nolan Ryan fastball.
- After I hugged Aunt Ruth, I felt *like* I had been run over by a truck.
- She ran around the track faster *than* greased lightning.

Subjunctives

27 *Aunt Ruth Hunts the Subjunctive Beast*

> **Rule:** Use subjunctives with a wish, doubt, or demand.

- I wish I were back home.
- ☹ I wish I was back home.
- I wish I were king for a day.
- ☹ I wish I was king for a day.
- I wish that he were going to the ball game.
- ☹ I wish that he was going to the ball game.
- He required that we all be grammar experts.
- ☹ He required that we all are grammar experts.

> **Rule:** Use subjunctives in a false or hypothetical situation.

- If my cow **were** blue, what color would the milk be?
- ☹ If my cow was blue, what color would the milk be?
- If she **were** cloned, she would be beside herself.
- ☹ If she was cloned, she would be beside herself.
- If I **were** playing the tuba last night, you wouldn't have fallen asleep.
- ☹ If I was playing the tuba last night, you wouldn't have fallen asleep.

> **Rule:** Use subjunctives for a future, unknown situation.

- If Jupiter **were** someday to crash into Earth, all literature containing grammar errors would be destroyed. (We don't know whether Jupiter will someday crash into Earth. We hope not, but then again, the idea of cleansing society of grammar errors is enchanting.)
- ☹ If Jupiter **was** someday to crash into Earth …

Superlatives (see Comparatives)

Synonyms

41 *Aunt Ruth and the Synonym Bun*

> **Rule:** Synonyms are words that have the same (or very nearly the same) meaning: [difficult / hard], [simple / easy], [fast / speedy], and [big / large] are all pairs of synonyms.

Than

1 *Aunt Ruth Loves Chocolate More Than Me*

> **Rule:** *Than* can always be used as a conjunction, but it is seeing more frequent use in casual English as a preposition. When used as a conjunction, *than* connects an independent clause with another independent clause.

- She likes ham biscuits more than I. (Here, the independent clause *She likes ham biscuits* is connected in a comparative relationship to *I* (implied *I do*, or *I do like ham biscuits*).

> **Rule:** When *than* is used as a preposition, the object pronoun in the sentence may very well be the object of the preposition.

- She likes ham biscuits more than me. (Here, *me* is the object of the preposition. What this is saying is that shes likes ham biscuits more than she likes me.)

> **Advice:** Because there may be some confusion when *than* is used as a preposition—and because it may result in the casting of a furtive brow from the grammar police—it is best to avoid using *than* as a preposition in formal writing. It is perfectly fine, however, for sidewalk graffiti and tattoos.

That and Other Relative Pronouns

35 *The Aunt Who Baked the Fruitcake*

> **Rule:** *That, which,* and *who* are *relative pronouns* that modify or elaborate on another noun or noun phrase in the sentence. Use *that / which* when referring to a non-person; use *who* when referring to a person.

- The aunt *who* gives me headaches needs to get her head examined.
- The dog *that* bit me meant to bite my aunt instead.

> **Rule:** Use *that* when the relative clause is essential to the meaning of the sentence (also called a *restrictive clause*). Use *which* when the relative clause contains additional information that is not essential. Use commas to separate the non-restrictive clause.

- I need you to paint my car that I've had for 15 years yellow. That is, don't paint my new car, and don't paint the old Model-T that's sitting in the garage. Paint this specific car yellow.
- I need you to paint my car, which I've had for 15 years, yellow, i.e., I've had this car a long time and its paint is flaking, but it's still a good car, and I'm going to continue using it a while longer.

> **Rule:** Use *who* when the relative pronoun is the subject of the relative clause; use *whom* when the relative pronoun is the clause's object. The same applies to *whoever / whomever*.

- I spilled a cup of prune juice on the lady *who* had kicked me in the shins.
- I inadvertently knocked over the guy *whom* I had met at the annual English Grammar Shindig.
- Aunt Ruth will gladly yield her super-grammar powers to *whoever* is willing to accept the pressure of fame. (Here, the object of preposition "to" is implied; you could replace *to whoever* with *to one who*.)

- I decided it was in my best interest to give the pet iguana to *whomever* the king chose.

- I am he *who* shall remain nameless.

- The porcupine salesman gave the free pen to him, *who* had paper but no quill. (Here, the relative clause *who had paper but no quill* is non-restrictive (i.e., it is non-essential to the meaning of the sentence). You could replace that relative clause with another, such as *the guy wearing the straw hat*, and it would not change the tenor of the sentence. The comma after *him* is the clue that the clause is non-restrictive.)

- The porcupine salesman gave the free pen to him *who* had paper but no quill. (Here, the relative clause is essential because there is no comma. However, the "*him who*" juxtaposition screams to our grammatical sensibilities, "Awkward!" Quick, get out the smelling salts! One solution to such a dilemma is to substitute another word or phrase for *him*, such as *the one* or *the person*.)

Transitive Verbs

20 *Aunt Ruth Loves Her Transitive Radio*

> **Rule:** Transitive verbs perform actions on direct objects. If no object receives the action, the verb is intransitive.

- I *saw* the hamburger; I *grilled* the hamburger; I *ate* the hamburger. The verbs *saw, grilled,* and *ate* are transitive. The direct object for all three is *hamburger* (and yes, it was delicious).

- I will be eating the hamburger; I was eating the hamburger; and now I am eating the hamburger.

- ☹ Rip van Winkle napped. The verb *napped* is intransitive.

- ☹ Mrs. Whigglethorpe sang in the shower. The verb *sang* is intransitive in this example. The noun *shower* is the object of the preposition *in* and is not a direct object.

- Mrs. Whigglethorpe sang a song in the shower. The verb *sang* is transitive in this example because *song* is a direct object.
- Henrietta kissed the frog. The verb *kissed* is transitive, and the direct object is *frog*.
- Henrietta gave a kiss to the frog. The verb *gave* is transitive, and the direct object is *kiss*. The noun *frog* is the object of the preposition *to* and is not the direct object.
- Henrietta gave the frog a kiss. The verb *gave* is transitive, and the direct object is *kiss* (a kiss is the object she gave). The noun *frog* here is an indirect object, the recipient of the thing being given.

Verb Tenses

24 *Aunt Ruth and a (Verb) Tense Predicament I, II*

Advice: Learn these irregular verbs!

Irregular Verbs			
Verb	**Past**	**Past Participle**	**Present Participle**
awake	awoke	awoken	awaking
be	was, were	been	being
beat	beat	beaten	beating
become	became	become	becoming
begin	began	begun	beginning
bend	bent	bent	bending
bet	bet	bet	betting
bid	bid	bid	bidding
bite	bit	bitten	biting
blow	blew	blown	blowing
break	broke	broken	breaking

Irregular Verbs			
Verb	**Past**	**Past Participle**	**Present Participle**
bring	brought	brought	bringing
broadcast	broadcast	broadcast	broadcasting
build	built	built	building
burn	burned(t)	burned(t)	burning
buy	bought	bought	buying
catch	caught	caught	catching
choose	chose	chosen	choosing
come	came	come	coming
cost	cost	cost	costing
cut	cut	cut	cutting
dig	dug	dug	digging
do	did	done	doing
draw	drew	drawn	drawing
dream	dreamed(t)	dreamed(t)	dreaming
drink	drank	drunk	drinking
drive	drove	driven	driving
eat	ate	eaten	eating
fall	fell	fallen	falling
feel	felt	felt	feeling
fight	fought	fought	fighting
find	found	found	finding
fly	flew	flown	flying
forget	forgot	forgotten	forgetting
forgive	forgave	forgiven	forgiving
freeze	froze	frozen	freezing
get	got	got or gotten	getting
give	gave	given	giving
go	went	gone	going

Irregular Verbs			
Verb	Past	Past Participle	Present Participle
grow	grew	grown	growing
hang	hung	hung	hanging
have	had	had	having
hear	heard	heard	hearing
hide	hid	hidden	hiding
hit	hit	hit	hitting
hold	held	held	holding
hurt	hurt	hurt	hurting
keep	kept	kept	keeping
know	knew	known	knowing
lay	laid	laid	laying
lead	led	led	leading
learn	learned(t)	learned(t)	learning
leave	left	left	leaving
lend	lent	lent	lending
let	let	let	letting
lie	lay	lain	lying
lose	lost	lost	losing
make	made	made	making
mean	meant	meant	meaning
meet	met	met	meeting
pay	paid	paid	paying
put	put	put	putting
read	read	read	reading
ride	rode	ridden	riding
ring	rang	rung	ringing
rise	rose	risen	rising
run	ran	run	running
say	said	said	saying

Common Rough Spots in English

Irregular Verbs			
Verb	Past	Past Participle	Present Participle
see	saw	seen	seeing
sell	sold	sold	selling
send	sent	sent	sending
shine	shined or shone	shined or shone	shining
show	showed	showed or shown	showing
shut	shut	shut	shutting
sing	sang	sung	singing
sink	sank	sunk	sinking
sit	sat	sat	sitting
sleep	slept	slept	sleeping
speak	spoke	spoken	speaking
spend	spent	spent	spending
stand	stood	stood	standing
stink	stank	stunk	stinking
sweep	swept	swept	sweeping
swim	swam	swum	swimming
take	took	taken	taking
teach	taught	taught	teaching
tear	tore	torn	tearing
tell	told	told	telling
think	thought	thought	thinking
throw	threw	thrown	throwing
understand	understood	understood	understanding
wake	woke	woken	waking
wear	wore	worn	wearing
win	won	won	winning
write	wrote	written	writing

Verb Tenses

Present Progressive (also called **Present Continuous**): This is what is happening right now. Use Present Tense of **TO BE** and the **Present Participle**.

- I *am seeing* things.
- She *is raiding* the fridge.
- We *are throwing* the ball.
- They *are flying* and *hoping* to find a place to land. (The verb phrase can also be *are flying and are hoping*, but the second *are* is redundant.)

Past Progressive (also called **Past Continuous**): This is what was happening earlier. Use Past Tense of **TO BE** and the **Present Participle**.

- I *was seeing* clearly yesterday.
- She *was raiding* the fridge when the phone rang.
- We *were throwing* the ball last night.
- They *were flying and hoping* to find a place to land.

Future Progressive: This is what will be happening in the future. Use **WILL BE** and the **Present Participle**. (Alternatively, you can use Present Tense of **TO BE**, followed by **GOING TO BE** and the **Present Participle**.)

- I *will be seeing* you tomorrow for breakfast.
- I *am going to be seeing* you tomorrow for breakfast.
- She *will be raiding* the fridge sometime tonight.
- I *will be throwing* with Jimmy at the park.
- I *am going to be throwing* with Jimmy at the park.
- They *will be flying and hoping* to find a place to land.

Present Perfect: This is what has been completed, participated in, or done as of right now. Use **HAS / HAVE** and the **Past Participle.**

- I *have seen* the movie before.
- He *has sung* that song.
- We *have drunk* all the lemonade.
- They *have chosen* where they want to go.

Past Perfect: This is what has been complete, participated in, or done in the past. Use **HAD** and the **Past Participle.**

- I *had seen* the movie the first time it came out.
- He *had sung* that song a million times before I stopped him.
- We *had drunk* all the lemonade, but the burgers weren't done.
- They *had chosen* where, but we changed their minds.

Future Perfect: This is what will be completed, participated in, or done before some future date or event. Use **WILL HAVE** and the **Past Participle.** (Alternatively, you can use Present Tense of **TO BE**, followed by **GOING TO HAVE** and the **Past Participle.**)

- I *will have seen* the movie ten times before the year is out.
- I *am going to have seen* the movie ten times before ….
- He *will have sung* that song to death before the night is over.
- He *is going to have sung* that song to death before ….
- We *will have drunk* all the lemonade by the time they get here.
- We *are going to have drunk* all the lemonade by then.
- They *are going to have chosen* a new place to camp by then.
- They *will have chosen* a new place to camp by then.

Present Perfect Progressive: This is what has been done in the past and/or is still currently underway. Use **HAS / HAVE**, followed by **BEEN** and the **Present Participle**.

- I *have been yodeling*.
- She *has been yodeling* for seven years, but not all at once.
- Don't tell me that you *have been yodeling* too!
- We *have been yodeling* non-stop for three hours!

Past Perfect Progressive: This is what had been done or was underway in the past, up to a certain point in time. Use **HAD BEEN** and the **Present Participle**.

- I *had been yodeling* for ten weeks before the arrest.
- She *had been yodeling* to earn money on the side.
- They *had been yodeling* for less than an hour before the lonely goatherd was scared away.
- Aunt Ruth said you *had been yodeling* until you turned five.
- We *had been yodeling* at local yodeling clubs when we met.

Future Perfect Progressive: This is what will be done or underway by a certain point in time in the future. Use **WILL HAVE BEEN** and the **Present Participle**. (Alternatively, use present tense of **TO BE**, followed by **GOING TO HAVE BEEN** and the **Present Participle**.)

- I *will have been yodeling* for weeks by the time she gets here.
- I *am going to have been yodeling* for ten years in May.
- He *will have been yodeling* all night long.
- She *is going to have been yodeling* for four decades!
- We *are going to have been yodeling* together for two years.

Verbs Ending in -T or -ED

15 *Aunt Ruth Burned or Burnt the Toast?*

Rule: There are many verbs whose past tense ends in "t" in England but ends in "ed" in (most of) America.

burned / burnt	leaped / leapt
dreamed / dreamt	smelled / smelt
kneeled / knelt	spilled / spilt
leaned / leant	spoiled / spoilt

Note that there are also many verbs that have a past tense ending in -t but not in -ed.

sent (not sended)	kept (not keeped)
meant (not meaned)	swept (not sweeped)
slept (not sleeped)	lost (not losed)
left (not leaved)	bent (not bended)

- I *burned* the grilled cheese sandwich that I made for Aunt Ruth. That wouldn't have been bad in itself, but I also forgot to take the plastic wrap off the cheese and the whole mess *smelled* simply atrocious.
- I *dreamt* last night that I had become a writer of grammar books. I'm glad I awoke because it was too tense.
- I fell asleep watching GrammarTube on the couch last night and *slept* straight through until five o'clock this morning.
- The Boston Red Sox *swept* the 2004 World Series against the St. Louis Cardinals, winning four games and losing none.
- He *kneeled* and put his ear to the ground; it was either Aunt Ruth or Mrs. Thornborough's hippopotamus that was just around the corner, but he couldn't tell which.

Wait for / Wait on

45 *Aunt Ruth and the Train to Gettysburg*

> **Rule:** To *wait on* someone is what a waiter or waitress does. To *wait for* something is to be ready or in some state of preparedness for something.

- I've been *waiting for* Grandma to finish her breakfast so that I can borrow her teeth.
- ☹ I was *waiting on* you for over three hours at the airport, but then I realized I was in the wrong city.
- I've been *waiting on* Grandma this week. She has a bell. One ring means bring water. Two rings mean bring food. Three rings mean she wants me to read her another Aunt Ruth story.
- ☹ I *waited for* Table 47 this morning; they ordered seventeen cheeseburgers, twelve orders of fries, and a small diet soda. (This should be *waited on*.)

Way and Ways

45 *Aunt Ruth and the Train to Gettysburg*

> **Rule:** When referring to distance, one place is a long *way* from another place, not a long *ways*.
>
> In the U.S., it's not uncommon to see *ways* (e.g., she has a ways to go before she's done), even though the singular article "*a*" doesn't fit with plural noun "*ways.*" In British English, *ways* used like this is grammatically incorrect.

- We have *ways* of getting the grammatical information from him. (Here, *ways* does not refer to distance.)
- Lincoln is a long *way* from Miami. (Here, *ways* does refer to distance.)
- ☹ That's a long *ways* to walk! (Though accepted in the U.S., the preferred usage is *way*.)

While / Although

45 *Aunt Ruth and the Train to Gettysburg*

> **Rule:** *While* could mean *at the same time*, but it also could mean *although* or *whereas*. Be careful so that the meaning is not ambiguous.

- While Aunt Ruth enjoys playing hide-and-seek, she doesn't like to play board games.

Does this usage of while mean *although*? That is, perhaps Aunt Ruth asked me to play hide-and-seek because she doesn't like playing Monopoly.

The alternative meaning is that she doesn't like to play board games at the same time that she is playing hide and seek. That is certainly reasonable. There is some ambiguity in this sentence. Therefore, I would probably use *although* or *whereas* in this example.

Whoever and Whomever (see That and Other Relative Pronouns)

47
Relevant Grammar Points in Each Story

1 *Aunt Ruth Loves Chocolate More Than Me*
   • than: conjunction or preposition? (i.e., "than I" vs "than me")

2 *Aunt Ruth, QE-II*
   • "into" vs "in to"

3 *Aunt Ruth and Lou Gerund's Practicing*
   • gerunds

4 *Aunt Ruth's Go-Cart Has Gone*
   • conjugation of go (go / went / gone), bring (bring / brought / brought) and other irregular verbs

5 *Aunt Ruth Herself Meets Henry VIII*
   • myself, herself, yourself, and other -self words

6 *Aunt Ruth Is a Superlative Super Relative*
   • comparatives and superlatives

7 *Aunt Ruth Is a Historic Anomaly*
   • articles with H- words

8 *Aunt Ruth Brings It*
   • bring and take

9 *Aunt Ruth and the Okay Chorale*
   • use to / used to   • do: auxiliary
   • different of / different than / different from

10 *Aunt Ruth Is Only in a Quandary*
   • only

11 *Frankly, My Dear Aunt Ruth*
- sentence adverbs

12 *Aunt Ruth and Metaphors*
- metaphors and similes

13 *Queen Ruth Borrows Your Ear*
- borrow / lend / loan
- could / couldn't care less
- linking verbs

14 *Aunt Ruth: Fishes Tight, Fishes Deep*
- adjectives that can be used as adverbs

15 *Aunt Ruth Burned or Burnt the Toast?*
- verbs ending in -ed and -t

16 *Aunt Ruth and Double Negatives*
- double negatives

17 *Aunt Ruth Passes the Pasta Pesto Test*
- pass / passed and past / present

18 *Aunt Ruth by the Numbers*
- using numbers

19 *Aunt Ruth Fragments*
- sentence fragments
- eminent and imminent
- ingenuous and ingenious
- masterful and masterly
- duplicity

20 *Aunt Ruth Loves Her Transitive Radio*
- transitive and intransitive verbs

21 *The Ripcord Was Pulled by Aunt Ruth*
- active and passive voice

22 *Intransitive Verbs Rock*
   - intransitive verbs

23 *Aunt Ruth and Verbs Ala Mode*
   - indicative, imperative, and subjunctive moods

24 *Aunt Ruth and the Tense Predicament, Part I*
   - verb tenses / conjugation

25 *Past Participle Guilt (Intermission)*
   - irregular verb tenses / participles

26 *Aunt Ruth and the Tense Predicament, Part II*
   - verb tenses / conjugation

27 *Aunt Ruth Hunts the Subjunctive Beast*
   - verbs (subjunctive mood)

28 *Aunt Ruth Wants a Cheeseburger Bad*
   - bad / badly

29 *Aunt Ruth and the Comma Splice*
   - comma splices
   - sentence fusion
   - independent clauses

30 *Aunt Ruth and the Lost Commas*
   - comma usage
   - independent clauses
   - subordinate clauses and appositives
   - conjunctive adverbs

31 *Aunt Ruth and the Independent Santa Clause*
   - semi-colon and colon usage
   - independent clauses

32 *Aunt Ruth is a Short Short-Order Cook, etc.*
   - usage of etc. and abbreviations

33 *Aunt Ruth Is Spaced Out*
- either / or, neither / nor

34 *Aunt Ruthii*
- plurals ending in -i or -ii

35 *The Aunt Who Baked the Fruitcake*
- double subjects
- that / which
- that / who

36 *Aunt Ruth and the Queen's Baseball Card*
- double possessives

37 *Aunt Ruth Is Non-Nonplussed*
- usage of nonplussed
- whoever and whomever

38 *Bored of Aunt Ruth*
- bored of / bored by / bored with

39 *Aunt Ruth and the Solar ... Ellipsis*
- using ellipses (...)

40 *Aunt Ruth Letters from Aunt Iquity*
- drier / dryer
- breath / breathe
- lightening / lightning

41 *Aunt Ruth and the Synonym Bun*
- homographs, homophones, and homonyms
- synonyms   • antonyms

42 *Aunt Ruth Has Got to Be Kidding*
- get, got, have got / have gotten

43 *Aunt Ruth and the Peach Cobbler's Kitten*
- possessives with appositives

44 *Aunt Ruth in the Oval Office*
- Let's

45 *Aunt Ruth and the Train to Gettysburg*
- adverse / averse
- beside / besides
- precede / proceed
- while / although
- anxious / eager
- plus
- way / ways

48

Find the Story for Each Grammar Point

Active voice	Chapter 21
Adjectives used as Adverbs	Chapter 14
Adverbs (Sentence)	Chapter 11
Adverse and Averse	Chapter 45
Antonyms	Chapter 41
Anxious and Eager	Chapter 45
Bad and Badly	Chapter 28
Beside and Besides	Chapter 45
Bored of / Bored with	Chapter 38
Borrow and Loan	Chapter 13
Breath and Breathe	Chapter 40
Bring and Take	Chapter 8
Colons	Chapter 31
Comma (Appositives)	Chapter 30
Comma (Splice)	Chapter 29
Comma (Subordinate Clause)	Chapter 30
Comma (Independent Clause)	Chapter 29-31
Comparatives and Superlatives	Chapter 6
Could and Couldn't care less	Chapter 13
Different of / from / than	Chapter 9
Do: Auxiliary	Chapter 9
Double negatives	Chapter 16
Double possessives	Chapter 36
Double subjects	Chapter 35
Drier and Dryer	Chapter 40
Duplicity	Chapter 19
Either / Or	Chapter 33
Ellipses (...)	Chapter 39
Eminent and Imminent	Chapter 19
Etc.	Chapter 32
Fragments	Chapter 19

Gerunds	Chapter 3
Get, Got, Have got / Have gotten	Chapter 42
Go / Went / Gone and other Irregular Verbs	Chapter 4, 25
H-words with Articles	Chapter 7
Herself, Himself	Chapter 5
Homonyms	Chapter 41
Hopefully (and other Sentence Adverbs)	Chapter 11
Imminent and Eminent	Chapter 19
Imperative Mode / Mood	Chapter 23
Indicative Mode / Mood	Chapter 23
Ingenuous and ingenious	Chapter 19
Into vs in to	Chapter 2
Intransitive Verbs	Chapter 20, 22
Irregular Verbs and Past Participles	Chapter 4, 25
Let's	Chapter 44
Lightening and Lightning	Chapter 40
Linking Verbs	Chapter 13
Masterly and masterful	Chapter 19
Metaphors	Chapter 12
Myself and Other -Self Words	Chapter 5
Neither / Nor	Chapter 33
Nonplussed	Chapter 37
Numbers	Chapter 18
Only	Chapter 10
Passive voice	Chapter 21
Past and passed	Chapter 17
Past Participles	Chapter 4, 25
Plurals ending in ii	Chapter 34
Plus	Chapter 45
Possessives with Appositives	Chapter 43
Precede and Proceed	Chapter 45
Relative Pronouns	Chapter 35
Semi-colons	Chapter 31
Sentence Adverbs	Chapter 11
Sentence Fragments	Chapter 19
Similes	Chapter 12
Subjunctive Mode / Mood	Chapter 23, 27
Superlatives and Comparatives	Chapter 6

Synonyms	Chapter 41
Than	Chapter 1
That and Which	Chapter 35
That and Who	Chapter 35
Transitive Verbs	Chapter 20
Use to / Used to	Chapter 9
Verbs (General)	Chapters 20-27
Verbs (Imperative)	Chapter 23
Verbs (Indicative)	Chapter 23
Verbs (Intransitive)	Chapter 20, 22
Verbs (Modes / Moods)	Chapter 23
Verbs (Subjunctive)	Chapter 23, 27
Verbs (Tenses)	Chapter 24-26
Verbs (Transitive)	Chapter 20
Verbs (Voices - Active and Passive)	Chapter 21
Verbs ending in -t or -ed	Chapter 15
Wait for / Wait on	Chapter 45
Way and Ways	Chapter 45
While and Although	Chapter 45
Whoever and Whomever	Chapter 37
Will versus Going To	Chapter 26
Word Fun: Quandary	Chapter 10
Passed / Past	Chapter 17

www.ingramcontent.com/pod-product-compliance
Lightning Source LLC
Chambersburg PA
CBHW020640300426
44112CB00007B/178

In Praise of
Aunt Ruth: The Queen of English and Her Reign of Error

"Nobody is better than Joel Schnoor when it comes to presenting grammar dressed up to have fun."
— Richard Lederer, author of *Anguished English*

"An answer to the prayers of English teachers!"

Joel Schnoor's *Aunt Ruth: The Queen of English and Her Reign of Error* is truly a language lover's delight. Joel may have been prompted to write the book in the belief that, metaphorically speaking, "The integrity of our language is crumbling; the foundation of our Grammar Castle is being undermined by giant serpents of ignorance."

Following the format of his first book, *I Laid an Egg on Aunt Ruth's Head*, each chapter deals with one or more glaring errors in English grammar, usage, or mechanics—errors that make a language teacher's hair stand on end and make the book's author grab his laptop and add another tale to his hilariously entertaining Aunt Ruth stories.

Masterfully written in Joel's comfortable, easy-to-read style, the book combines practical examples, humor, creative description, and figurative language to produce memorable passages, characters or scenes: "he looked like an overweight Charlie Chaplin doing a poor imitation of a constipated hula dancer demonstrating the Macarena," or "her jowls were flapping in the air like a basset hound driving a convertible through a wind tunnel."

Aunt Ruth: The Queen ... will be enjoyed by those pleasure-reading grammar gurus interested in recognizing and avoiding the pitfalls of language abuse. The book is also an answer to the prayers of English teachers looking for a new creative approach to helping students use troublesome aspects of language in correct, effective communication. As the narrator says to Bill the Grammar Fairy, "Please call it [the book] a grammar story, not a grammar lesson. We don't want the reader suspecting that he or she may be both enjoying the story and learning grammar concurrently."

Because of its episodic structure, where Aunt Ruth's character changes by chapter from race car driver to safari hunter to mountain climber to time traveler to ..., and the language lessons vary from sentence fragments to verb tense to modifiers, to pronouns, to commas, to figures of speech to ..., the forty-five short, zany, adventure-filled chapters can be included, omitted, or presented in any order the teacher chooses to best meet the specific abilities or needs of his or her students.

If you chuckled as you read *I Laid an Egg on Aunt Ruth's Head*, you will howl as you read *Aunt Ruth: The Queen of English and Her Reign of Error*. It's another five-star accomplishment of a proven author. And it leaves the reader anxiously awaiting Joel's next release.

—Jerry Laffey, English teacher, National Federation Outstanding Interscholastic Speech and Debate Award for Iowa, I.H.S.S.A. Hall of Fame

"So much here to love!"

"Rambunctious Aunt Ruth and her notable nephew are delightful! Their inherent individual charm as characters makes for a good read even if you don't need new grammatical insight. But Mr. Schnoor knows well that when the indomitable spirit meets the intellectual perfectionist, there is context for the kind of witty conversation that makes those slippery points of English grammar stick a whole lot better. So much here to love!"

—Kristi Eskelund, English teacher, storyteller, and grammar enthusiast